A GUIDE TO
BIRDING

A GUIDE TO
BIRDING

JOSEPH FORSHAW, STEVE HOWELL,
TERENCE LINDSEY, RICH STALLCUP

CONSULTANT EDITOR
TERENCE LINDSEY

FOG CITY PRESS

Published by Fog City Press
814 Montgomery Street
San Francisco, CA 94133 USA

Copyright 1994 © US Weldon Owen Reference Inc.
Copyright 1994 © Weldon Owen Pty Limited
This edition 2002
Reprinted 2002, 2003, 2004

CHIEF EXECUTIVE OFFICER John Owen
PRESIDENT Terry Newell
PUBLISHER Lynn Humphries
MANAGING EDITOR Janine Flew
DESIGN MANAGER Helen Perks
EDITORIAL COORDINATOR Jennifer Losco
EDITORIAL ASSISTANT Helen Flint
PRODUCTION MANAGER Caroline Webber
PRODUCTION COORDINATOR James Blackman
SALES MANAGER Emily Jahn
VICE PRESIDENT INTERNATIONAL SALES Stuart Laurence

PROJECT EDITOR Scott Forbes
EDITORIAL CONSULTANT Paul Lehman
COPY EDITOR Gillian Hewitt
EDITORIAL ASSISTANTS Greg Hassall, Vesna Radojcic
PROJECT ART DIRECTOR Hilda Mendham
DESIGN ASSISTANT Stephanie Cannon
JACKET DESIGN John Bull
PICTURE RESEARCH Connie Komack, Pictures & Words,
Rockport, Massachusetts; Terence Lindsey; Gillian Manning

ISBN 1 877019 34 8

Color reproduction by Mandarin Offset, Hong Kong
Printed by Kyodo Printing Co. (S'pore) Pte Ltd
Printed in Singapore

A Weldon Owen Production

Do you ne'er think what wondrous beings these?
Do you ne'er think who made them, and who taught
The dialect they speak, where melodies
Alone are the interpreters of thought?
Whose household words are songs in many keys,
Sweeter than instrument of man e'er caught!

The Birds of Killingworth,
HENRY WADSWORTH LONGFELLOW (1807–82), American poet

CONTENTS

FOREWORD

People love birds. They celebrate birds in poetry and in song; they spend thousands of dollars and hours providing food, shelter, and water for birds; they purchase expensive optical equipment to obtain a clearer view of birds; they buy dozens of books to increase their understanding of birds; and they travel long distances in order to see as many birds as possible.

Why birds? Of all the creatures of the world, birds share our perceptual space the most. They sing and call at frequencies most of us can hear, and they display colors and behaviors that we can easily see and enjoy. Thus, we are able to identify with birds and share in their lives to a greater extent than we can with most of the other creatures with which we share our planet.

At the same time, birds are exotic. Above all, they fly. They fly quickly, they fly high, they hover, they fly backwards, and—amazingly—they fly thousands of miles in a few weeks, disappearing in the fall and reappearing on our doorstep the next spring.

A Guide to Birding is your guide to the world of birds. Read it through at least once for an excellent introduction to this delightful pastime and to the birds you will encounter. Then refer to it again and again to learn more about what you observe outdoors. Enjoy *Birding*, and enjoy the birds!

Greg Butcher

GREG BUTCHER
Executive Director,
American Birding Association

INTRODUCTION

For centuries, birds have been used in art, folklore, and mythology to symbolize wisdom and truth, strength and power, birth and death. However, nothing about birds has tantalized humans more than the gift of flight. There are birds that "fly" through water, and others that can attain incredible speeds while swooping on prey. Some, such as the hummingbirds, are extraordinarily agile and can even fly backward. However, what unites and defines these creatures is not their ability to fly—for, curiously, some cannot fly at all—but the possession of feathers on their bodies.

Like so many members of the natural world, birds are under threat. Humans have been responsible for the extinction of many species, and with the continued destruction of their habitats, many more birds will fall victim to the pressures imposed by the modern world. It is only by understanding these creatures that we can save them from this fate. This book aims to inform and inspire, and features text by international experts and beautiful color photographs, maps, and illustrations. It examines the origins, anatomy, classification, and behavior of birds. There is advice on attracting birds to your garden, and on observing them there and in the wild. Also included is a field guide to 148 species of birds, grouped according to their habitats. For beginner and experienced birders alike, *A Guide to Birding* provides a concise and authoritative guide to the fascinating world of birds.

THE EDITORS

In a world that seems so very puzzling is it any wonder birds have such appeal? Birds are, perhaps, the most eloquent expression of reality.

ROGER TORY PETERSON (b. 1908),
American ornithologist

THE WORLD *of* BIRDS

Step out of your door, almost anywhere in the world, and, within minutes, you will see birds of one kind or another.

Dark-eyed Junco

Birds are among the most mobile of all animals. There are other animals that roam widely, but birds alone can, at least in principle, go anywhere they please on the earth's surface.

Although most numerous in marshes, woodlands, and rainforests, birds inhabit the most inhospitable of deserts, and have been seen within a few miles of both poles. Some never stray from home in their entire lives, but others can, and frequently do, span entire oceans or continents, sometimes in a single flight.

There are about 9,300 species of birds in the world, and they range from the tiny Bee Hummingbird, which weighs little more than a dime, to the imposing Ostrich, which stands taller than a man and weighs over 300 pounds (136 kg). Among these species can be found almost any color of the rainbow. These colors may be arranged in the dazzling patterns found in breeding peacocks or in the astonishingly effective camouflage of birds such as the Tawny Frogmouth, which evades predators by imitating a dead tree stump.

Some birds hover on the brink of extinction; on the other hand, there are far more domestic chickens on earth than humans.

Golden-plovers, taking off with a load of fuel almost equal to their own weight, fly nonstop from Alaska to Hawaii and back each year, while Peregrine Falcons reach speeds approaching 200 miles (320 km) per hour as they dive upon their winged prey. In contrast to these masters of the air, there are a few birds —the Ostrich, for example— that cannot fly at all.

Peregrine Falcon

Ostrich

Tawny Frogmouth

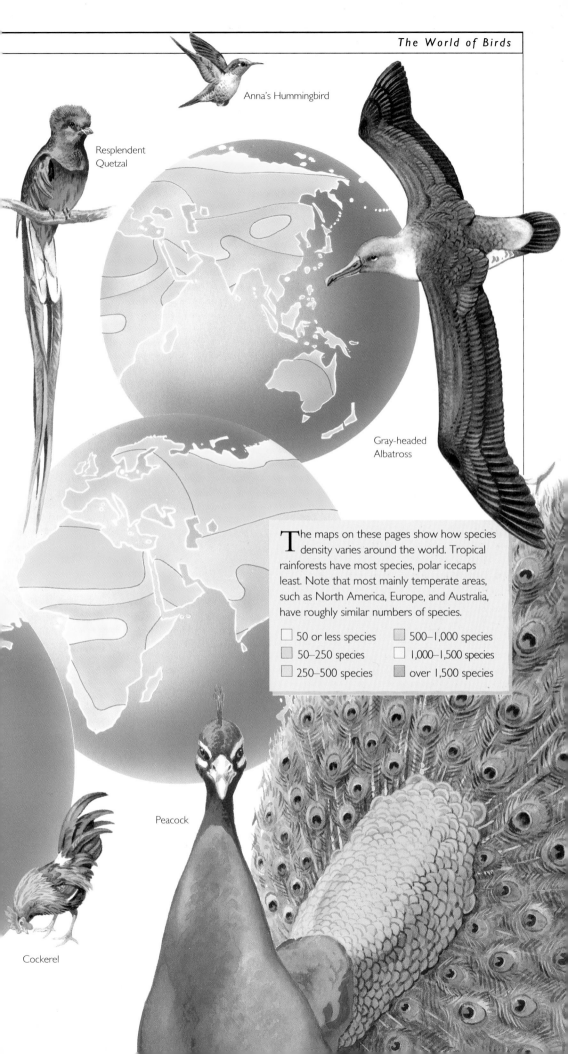

Anna's Hummingbird

Resplendent
Quetzal

Gray-headed
Albatross

The maps on these pages show how species
density varies around the world. Tropical
rainforests have most species, polar icecaps
least. Note that most mainly temperate areas,
such as North America, Europe, and Australia,
have roughly similar numbers of species.

☐ 50 or less species   ☐ 500–1,000 species
☐ 50–250 species   ☐ 1,000–1,500 species
☐ 250–500 species   ☐ over 1,500 species

Peacock

Cockerel

BIRDS, REAL *and* IMAGINARY

From the Phoenix rising from the ashes to the sacred Garuda, king of the birds,

from the dove of peace to the bluebird of happiness, birds real and imaginary

have featured prominently in the human imagination.

THE ROC *One of the oldest and most widespread bird myths concerns this giant bird that feeds on elephants. In this scene from The Arabian Nights (left), merchants pull a roc chick from its egg.*

It is, perhaps, not surprising that birds, being among the most easily observed of all animals, have captured the human imagination. Their attributes and habits have proved a rich source of inspiration to us since prehistoric times.

Bird song, for example, has inspired some of the finest poetry in the English language, and for centuries the power of flight was the envy of humankind.

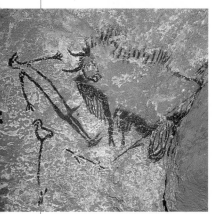

BIRD-MAN *One of the earliest images of a bird—dating from over 15,000 years ago—is to be found in the Lascaux caves in France. It depicts a bison, a bird, and what seems to be a bird-headed human.*

Throughout history, birds have been used to symbolize particular qualities and states: the wise owl, the dove of peace, the bluebird of happiness, and so on. And deep in our past lurk myths and legends about birds, some of uncertain origin.

CLASSICAL MYTHS
One of the most enduring of bird myths is that of the Phoenix. This legendary bird was well known to Greek and Roman scholars more than 2,000 years ago, and elements of its story can be traced to the ancient Egyptians, several thousand years earlier.

In most legends, the Phoenix is a bird of great beauty that lives for 500 or 600 years in the Arabian desert. It then burns itself to ashes on a funeral pyre, from which it emerges with renewed youth.

Through the Dark Ages, this story was commonly used as a metaphor for the resurrection of Christ, and there are many references to the Phoenix in literature. The Phoenix is still referred to

today, to symbolize a new structure or idea arising from the ruins or ashes of its predecessor.

Another story of uncertain origin is the Greek myth of the halcyon. This bird, often associated with the kingfisher, floated its nest on the open sea. Aeolus, god of the winds, decreed that all storms must cease while the halcyon's young were reared. This fable gave rise to the expression "halcyon days", which is used to describe any interlude of peace and serenity.

Now I will believe...

that in Arabia,

There is one tree, the

phoenix' throne,

one phoenix, At this

time reigning there.

The Tempest,
WILLIAM SHAKESPEARE (1564–1616),
English playwright

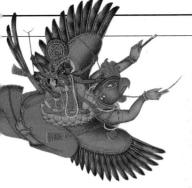

SYMBOL OF POWER

Few birds have impressed humankind as much as the eagle. Its powerful flight was noted in The Song of Solomon, and an eagle was the emblem of the Babylonian god Ashur. An eagle adorned the scepter of Zeus, supreme god of the ancient Greeks.

In Hindu mythology, it was an eagle that brought to humankind the sacred drink soma, and in the old Norse sagas, Odin, king of the Gods, often took the form of an eagle. The warbonnets of American Plains Indians were dressed only with eagle feathers. The double-headed eagle was a common Byzantine motif, and eagles were adopted as imperial symbols by a number of nations, including Austria, Germany, Poland, and Russia.

Today an eagle occurs on the Mexican coat of arms and is the national symbol of the United States of America.

EASTERN LEGENDS

Myths involving birds of supernatural proportions are common around the world. One of the most monstrous of all birds, real or imaginary, is Garuda, sacred to the Hindu god Vishnu, preserver of the world. King of birds and herald of storms, Garuda is a huge winged monster that feeds on snakes. Its image can be seen wherever the Hindu religion has spread, and has been adopted as the symbol of Indonesia's national airline.

The roc, or rukh, entered Western folklore from a fifteenth-century collection of Arabian tales called *The Arabian Nights*. The central character, Sinbad the Sailor, is wrecked on an island in the Indian Ocean, where he encounters a bird so enormous that it feeds its young on elephants.

An almost identical story is found in ancient Chinese literature, and the bird was even mentioned by Marco Polo, who recorded that a roc's feather was presented to the Mongul ruler Genghis Khan.

AMERICAN MYTHS

Most of the native peoples of North and South America have myths of monstrous birds. The Thunderbird, for example, is an eagle-like bird so huge that lightning flashes when it blinks and

MYTHICAL BIRDS *The Hindu god Garuda (top); and the Thunderbird of Native American legend (right), depicted as part of a totem pole.*

SELF-SACRIFICE *A pelican feeding its young on its own blood, in a woodcut from Ulisse Aldrovandi's* Ornithologiae *(1559–1603).*

Ornithologiæ. Lib. XIX. 47
Pelicanus Pictorum & vulgi.

thunder rolls at the slightest movement of its wings. This fabulous bird is known to the Athapascans, Inuit, and Hopi among others. According to the Tlingit tribe, of the Pacific Northwest, it carries a lake of water in the hollow of its back that, spilling out as it flies, produces torrents of rain.

MYTHICAL QUALITIES

Alongside stories of imaginary birds, legends relating to real birds have been common too.

In ancient China, the pheasant was regarded as a symbol of harmony and heaven's favor. The "love-pheasant" was, in fact, one of the four chief supernatural creatures of Chinese mythology, ranking equally with the tortoise, the unicorn, and the dragon.

In medieval Europe, it was widely believed that the pelican fed its young on its own blood, and the bird became a common symbol of Christian piety.

Today, among Aboriginal people in Australia, the Willie-wagtail, a small songbird, is widely regarded as a tattler. It is said to hang around the mens' councils picking up secrets that it then carries to the women.

In many countries in Europe, the woodpecker is believed to call up rain.

THE ORIGINS *of* BIRDS

Contrasting markedly with our comprehensive knowledge of living birds is our tentative, piecemeal understanding of their origins.

Birds are poorly represented in fossil deposits for a variety of reasons. Bird bones are fragile and many are hollow, so they are easily broken and fragmented. In addition, few landbirds die where their remains can be buried in waterlaid sediments, the richest source of fossils. It also seems likely that many ancient birds, like birds today, were preyed upon by carnivorous animals.

IMAGES IN STONE *Both nature and humankind have created images of birds in stone. This Egyptian carving (left) dates from the eighth century.*

It has been estimated that between the time of *Archaeopteryx*, the earliest known bird, and the present, between 1.5 million and 2 million species of bird have existed. Of these, we have specimen evidence for the existence of fewer than 12,000 species!

"FEATHERED DINOSAURS"

The exact origins of birds are still uncertain, but it has long been thought that they evolved from reptiles. One popular theory links birds to a specific subgroup of dinosaurs called theropods, which were common approximately 200 million years ago.

Archaeopteryx provided what is still the most important evidence of the link between birds and dinosaurs. *Archaeopteryx* was certainly a bird, as it clearly possessed feathers and a U-shaped "wishbone", but it also had prominent reptilian characteristics, including teeth and clawed digits on the forewing.

About the size of a crow, *Archaeopteryx* was a predator, and probably caught insects or small vertebrates, such as lizards. Recently, there has been much debate about its flight capabilities, and whether it was terrestrial or arboreal in its habits. Some authors claim that it would have been a weak flier, while others argue that it would have been capable of sustained flight.

THE EARLIEST KNOWN BIRD

In the Jurassic cycad forests of Europe, about 150 million years ago, a group of dinosaurs was browsing on plants along the shoreline of a Bavarian lake, while in the taller vegetation strange bird-like creatures were clambering among the branches and fluttering from tree to tree. Perhaps in a frantic effort to escape capture by an arboreal predator, one of these creatures lost its balance and fell into shallow waters at the lake's edge, where it drowned and sank into sedimentary silt.

Some time in the first part of the nineteenth century, a worker in a quarry near Solnhofen, in Bavaria, Germany, found a fossilized feather. Then, in 1861, in the same quarry, the incomplete fossilized skeleton of the bird-like creature was found. German paleontologist Hermann von Meyer examined these remains and made a formal description of them, naming this earliest known fossil bird *Archaeopteryx lithographica*.

FOSSILS *(above) have provided us with a fairly clear idea of what* Archaeopteryx *must have looked like (above right).*

HESPERORNIS, *a flightless fish-eating bird, first appeared over 100 million years ago during the Cretaceous period. Many present-day waterbirds, including the pelican (below right), have their origins in this era of prehistory.*

An important piece of evidence for this link is a U-shaped furcula or "wishbone" found both in birds and in some theropods. In birds, this feature plays an important role in flight. In the dinosaurs it probably evolved as a support for the short forelimbs that they used for catching prey.

CRETACEOUS BIRDS

Though only slightly younger than *Archaeopteryx*, birds of the early Cretaceous period (about 130 million years ago) were much more like modern birds. Most were undoubtedly strong fliers.

Probably the most famous of the many Cretaceous fossil birds are *Hesperornis* and *Ichthyornis* from North America. Both are notable in that they possessed teeth, a primitive condition prominent in *Archaeopteryx* and its theropod ancestors. *Hesperornis* was a flightless, fish-eating, diving-bird, whereas *Ichthyornis* was a strong flier.

THE PLEISTOCENE EPOCH

Fossils of the Pleistocene epoch (2 million to 10,000 years ago) include many species that are alive today, as well as numerous species that are now extinct.

A rich source of these fossils are the Rancho La Brea tarpits in California. These have yielded specimens of birds like the *Teratornis*, which used its 12½-foot (3.8-m) wingspan to soar across the skies of North America.

MODERN BIRDS

Present-day birds really are not so "modern", since most of the species we know today have been around for thousands of years. Indeed, about 11,500 species probably occurred during the Pleistocene— approximately 1,500 more species than exist today. Bird species probably reached a peak from 250,000 to 500,000 years ago, and have been in gradual decline ever since.

In times prehistoric, 'tis easily proved… That birds and not gods were the rulers of men.

The Birds,
ARISTOPHANES (c. 448–380 BC),
Greek dramatist

TERATORNIS *Many fossils of this large, vulture-like predator that lived in western North America in the Pleistocene epoch have been found in the Rancho La Brea tarpits in California.*

NAMING *the* BIRDS

The spectacular diversity of birds is a delight, but it presents us with the challenge of establishing which birds are related and how best to classify them.

The science of classifying living things is called taxonomy. Early taxonomists based their classifications of birds almost entirely on external appearances, in the way that a child might organize building blocks according to size, shape, and color. These methods frequently resulted in birds that were not related being linked and some that were related being kept apart.

Advances in scientific procedures have led to new techniques being applied to determining alliances between kinds of bird, and the systems of classification have become increasingly sophisticated. Taxonomy now draws on a synthesis of data from many fields of biology, including paleontology, ecology, physiology, behavior, and DNA and protein analysis.

SYMBOLS AS NAMES *The ancient Egyptians used several birds in their system of hieroglyphics. The falcon (left), for example, represented the god Horus, personal god of the ruling pharaoh.*

THE SPECIES CONCEPT

The keystone of modern taxonomy (and the focus of bird identification) is the species. A species is defined as a population whose members do not freely interbreed with members of other neighboring populations (although this is sometimes difficult to establish one way or the other).

Within a species, there are often groups or populations which differ in minor ways, such as in size or plumage coloration. These inter-breeding groups are recognized as subspecies or races. Populations separated by geographical barriers (such as mountain ranges and oceans) are also known as isolates.

HIGHER CATEGORIES

All birds are related to some extent and the practice and procedures of taxonomy operate to establish different levels of relationship. Above species level, related species are grouped into genera, related genera are grouped into families, and related families into orders. Some intermediate categories are used by taxonomists to express fine distinctions, but these need not concern the beginning birder.

Together, birds form a class, Aves, and, along with other classes of backboned animals, this class is part of the Subphylum Vertebrata (the vertebrates) and the Animal Kingdom.

WHAT'S IN A NAME?

Most animal species have a common name—the English name in English-speaking countries—and a scientific name. The latter consists of two main elements: the genus and the specific name. Where there are subspecies, the subspecies name is sometimes included as a third element.

The scientific name is latinized and highlighted in a different type (normally italic). Only the generic name is capitalized.

FAMILY TIES *The close relationship between the three bluebird species—Mountain Bluebird (left), Eastern Bluebird (above right), and Western Bluebird (far left) is described taxonomically by* their inclusion in the genus Sialis. *The American Robin (opposite), on the other hand, is obviously related, yet not closely enough to share the same genus. It belongs to the genus Turdus. Both genera are members of the family Turdidae.*

CAROLUS LINNAEUS

The system of biological nomenclature used today was devised by the Swedish botanist, Carolus Linnaeus (1707–78).

Linnaeus was born in South Rashult in Sweden. From an early age, he loved plants, and this led him to a career in botany. In the course of his studies, he became aware that every organism needed to have a unique scientific name that could be used and understood by people of all nationalities. He therefore developed a system using Latin names, Latin being the language used by scholars throughout Europe at the time. This system, still referred to today as the Linnaean system, was presented to the scientific community in the *Systema Naturae*, published in 1735.

In 1741, Linnaeus was appointed to the chair of medicine at Uppsala University, but in the following year he exchanged this for the chair of botany. In 1761, he was granted a patent of nobility, becoming

Carl von Linné. During his lifetime, Linnaeus published more than 180 works. It was in editions of the *Systema Naturae* that many species of birds were first formally named.

The purpose of scientific names is to provide an internationally recognizable system of classification. A single species' common name may vary between languages and countries, but its scientific name will always be the same. Conversely, one or more birds may have the same common name in different countries but not be related at all. For example, we often talk about "robins" in America, but the "robins" of the UK and Australia are quite different birds. Use of the scientific name eliminates any confusion.

THE CODE OF LIVING THINGS

A computer simulation of the structure of DNA (below), showing its intricate double-spiral structure.

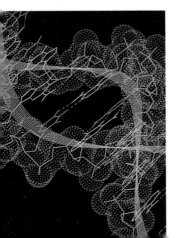

DNA CLASSIFICATION

Recent work in the field of biochemical research, especially analyses of DNA (deoxyribonucleic acid)—the essential genetic material—has proved a powerful tool in clarifying the relationships of birds.

Pioneered by Charles Sibley and Jon Ahlquist at Yale University, this research started out using protein material from blood and egg-white for analysis. It has now reached the point where the scientists are able to examine the DNA itself and measure relatedness in an extraordinarily precise manner.

Some fascinating results have emerged from these studies, and Sibley and Ahlquist's findings have allowed researchers to resolve a number of long-standing uncertainties in the field of taxonomy.

CLASSIFYING THE ROBIN

The purposes of taxonomy are twofold: to assign a unique name to each species and to place it within a structure of relation-ships. The American Robin, for example, is classified in the following way:

- Class Aves
- Order Passeriformes
- Family Turdidae
- Genus *Turdus*
- Species *migratorius*

Subspecies may also be named. Robins breeding in Texas, for example, are identified as *Turdus migratorius achrusterus*.

BIRD ANATOMY

Despite their external diversity, birds are remarkably uniform in basic structure. This similarity results chiefly from adaptations associated with flight.

Birds are the only living things with feathers. Also, they are ver-tebrates, which means that, just like reptiles, amphibians, fish, and mammals (including ourselves), they have a jointed internal skeleton with two forelimbs and two hindlimbs; the brain is encased in a strong bony container (the skull); and the main nerve route in the body is carried down the center of the back inside a flexible column of bones (the spine).

If you compare the skeleton, muscle, and organ systems of a bird with those of a human, you will find many points of similarity. Broadly speaking, the same basic elements—eyes, ears, skull, ribs, lungs, heart, and so on—are found in corresponding places in both and serve comparable functions.

SKELETAL SYSTEM

Almost all of the differences between human and bird skeletons are the result of profound modifications in birds to enable sustained flight. The sternum, or breastbone, for example, lies in the same relative position and serves the same basic function as the sternum in our own bodies. However, in birds it is much bigger in relative terms and bears,

skull

radius

furcula (half of "wishbone")

carpometacarpus

synsacrum

femur

pygostyle

ulna (attachment of secondaries)

keel of sternum

tibiotarsus

tarsus

HOLLOW BONES *Many of the larger bones in a bird's skeleton are thin-walled and hollow, to minimize weight, but intricately braced and strutted inside, to maximize strength.*

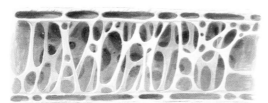

FORMED FOR FLIGHT *A Northern Harrier (top left) soars through the open skies. The skeleton of a bird (above) could be described as a typical vertebrate skeleton that has undergone significant modification to support powered flight.*

projecting at right angles, the most obvious and distinctive of avian skeletal structures: a large flat keel (called the carina). This serves as a point of attachment for the huge pectoral muscles used to flap the wings.

Another unique feature of the avian skeleton is that in many birds the collarbones have fused to form a rigid brace for the wings: the furcula or "wishbone".

ORGAN SYSTEMS

The organ systems, too, are comparable to those of other vertebrates but are heavily modified to service the needs of powered flight. In particular, they support a far higher metabolism than that of most other animals. The large size of a bird's heart is an indication of this.

Birds have a highly specialized and remarkably efficient respiratory system. A multitude of empty spaces (called pulmonary sacs or air sacs) extend throughout the body, in

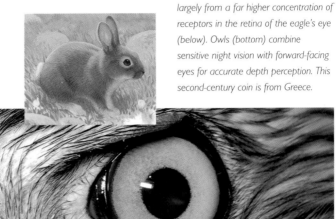

KEEN EYESIGHT *An image of a rabbit (left), as it might be seen by most animals, compared to the same rabbit as it might be seen by an eagle (below left). The much higher definition results largely from a far higher concentration of receptors in the retina of the eagle's eye (below). Owls (bottom) combine sensitive night vision with forward-facing eyes for accurate depth perception. This second-century coin is from Greece.*

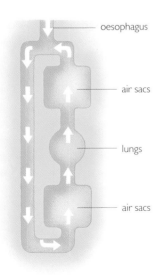

NEVER OUT OF BREATH *The net result of a bird's sophisticated respiratory system (below) is that air flows through the bird's lungs, rather than in-and-out as in humans and other animals.*

— oesophagus

— air sacs

— lungs

— air sacs

many birds extending even into the hollow bones. Air flows through this system of interconnected sacs almost like blood in the circulatory system. The lungs are located so that air flows through them, not in-and-out as in other vertebrates. Oxygen transfer to the blood is therefore a continuous process, taking place during both inhalation and exhalation. This system is so efficient that, paradoxically, birds get by with much smaller lungs than other vertebrates.

SENSORY SYSTEMS

Birds have poor powers of smell but acute hearing, and their eyes are among the most sophisticated sensory organs in the animal kingdom.

The eye of a large eagle, for example, is approximately the same size as a human eye, but has a far greater density of sensory elements (rods and cones) in the retina (the rear

inner surface of the eye on which the image is formed).

A unique feature of birds' eyes is the pecten, a highly vascularized structure that emerges from the retina. Despite numerous studies, its function is still unclear, but it is believed to play a role in improving the supply of oxygen and nutrients to the light-sensitive cells of the retina.

My heart in hiding

Stirred for a bird, —the

achieve of, the

mastery of

the thing!

GERARD MANLEY HOPKINS
(1844–1889), English poet

FEATHERS *and* PLUMAGE

Feathers define birds and are unique to birds—no other animal has feathers. The feather itself is a complex product of a bird's skin, and its structure is one of nature's great wonders.

One of the marvels of animal engineering, the feather is light, flexible, and strong. Feathers play a critical part in controlling a bird's internal temperature, and an obviously crucial role in flight.

MATERIAL AND DESIGN

The material from which the feather is built is keratin, the same substance that makes up our hair and fingernails. Along the length of the central stalk (rachis) of a feather, structures called barbs emerge in parallel and on one plane, in an arrangement

COLOR *Feathers come in all colors, from the sober shades of sparrows to the vibrant hues of the the American Flamingo (above) and the male Altamira Oriole (below).*

reminiscent of a plastic comb. Each barb in turn carries even smaller structures called barbules, arranged in the same manner along its length. The whole assembly is held together by a myriad of tiny hooks on the barbules which lock onto the barbules of the neighboring barb.

A bird spends part of each day making minor repairs to tears in its feathers (preening). Most repairs involve reattaching the hooks, rather like reclosing Velcro strips. The bird does this by nibbling along the barbs of each feather to bring the "Velcro" in contact again.

BARBS AND BARBULES *This electron microscope photograph (below) shows a barb and the barbules arranged along its sides. Each barbule bears tiny hooks (left) that lock the whole structure together.*

HOW A FEATHER GROWS *Each feather grows from a structure in a bird's skin roughly comparable to a hair follicle in humans. First, the old feather falls away. As a new one grows, it starts to look like a plastic drinking straw. Within this tube, or sheath, the feather itself develops, its barbs and barbules crammed in a tight-packed spiral. After some time, the tip of the sheath splits, allowing the feather to unfold, fan-like, into its final shape.*

sheath —

— barbs

— central stalk (rachis)

PLUMAGE

The mass of feathers on a bird's body constitutes its plumage. In most birds, feathers tend to clump in distinct tracts, known as pterylae (the spaces between the tracts are apterylae). As a general rule, birds' color patterns are built of these units—which is why it is valuable to know the details of a bird's surface "geography". Bird identification is simpler and more reliable if you can express pattern in terms of feather tracts.

Birds have many different kinds of feathers, but most of them are either contour feathers or flight feathers. Contour feathers are those that cover the body itself and are basically there to keep the bird warm. The flight feathers are those directly involved in the business of flying. These are considerably longer, stiffer, and less curved than contour feathers, and are aerodynamically shaped.

Other types of feathers include down feathers, which form a soft underlayer that further insulates the bird. Some birds also have specialized feathers called powder-down. These break down into a waxy powder that the bird spreads throughout its plumage during preening.

TYPES OF FEATHER *Most contour or body feathers (above left) are small, blunt and fluffy, whereas flight feathers (top and above) are larger, longer, stiffer, and more smoothly shaped.*

The total number of feathers on a bird varies widely, though it correlates, roughly, with body size. A typical hummingbird has about 1,000 feathers, whereas a swan has more than 20 times as many. Plumage represents a substantial proportion of a bird's total body weight. The frigatebird, for example, is outweighed by its own feathers. The feathers of a typical songbird are about one-third its body weight.

PLUMAGE FEATURES *Knowing the names of the different tracts of feathers will make identification simpler.*

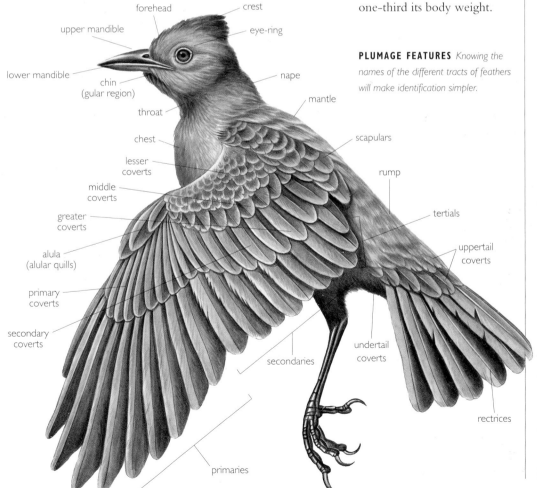

forehead
crest
upper mandible
eye-ring
lower mandible
chin (gular region)
nape
throat
mantle
chest
scapulars
lesser coverts
rump
middle coverts
greater coverts
tertials
alula (alular quills)
uppertail coverts
primary coverts
secondary coverts
undertail coverts
secondaries
rectrices
primaries

25

PLUMAGE CYCLES

As a bird matures, so its plumage changes. In addition, plumage varies from season to season in many species and will, at least once a year, be completely replaced in a process known as molt.

Despite preening and constant care, the marvelously intricate structure of the feather inevitably wears out. All adult birds molt their feathers at least once a year, and if you carefully study the birds you see around you, you will learn to recognize the frayed, ragged appearance of feathers that are nearing the end of their useful life.

Molting is one of the most intricate things a bird does in its annual life cycle. Two distinct processes are involved. The first step is when the old, worn feather is dropped, or shed. The second is when a new feather grows in its place. When each feather has been shed and replaced, then the molt can be said to be complete. This, however, is an abstraction that often does not happen: incomplete, overlapping, and arrested molts are quite common.

TIMING

Molt requires that a bird find and process enough protein to rebuild around one-third of its body weight, so it is not surprising that a bird in heavy molt often seems listless and unwell. But far from being random and ad hoc, molt is controlled by strong evolutionary forces that have established an optimum time and duration.

Generally, molt occurs at the time of least stress on the bird. Many songbirds, for instance, molt in late summer, when the hard work of breeding is done but the weather is still warm and food still plentiful. This is why the woods in late summer often seem so quiet, when compared with the exuberant choruses of spring.

INTRICACIES OF MOLT

Molt of the flight feathers is the most highly organized part of the process. Some species, for example, begin by dropping the outermost primary on each side (to retain balance in the air) and

wait until the replacement feathers are about one-third grown before shedding the next outermost, and so on. Others always start with the innermost primary and work outward. Yet other species begin in the middle and work outward on both sides. Most ducks shed all their wing feathers at once, and remain flightless for two or three weeks while the replacement feathers grow.

DURATION

Molt may be overlapped, extended, incomplete, or interrupted, so it is almost impossible to generalize about the time it takes. Furthermore, the process is strongly influenced by the season, and the age and general health of

THERMAL UNDERWEAR *A Pine Grosbeak fluffs up its contour plumage to keep out winter cold.*

YEAR-ROUND CAMOUFLAGE *In Willow Ptarmigan, molt changes the bird's appearance so that its camouflage is effective in winter (below) and throughout the rest of the year (left).*

the bird. On the whole, a songbird takes around three weeks to complete its molt.

IDENTIFICATION AND MOLT

A basic understanding of the molting process can be very useful in birding. As color and pattern are very strongly influenced by feather wear, and of course completely changed by molt, you may often find that the bird you are looking at through your binoculars looks quite different from its picture in your field guide.

This is often the case, for example, with migratory shorebirds. In a process known as arrested molt, they replace their flight feathers quickly after nesting, then put the rest of the molt on hold until they have completed their migration. As a result, they spend much of the year in a plumage that is neither "breeding" nor "non-breeding", but some-where in between.

PLUMAGE SEQUENCES

When a bird first hatches from the egg, it may be nearly naked, as in a typical song-bird, or covered in down, like a baby chicken or a duckling. In either case, development of the ability to fly is generally the point at which the young bird reaches independence.

The juvenile plumage of a bird is defined as the first plumage state in which true contour feathers are present, but for most practical purposes it can be viewed as the first set of feathers with which flight is possible. Any subsequent plumages (there may be several) between the juvenile plumage and full sexual maturity are referred to as immature plumages.

In most birds, first breeding marks the point at which an adult cycle of plumages

is attained, which will then continue throughout life. In many American birds, this involves a continuous cycle of two alternating plumages: winter and summer, or breeding and non-breeding.

Not all birds breed in summer, however, and some birds court and form pair bonds in their "breeding" plumage but molt out of it before they actually breed. These terms are therefore not always precise. Many specialists evade such difficulties by referring to the winter or non-breeding plumage as the "basic" plumage, and any other plumage states (such as breeding) as "first alternate", "second alternate", and so on.

DRESSED TO IMPRESS *In birds such as the Wood Duck, molt alternates a dull winter plumage with a bold breeding plumage (left).*

FLIGHT

The size and shape of a bird's wing can tell you a great deal about its lifestyle and feeding requirements.

I n the same way that air-craft are designed with different wing shapes according to their function, so evolution has ensured that the forms of birds' wings exactly suit their lifestyle.

In both birds and aircraft, lift, thrust, and maneuverability all depend on the form of the wing and tail, and these properties are related in such a manner that improvement in any one can generally be achieved only by some sacrifice of performance in the other two.

HUMMINGBIRDS *achieve the ultimate in avian maneuverability: they can fly in any direction without needing to turn in that direction first. All other birds, such as this Eastern Bluebird (above left), are limited to flying forwards.*

IN CONTROL *Just as a pilot uses flaps on the wings of an aircraft (top) to control its speed, so a bird employs certain wing feathers to do the same. Here, a gull uses its alulas to slow itself down during descent.*

EFFICIENCY AND FORM

The most significant feature in relation to flight is of course the wing shape. Generally, a long, narrow wing is more efficient than a short, blunt wing—for purely aerodynamic, non-biological reasons that are well under-stood by aircraft designers. So birds that spend much time in the air, such as swallows, swifts, and migratory shore-birds such as Golden-Plovers, have long, narrow wings that provide maximum efficiency.

But, for a bird, flapping long wings is harder work than flapping short ones.

Many ground-dwelling birds, such as quail and partridges, need flight for little more than escape from predators. What matters for these birds is rapid acceleration; efficiency is less significant because their flights are generally of short duration. The best possible configu-ration is therefore a short, blunt wing.

Tail shapes also have a bearing on flight perfor-mance and vary for similar reasons. A short tail is aerodynamically efficient but a long tail can improve maneuverability.

WATERFOWL *fly fast in a direct line, flapping their wings at a steady rate to maintain speed.*

VULTURES *use rising air currents to propel them in an upward spiral.*

WOODPECKERS *alternately flap their wings to gain speed and glide to conserve energy.*

MODES OF FLIGHT

This close relationship between lifestyle and wing and tail configuration is manifest in most birds.

Like fighter aircraft, falcons have narrow, backswept wings that provide a high level of performance in open skies. Some other raptors, such as accipiters, operate in more cluttered environments, such as woodlands, and rely heavily on surprise. They have broad wings and long tails, offering maximum agility and acceleration.

Large birds of prey, such as vultures and eagles, ride thermals all day to conserve energy. They therefore have little need to flap their wings, which consequently tend to be long and broad, providing maximum lift.

Hummingbirds, on the other hand, flap their wings at an incredible rate that requires a high expenditure of energy. Their wings have more in common with helicopter rotor blades than with conventional aircraft wings, and they share many of the same flight characteristics,

DREAMS OF FLIGHT *From the legend of Icarus (right) to Leonardo's designs for flying machines (below right) and more recent visions of "bird-men" (below left), the idea of flight has captured the imagination of humans through the centuries.*

especially in the sacrifice of speed and range in return for a significant gain in precision. Like helicopters, humming-birds can hover in midair, or fly backwards or forwards with almost equal ease.

O that I had wings like a dove, for then I would fly away and be at rest.

Psalms, 55: 6

LEONARDO AND THE DREAM OF FLIGHT

The quest for flight is one of humankind's oldest passions. From the fable of Daedalus and Icarus, through the tower jumpers of medieval times and the "bird-men" of later centuries, history is filled with accounts of people building wings and leaping from hillsides and towers, in the vain effort to fly like a bird.

Among the most noted of early bird-men was the Italian Renaissance artist and engineer, Leonardo da Vinci (1452–1519), whose theories and designs formed the basis and stimulant for actual flight, generations later.

The fundamental idea that Leonardo followed was that human flight could be achieved by studying and imitating bird flight. Based on this, he evolved a series of machines, with flapping wings, called ornithopters. "Write of swimming in the water and you will have the flight of the bird through the air" he wrote. His fecund imagination also generated the first designs for a parachute and a helicopter.

Leonardo's obsession with flight is reflected in his notebooks, which were filled with sketches of bird flight and flying machines. The most famous of these works, *Sul volo degli uccelli* (On the Flight of Birds), was published in Florence in 1505.

HABITATS *and* NICHES

The bird species that have survived the process of evolution are those that have most effectively exploited a niche within a specific habitat.

To a certain extent, we are all familiar with the concept of habitat in relation to birds. We normally associate ducks, for example, with wetland areas, and gulls with seashores. But a bird's habitat is more than just a place: it is a complex web of relationships between the bird species that occupy it, the vegetation, the climate, the food supply, and predators.

Birds are versatile animals and have come to occupy almost all habitats from frozen wastelands to deserts, and from swamps to dense forests.

ECOLOGICAL NICHES

Bird species have specialized to such an extent in order to survive that not only do they favor a particular habitat but also a specific slot, or ecological niche, within that habitat. This niche is often associated with the means of gathering food.

Let's take as an example a group of insect eaters that may be found together in American woodlands. Among them, Rufous-sided Towhees spend much time on the forest floor, where they search for prey in the leaf litter. In the understory, Carolina Wrens flit from shrub to shrub in search of insects. Brown Creepers climb tree trunks extracting insects from the bark, while Hairy Woodpeckers peck repeatedly at the trunks to get at wood-boring insects. From their perches under the canopy, Acadian Flycatchers dart out to seize flying insects. High in the canopy, Yellow-throated Warblers creep methodically along the branches in search of prey, while Chimney Swifts pursue flying insects in the air above.

All these birds occupy the same habitat and share the same basic diet (insects). They differ, however, in the equipment and the techniques they use to obtain their food. These differences define each bird's position—its niche—within its community.

HABITAT PREFERENCES *The subtle distinction between habitat and niche becomes most evident in highly specialized birds, such as the Roseate Spoonbill (above right) and the Brown Creeper (right). Both inhabit very different environments, and both exploit their habitats in very particular ways.*

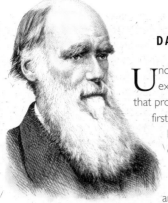

DARWIN'S FINCHES

Undoubtedly the most famous example of niche adaptation is that provided by a group of finches first discovered in the Galapagos Islands by Charles Darwin (left) during his voyage on the HMS Beagle in 1835.

All the finches on the islands are descended from one species—a seed-eating ground finch. Some of the finches have taken up typical seed-eating niches, but others have evolved in quite different ways to take advantage of the niches that were originally available to them in the absence of other land birds.

One species has developed a longer bill for feeding on cactus flowers and fruits as well as seeds. Other tree-dwelling finches have adapted to feeding on fruits, seeds, and insects. Another species—the Warbler Finch—has adopted the habits of a warbler and gleans insects from foliage.

The Woodpecker Finch, on the other hand, has learned to use a twig or cactus spine to dislodge insects from beneath bark or from cracks in rotten wood. Perhaps the most remarkable of all these finches, however, is the Sharp-billed Finch, which pecks at the bases of wing and tail feathers of molting seabirds and then drinks the oozing blood!

FOOD THAT FITS THE BILL

Bill shape often betrays diet more obviously than any other feature. If you guess from its bill shape that whatever the avocet (below, top) feeds on, it must be very small and agile, you would be right—it eats tiny shrimps living in shallow water. Similarly, finches (upper center) have deep, short conical bills for crushing the husks of seeds; eagles (lower center) have hooked bills that are ideal for tearing flesh; and herons (bottom) have bills that resemble spears in function as well as shape.

MORPHOLOGICAL ADAPTATIONS

Of all the characteristics that relate to a bird's niche and how it obtains its food, the most obvious are the sizes and shapes of the bill and feet. Indeed, the shape of a bird's bill and feet can tell you a good deal about what and how it eats.

Returning to the insect-eating birds of our American woodlands, we can link physical characteristics to foraging strategies. The Rufous-sided Towhee has large, strong feet, ideal for kicking leaves aside to reveal insects. The fine, pointed bill of the Carolina Wren is suited to gleaning insects from underbrush foliage.

Both the Brown Creeper and the Hairy Woodpecker have short legs with long claws adapted for grasping the surface of tree trunks, and stiffened tail feathers that serve as props, but their bills reflect different ways of capturing their prey. The straight, stout bill of the woodpecker is used for hammering the trunk to remove bark, whereas the fine, downward-curving bill of the creeper serves to probe beneath the bark or into fissures.

Long, pointed wings enable the Chimney Swift to stay aloft most of the day, and its short, triangular bill with a broad gape is ideal for capturing and swallowing flying insects.

In the introduction to each habitat in the Habitat Bird-finder section of this book (p. 84), you will find further illustrations of the way birds interrelate with their environment.

LIFE CYCLE

Once it reaches adulthood, a bird follows

an annual cycle of events for the rest of its life.

After fledging and leaving its parent's territory, a typical young bird begins a nomadic period that may last several years. If the bird is a male, he probably will not be able to establish a territory (and therefore breed) for some time because most suitable territories will already be occupied by resident males that he has little chance of ousting. He therefore can only slip inconspicuously from one territory to another, always risking hostility from the occupier.

Mortality is generally high during this period. But if the bird can survive long enough, sooner or later he may stumble upon a territory that has been recently vacated by its occupier. He can then establish the territory as his own, attract a mate, and begin his own breeding cycle.

THE ANNUAL CYCLE OF THE YELLOW WARBLER
The chart on these pages shows the annual cycle of a Yellow Warbler (see also p. 144) that winters in Costa Rica and breeds in the northeastern United States. This chart is obviously a generalization, even for this species, but it is fairly typical of most North American songbirds. Further information on each phase of this cycle is provided elsewhere in this chapter.

LEAVE COSTA RICA
Warblers migrate by night, covering around 120 miles (200 km) each day.

APR

MAR

FEB

JAN

ARRIVE AT BREEDING GROUND
Timing is critical during spring migration. Fish-eating birds, for example, cannot arrive until lakes and rivers are clear of ice.

DEPART BREEDING GROUND
Timing is less significant in fall than in spring. In fall, departure and travel therefore tend to be spread over a broader time frame.

SEPT

MOLT *This may last up to two weeks. It precedes migration in most landbirds, but in many other birds may be delayed until after migration.*

AUG

JULY

JUNE

ESCORT YOUNG, YOUNG DEPART
Having left the nest, juveniles remain with the adults for only a few days before dispersing (right).

SING, ATTRACT MATE *Small songbirds often begin breeding in their first spring, but larger birds often take longer to reach sexual maturity: some albatrosses, for example, may not breed until their seventh year. Small migratory songbirds form their pair bonds on arrival at their breeding grounds, but many larger birds, such as wildfowl, mate at their wintering grounds then migrate north together.*

BUILD NEST *The forms of nests seem to have a bearing on mortality rates. Song Sparrows, for example, build open nests, and successfully raise to fledging only about 41% of total eggs laid, whereas cavity-nesting birds like the House Wren may raise about 79%.*

FEED YOUNG *Typically, this is when male birds get more involved in the process, foraging and supplying food to the hungry young (below).*

MAY

LAY EGGS, INCUBATE EGGS *Among most birds, average breeding success (that is, the number of young raised to independence against the number of eggs laid) tends to rise slightly after the first year or two, showing that learning and experience often play a part in the nesting cycle.*

JUNE

NOV DEC

RETURN TO COSTA RICA *Losses during migration are frequently very heavy, particularly among young birds and during water-crossings. However, average life expectancy tends to stabilize after the first successful crossing.*

THE TIMING *of the above events will vary among Yellow Warblers according to where in North America the birds breed and how long they spend there. The duration of each phase, however, is relatively consistent. For example, the following timescales will hold true for most Yellow Warblers:*

Nest construction	4–5 days
Egg laying *(clutch size: 3–6 eggs)*	5–7 days
Incubation	11 days
Fledging *(from hatching to departure of young)*	9–12 days

Photographs, clockwise from the top of page 32: female Yellow Warbler incubating eggs; juvenile bird shortly after leaving nest; collecting nest-building materials; male Yellow Warbler bathing.

LIFE EXPECTANCY *As mortality is high in the first months (75% in some cases), figures for average life expectancy are low. As indicated below, larger birds tend to live longer.*

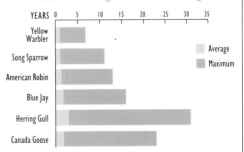

YEARS 0 5 10 15 20 25 30 35

Yellow Warbler
Song Sparrow
American Robin
Blue Jay
Herring Gull
Canada Goose

Average
Maximum

DISPLAYS

Like humans, and unlike most other animals, birds respond strongly to visual signs. Much of their communication therefore involves displays, and these convey a wide range of messages.

COURTSHIP DISPLAYS *Displays in sexual contexts often involve plumage features. One of the most remarkable of these features is the male peacock's tail, portrayed here in a Roman mosaic from Ravenna in Italy.*

In the course of evolution, certain actions by birds have come to have a communicative function. Song, of course, is one such action but most other communication between birds is visual and often involves plumage displays.

PLUMAGE AS DISPLAY

Plumage patterns and colors are among birds' most appealing features, and we rely strongly on them for field identification. Among the birds themselves, plumage plays a significant role in communication. When Dark-eyed Juncos fly up, for example, they flash their white outer tail feathers. This says "follow me" to other birds in the flock.

A wide variety of birds have developed plumage colors and patterns that send messages at

certain times of the year. The most common manifestation of this is the colorful breeding plumage that many acquire each spring, often extending to elaborate features that may be used in specific displays. Such features take a variety of forms and usually occur on the most visible parts of the body, especially the head, neck and breast, upper wings, or tail. For example, they may be specialized feathers. Male egrets develop elaborate and colorful plumes, and male hummingbirds have iridescent gorgets and crowns that change color as they move. Possibly the most spectacular feather display of all is the fanning of raised upper tail-coverts by a male peacock.

In some cases the combination of color and pattern is particularly important. The male Wood Duck, for example, has glossy, brightly colored plumage with a sleek

TERRITORIAL DISPLAYS *A Red-winged Blackbird uses song to announce its territory. In many other birds, displays may be visual rather than vocal or they may use a combination of both.*

crest or hood. This crest can be depressed tightly against its neck and spread to one side to accentuate its appearance.

More bizarre features have evolved, purely for display, in other species. For example, the neck feathers of some grouse and prairie-chickens can be erected during courtship to reveal large, inflated air sacs with brightly colored skin.

DISPLAY BEHAVIOR

Displays are not confined to the appearance of the bird. While they may be given in conjunction with plumage displays, they can also take other forms.

The male Peacock performs as he fans his extraordinary tail. Breeding egrets posture to show themselves to best effect. If you watch male Wood Ducks in the breeding season, you may note that they always parade past the female in the same posture and at the same angle, showing only their best side!

Sometimes the behavioral component in the display dominates. Displays by raptors, for example, are almost entirely behavioral, and usually involve some kind of demonstration of aerial agility or power.

A number of other birds also give display flights, including hummingbirds,

SEXUAL DISPLAYS *In the breeding season, male Sage Grouse (top) indulge in elaborate displays that are essentially one-way. Other displays may be mutual, male and female performing them together. Examples include the "rushing" displays of Western Grebes (above), the "greeting" ceremony of Northern Gannets (right), and the dancing displays of Sandhill Cranes (above right).*

woodcock, snipe, and larks. These flights are often accompanied by singing.

THE FUNCTIONS OF DISPLAY

Most displays, particularly the more elaborate ones, are sexual—they are designed to attract potential mates—and the male bird generally takes the initiative. Males therefore have more colorful plumage and perform most of the display routines (though there are exceptions).

There are various other types of display, such as actions of greeting, threat, and submission, and some birds, such as the Killdeer, use displays to distract predators.

35

SONGS *and* CALLS

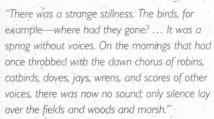

Down through the ages, humankind has delighted in the charm of birdsong, but only recently have we acquired the technology to find out what these songs and calls signify.

The joyous sound of birdsong is not only a source of pleasure and inspiration, it is also a valuable aid to field identification, and many birders rely on songs and calls to name more reclusive species in the field.

HOW BIRDS SING
In birds, as opposed to mammals, the larynx lacks vocal cords. Instead, vocalization is produced by the syrinx, a specialized organ found only in birds that is situated at the base of the windpipe or trachea. The syrinx is remarkably sophisticated, having two chambers which the bird can use simultaneously to produce extremely complex sounds.

CALLS
Vocalizations are commonly divided into calls and songs. These terms are useful, but they are difficult to define precisely. Generally, songs are used in sexual contexts and calls are used for all other types of vocal communication.

There are calls covering most aspects of social behavior, including threat, alarm, flight, begging, and so on, and some species have calls that have specialized functions. Cave-dwelling swifts, for example, emit a series of echolocating clicks when flying in the dark.

Although calls are relatively short and simple, there is evidence that they transmit information about the identity of the calling bird.

SONGS
Generally, the male does the singing (but there are exceptions) and the songs function as either territorial announcements or as sexual attractants.

Although each species has a distinctive song, some birds incorporate mimicry of other species in their repertoires. Sometimes a song includes contributions from two individuals, usually a mated pair. This is known as duetting and, at times, the co-ordination between the two singers is remarkable.

Experiments show that while some birds are born with their songs, others learn them from their parents. As with human languages, local dialects occur, with certain characteristics of songs in one population differing from those in other populations. Some first-year males sing a

RACHEL CARSON

"There was a strange stillness. The birds, for example—where had they gone? … It was a spring without voices. On the mornings that had once throbbed with the dawn chorus of robins, catbirds, doves, jays, wrens, and scores of other voices, there was now no sound; only silence lay over the fields and woods and marsh."

So wrote Rachel Carson (1907–64) in her historic book *Silent Spring*, published in 1962, which alerted the public to the disastrous consequences of the uncontrolled use of chemical pesticides.

A lifelong birder, Carson conjured images of a countryside without birdsong—a frightening picture of nature in deathly silence. Even people who generally pay little attention to conservation issues are concerned at the thought of losing the concertos and symphonies of nature that emanate from gardens and parklands as winter gives way to spring.

In her warnings, Rachel Carson confirmed birdsong as a precious part of our natural world.

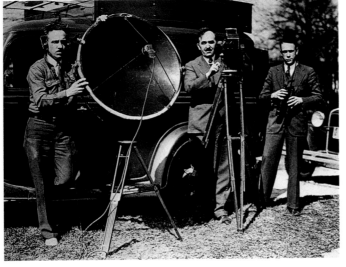

SOUNDING OUT THE BIRDS *Most bird sounds are vocal, as in the songs of the Yellow-headed Blackbird (above) and the Eastern Meadowlark (far left). Exceptions include the Ruffed Grouse (top), which uses wingbeats to produce a sound like distant thunder. Scientific study of bird sounds was made possible by the work of Dr Arthur Allen (left, in the center) and his associates. Today a common research tool is the sonogram (inset, above left). This one portrays the call of a Common Loon.*

little differently from adult birds, and different songs may be sung as the breeding season progresses.

Overall, the complexity of vocalizations varies widely. There are, however, a few birds, such as the stork, that never vocalize at all.

OTHER BIRD SOUNDS

Sounds other than songs and calls are also created by birds in a number of ways.

Some species produce loud, distinctive sounds by diving at high speed so that air passes rapidly through stiffened or modified wing and tail feathers. Others, including most grouse and prairie-chickens, use air sacs on the neck to produce loud booming sounds.

SCIENTIFIC STUDY

Only relatively recently have we been able to study bird vocalization scientifically.

The first ever recording of a bird was made by Ludwig Koch in Germany in 1889, and Sylvester Judd, a biologist, was the first person to achieve this in America, in 1898. But it was not until 1932 that scientists at Cornell University, led by Arthur Allen, perfected the techniques and equipment required to successfully record birdsong in the field.

This pioneering work allowed scientists and students of ornithology to study and compare the songs of different species. The subsequent evolution of technology has enabled ornithologists to not

only record bird songs and calls but also modify them electronically and play them back to birds in order to study how they react. Scientists are also able to reproduce bird sounds in graphic form as sonograms: charts that plot frequency, or "pitch", (vertical scale) against time (horizontal scale).

Among the artistic hierarchy, birds are probably the greatest musicians to inhabit our planet.

OLIVIER MESSIAEN (1908–92), French composer. Messiaen's music was strongly influenced by birdsong.

TERRITORY *and* PAIR FORMATION

Whether it be a large tract of land or a few inches of a branch for roosting, the quality of a bird's territory plays a crucial role in its breeding success.

For a bird, a desirable territory is an area that provides all that it requires in the way of food, shelter, and a nesting site, either for its general survival or for breeding. All territories are defended, usually against other birds of the same species, but also—particularly where there is a valuable food resource or nesting site at stake—against other species.

TYPES OF TERRITORIES

Those territories that provide all the necessary resources will be occupied by a pair of birds throughout the breeding season, or even throughout their entire lives. Other territories may be used for particular purposes, notably roosting and feeding.

Most territories are well-defined areas, with only minor boundary changes taking place from time to time, but birds may also defend additional territories—a foraging resource such as a berry bush, for example—that are outside their main territory.

Colonial nesters, such as seabirds, herons, egrets, and swallows, nest close to each other, and each pair will defend the immediate surrounds of the nest out to a distance at which pecking contact can be made with neighbors. Food may be gathered at a shared foraging site, such as in the sea or at a nearby swamp, or pairs may occupy and defend separate feeding territories.

Sizes of feeding territories usually depend upon the amount of food available. Nectar feeders, for example, require a certain number of flowers to produce sufficient nectar to meet the energy

SOUL MATES *The souls of the Pharoah Ani and his wife depicted as birds (left), from The Theban Book of the Dead, c. 1250 BC.*

requirements of each bird or pair of birds, and that number of flowers may be scattered over a wide area or found on a single bush.

TERRITORIES AND COURTSHIP

A variety of resources, the most obvious one being food, attracts females to territories held by males for breeding or specifically for courtship and mating. If a resource is scarce or unevenly distributed, then males with better-quality territories are likely to attract a greater number of females. For example, male humming-birds that defend the best

THE TERRITORY OF A SONGBIRD

nest site

* Saplings for roosting
* Tall trees for song perches
* Trees for foraging
* Brush for nest-building materials

BIRD TERRITORIES *may encompass only a single resource, such as the individual nest sites in this colony of gannets (right), or all the resources needed to sustain a breeding attempt, as in this diagram of a typical songbird territory (left). The highlighted area in the diagram indicates the extent of the territory, and the key indicates the uses of the resources within the territory.*

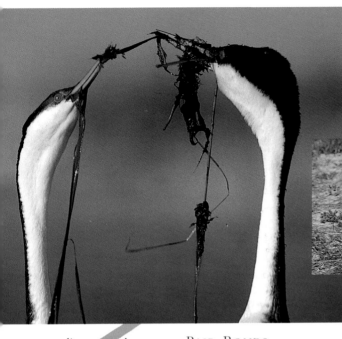

COURTSHIP *sometimes involves the transfer of a "gift" from one partner to the other, as in the "weed-swapping" display of Western Grebes (left) and the courtship feeding of Arctic Terns (below).*

nectar supplies attract the most females. Female Lark Buntings are more attracted to territories with shaded nest sites, for prolonged exposure to the sun often results in the death of nestlings.

Other types of territories play a part in courtship. For example, males of polygynous species (such as Sage Grouse) congregate at communal display areas, known as leks, where they compete for patches of ground. Males that win control of central territories are the ones that attract the most females.

FORMING A BOND

Generally, when a female first appears in a male's territory she is greeted as an intruder, but in response to submissive behavior on her part the male stops being aggressive and begins courting her. This may involve intricate social ceremonies. Courtship feeding, for example, is widespread. Not only is this a means of winning the female, but it also reflects her need for a high level of nutrition to support her through the demanding process of breeding and incubation.

PAIR BONDS

Some birds bond for life; some form new partnerships each breeding season; and some do not form pairs at all, the male mating with a number of females and taking no part in the rearing of the young.

Most songbirds form a pair bond for breeding, and the relationship may be resumed in subsequent breeding seasons. However, this may have more to do with convenience—the birds tend to return to the same area after migration and are thus likely to find the same partner again—than with any strong bond with a particular mate.

MARGARET MORSE NICE

One of the most influential studies of territorial birds was carried out in the 1930s by the renowned ornithologist Margaret Morse Nice (1883–1974). For eight years she observed a population of Song Sparrows living in an area at the back of her home near Columbus, Ohio. With painstaking attention to detail, she charted 39 acres (16 hectares), producing maps showing the location and movements of each bird.

Each spring, new maps had to be made almost every day to keep track of new arrivals. The resident sparrows were all trapped, weighed, and fitted with legbands for identification. Like many skilled birders, Nice was also able to recognize each individual bird by its song. One male bird was observed for over seven years as he established and defended his territory, attracted a mate, and reared successive broods.

Nice's pioneering work is widely regarded as one of the most significant contributions to our understanding of bird populations and their territories.

NESTS *and* EGGS

Most birds create a nest of one kind or another in preparation for the physically demanding process of egg-laying, incubation, and raising a brood.

As soon as a breeding pair has formed, work will begin on building a nest. This will serve as a cradle for the eggs and a temporary home for the developing chicks. Selection of the nest site and building the nest may be undertaken by the female alone or in co-operation with her mate.

Most nests are built for a single attempt at breeding. A few birds use nests at other times of the year for sleeping or shelter, but these dormitory nests are rarely used for raising young.

DIVERSITY OF NESTS

We usually think of nests as being constructed from twigs, leaves, and grass stems placed in a tree or bush. However, birds use an extraordinary

CRADLES FOR THE YOUNG *Nest materials and structures vary widely, from virtually none, as with this Black Skimmer nest (below right), to the intricate cobweb structures of humming-birds (above), and the mud-brick homes of certain swallows (below).*

range of techniques to create a wide variety of structures.

Some species, such as Ospreys and Bald Eagles, reuse their nests, each year adding new material to their platforms of sticks so that the structures grow larger and larger. Other birds reuse the nests of other species. Great Horned Owls, for example, often use old hawk nests, and many cavity-nesting birds use abandoned woodpecker holes.

EGG-LAYING AND EGGS

The batch of eggs laid in a single breeding attempt is known as a clutch and may take up to a week to lay. A complete clutch may comprise only a single egg, as in some seabirds and vultures, or up to a dozen or more in the case of quail, pheasants, and waterfowl. Some species will relay if their first nesting attempt fails, even if they normally produce only one clutch a season.

Many birds, especially the smaller songbirds, habitually lay two or more clutches a season, and these renestings can sometimes be so rapid that the male will still be feeding young from the first nesting while his mate is laying eggs in a second nest.

EGG COLOR

Most brightly colored eggs are laid where their owners can recognize them by daylight.

Where their brightness would stand out from the surround-ings, the eggs tend to be laid in deep nests or ones well hidden by foliage. Eggs laid in

A NEW LIFE *Using the tip of its bill to first puncture the tough inner membrane and smash a small opening in the hard outer shell, a baby bird struggles to free itself. This hatching process may last up to a day.*

open nests, particularly on or near the ground, are usually colored and patterned so that they blend in with their immediate surroundings. Eggs that are laid in hollows or burrows are generally white or near-white.

INCUBATION

In the breeding season, most female birds (and some males that share incubation) have brood patches. These bare patches of skin on the belly permit a more efficient transfer of heat from the bird's body to the eggs.

Incubation is hard work, and the incubating bird may have to double its thermal output. The period of incubation varies from a couple of weeks in smaller birds to over eight weeks in gannets, vultures, and eagles.

CARE OF THE YOUNG

The term altricial is used to describe chicks that are born blind and helpless. Chicks that hatch with their eyes open, are covered with down feathers, and are capable of leaving the nest shortly after emerging from the eggs are described as precocial. (Some chicks, however, have both altricial and precocial characteristics.)

During their development in the nest, altricial chicks are fed and cared for by the parents. This nestling period will last from an average of eight to twelve days for some small songbirds to more than a month for large woodpeckers and about five months for the California Condor.

Precocial chicks vary in their level of dependence on the parents. Some remain in the nest for a few days after hatching. After leaving the

KONRAD LORENZ AND IMPRINTING

For centuries, people have adopted ducklings, goslings, and other types of domesticated fowl as pets, giving little thought as to why the birds accepted them as foster parents. Only in 1935 was the process fully explained by the Viennese zoologist and ethologist, Konrad Lorenz (1903–89).

Lorenz had been interested in this question since childhood when he had adopted goslings as pets and found that he could get them to follow him as if he were their mother. In later experiments he was able to establish that there is a critical period immediately after the chick has hatched from the egg during which the first image that it sees will be imprinted in its mind and henceforth regarded as its parent.

Lorenz's work on this and other aspects of bird behavior provided ornithologists with a remarkable insight into the socialization of birds. He was awarded the Nobel Prize for physiology in 1973.

CHICK TYPES *Two broad groups can be distinguished among newly hatched birds. Altricial chicks (below) are naked, blind, and helpless. Precocial chicks (left) are alert, mobile, and covered in fluffy down.*

nest, chicks of certain species (grebe and rail, for example) are fed by the parents, whereas others, such as young gamebirds, are merely shown food by the parents. Other newly hatched birds may follow their parents, but find their own food, as do ducklings and young waders.

BROOD PARASITES

Some species have developed techniques to bypass the tasks of incubating and caring for their offspring. The most widespread are the brood parasites, which lay their eggs in the nests of other birds, leaving these eggs to be hatched and the chicks to be reared by the unwitting foster parents. In America, cowbirds are the best known brood parasites.

MIGRATION

In North America the flux of bird migration is greater than anywhere else, and the arrivals and departures of birds are major signs of seasonal change.

S ome sedentary birds remain in the same geographical area throughout their lives. However, nearly half the world's birds divide their year between two main localities and undertake annual migrations.

Most migrations result from seasonal fluctuations in the availability of a particular food. In temperate countries, there tends to be more food around in summer and fall than in winter and spring. Winter weather causes a reduction in the amount of food available and shorter days mean there is less time to gather it.

This situation is pro-nounced at higher latitudes in North America, where the availability of food de-clines dramatically in winter, particularly in deciduous forest. The only insect eaters that can remain in such areas are a few wood-peckers and nuthatches that are able to extract prey from the trunks of leafless trees.

While most birds travel alone, some migrate in flocks of one or more species. The benefits of traveling in flocks include greater protection against predation (particularly for daytime travelers), and, for younger migrants, in some cases at least (geese and cranes, for example), being guided by more experienced birds.

Some migrants travel by day, while many others journey by night. Typical day migrants include most waterfowl, the Chimney Swift, the Barn Swallow, and the American Robin. Night migrants include almost all warblers, vireos, grosbeaks, and buntings; many fly-catchers; and most sparrows.

ON THE WING *Many birds, such as cranes (top), travel mainly overland, but some of the most dramatic migrations involve ocean crossings by birds, such as shorebirds (above), that cannot land on water and must therefore complete their journey in a single flight. Migration studies have been greatly aided by the use of radar (top left), which can be used to track flocks of migrating birds.*

THE MYSTERY OF MIGRATION

For centuries, the annual disappearance of bird species perplexed humankind. Many primitive peoples considered the departure and return of birds to be a divine manifestation and there are many myths associated with migratory birds. Aristotle and his contemporaries proposed scientific theories to explain the disappearance of some species, suggesting, for example, that swallows (right) overwintered in burrows in the ground. Not surprisingly, many people believed that the birds that disappeared went into hibernation. As late as the sixteenth century, there was a theory that swallows formed tight balls under the surfaces of ponds, where they passed the winter.

MIGRATION ROUTES *Migrating birds traverse almost every part of North America. However, the flow (particularly of waterfowl) is heaviest along four main corridors: the Pacific, Mississippi, Central, and Atlantic flyways (below). At their northern end, these flyways overlap considerably.*

A B C D

A	Pacific
B	Central
C	Mississippi
D	Atlantic

NAVIGATION

Migratory birds are natural navigators with remarkable homing capabilities. In June 1952, a Manx Shearwater was taken from its burrow on Skokholm Island, off the coast of Wales, tagged with a leg band, and taken across the Atlantic to Boston. Here it was released, some 3,100 miles (5,000 km) from home. It was found safe in its burrow on Skokholm Island 12½ days later.

It is thought that most birds navigate by sight, using the sun to guide them during the day and the stars to lead them at night. Birds also have a built-in "chronometer", or innate time sense, that tells them when it is time to depart, how long the journey will take, and so on. But while these senses and abilities are present from birth, migrants also learn from experience, becoming familiar with territories and flyways.

Is it by thy wisdom that the hawk soareth and stretcheth her wings towards the south?

Book of Job, 39: 26

They also learn to follow certain air and sea currents, to use changes in temperature as guides, and to watch the passage flights of other birds.

STRATEGIES

Migration strategies vary widely. Most songbirds, for example, break their journey into short hops of 200 miles (320 km) or so and they may delay their journey in the event of severe or overcast weather. Large groups of birds often find themselves waiting together in one place for weather more conducive to traveling. Consequently, songbirds often migrate in waves, and the arrival of such a wave can be an incredible sight.

Other birds undertake epic nonstop journeys. The greatest globetrotter in terms of distance covered each year is the Arctic Tern. Terns that breed in Arctic and North Atlantic regions overwinter on the edge of Antarctica at the opposite side of the globe. From North America, the Barn Swallow makes annual journeys of up to 7,000 miles (11,300 km). The American Golden-Plover also makes nonstop transoceanic flights of thousands of miles from the

Atlantic coast of Canada to northeastern South America. This amazing journey is also made by one small landbird, the Blackpoll Warbler.

IRRUPTIONS

Not all movements of birds involve migration. Non-seasonal movements, mainly brought about by regular or irregular changes in food supplies, can result in a species appearing in areas well outside its normal range. Such movements are known as irruptions.

The Snowy Owl, for example, visits the United States from the American Arctic only when there is a drastic decline in the number of lemmings, its chief prey.

I sat in my sunny doorway from sunrise till noon, rapt in revery, amidst the pines and hickories and sumachs, in undisturbed solitude, while birds sang around or flitted noiselessly through the house.

Walden, HENRY DAVID THOREAU (1817–62),
American writer and naturalist

CHAPTER TWO
BIRDING *at* HOME

BACKYARD BIRDING

Whether you live in a downtown apartment with a shared backyard or a country cottage with an extensive garden, birding can begin at home.

Through the centuries, people have delighted in observing the activities of the birds frequenting the land around their homes. Their beauty has always been a source of joy and wonder, and at times a consolation.

Providing food, water, and nesting sites for birds in your yard will significantly increase opportunities for observing them. It will also help many species that in recent years have struggled to find suitable nesting and foraging habitats.

Once they have discovered your yard, many birds will keep coming back. Resident species, such as Song Sparrows and House Finches, may build their whole life cycle around a particular feeder station. Some migratory birds too, such as White-crowned Sparrows and Purple Finches, will return to spend winter in the same yard year after year.

FAST FOOD *Carefully presented food will attract many birds, especially in winter when smaller species often find it difficult to gather enough food by day to see them through the long nights.*

HENRY DAVID THOREAU

Some of the most interesting accounts of backyard birding can be found in *Walden or Life in the Woods*, written by the nineteenth-century essayist and philosopher, Henry David Thoreau. This series of 18 essays explores the relationship between humans and nature and features numerous, detailed notes on the activities of the birds found in and around Thoreau's wooded garden.

Rejecting the constraints and conformity of a commercial society, in 1845 Thoreau retreated to the woods to conduct an experiment in basic living. For two years, he lived in a cabin, which he had built on the shores of Walden Pond near Concord in Massachusetts. Here he spent many hours contemplating the wonders of nature. With little human contact during these years, the woodland birds became his constant companions and he devoted much of his writing to observations of their behavior.

In birds, he discovered kindred spirits, and he marveled at the simplicity and freedom of their lives. The experience at Walden gave rise to a lifelong fascination with birds and ultimately shaped Thoreau's philosophy on nature.

SETTING UP A FEEDER STATION

Birds have a number of basic requirements. They need food, water, protection from predators, and somewhere to nest. All these needs can be catered for in an average garden, even in urban areas.

For your feeder station to be as effective as possible it's important that you choose appropriate foods, present them in the right way, and make sure your visitors are well protected.

To further assist local birds and increase opportunities for observing bird behavior, you may also decide to put up a

BIRD GARDENS *Since antiquity, birds have been seen as a necessary adjunct to any fine garden, as shown in this mural from Pompeii.*

nestbox or two. And, if you have the space, cultivating trees and other plants will help turn your yard into a veritable wildlife refuge.

There is sufficient guidance in the following pages to get you started with backyard birding, but always try to learn from the birds themselves. Each area of the country has its own species, every species has different requirements, and individual birds will act in different ways. Creating the perfect environment for local birds will involve trial and error. Don't become discouraged. The rewards for both bird and birder are great.

OBSERVING BIRDS IN THE YARD

Backyard birding can provide you with a rich insight into the life cycle of birds.

PROJECT FEEDERWATCH

One way of putting your backyard birding experience to good use is to become involved in Project FeederWatch. This is run by the Laboratory of Ornithology at Cornell University. From November to March, participants all over North America record the species that visit their feeders each week.

This information is then collated at Cornell and provides scientists with a measure of the fluctuations in species populations around North America.

To participate, write to the address given for Cornell on page 278.

Birds generally follow a regular routine. They do the same things—feeding, preening, bathing—at the same time, and for the same length of time, each day. Even if you only attract a few common species, being able to watch them at different times of the day, for as long as you want is a great way to learn more about them.

Watching birds in the yard will also help you hone your identification skills. In the field, most songbirds move

quickly and keep their distance from humans. Difficult to see, they are even harder to name. Feeders and nestboxes bring the birds to the observer, and if the birds feel well protected, they will become confident enough to spend long periods close to buildings and people. This makes it far easier for you to identify them and learn more about them by consulting field guides like our Habitat Birdfinder (p. 84).

BIRD FOOD BASICS

*Knowing something about the eating habits
of birds in the wild will help you choose the right foods for the species
you wish to attract to your yard.*

In its natural habitat, each bird occupies a niche in the food chain based on the type of food it eats and the way it obtains this food.

Among seed eaters, sparrows, towhees, and juncos normally feed on the ground, scavenging seeds that have fallen or been blown there. House and Purple Finches, goldfinches, siskins, and Black-headed and Rose-breasted Grosbeaks harvest seeds from docks and thistles, and catkins from birch and alder trees. Crossbills and Evening Grosbeaks work seeds from pine, fir, and spruce cones.

The natural forage for warblers, vireos, titmice, chickadees, creepers, kinglets, wrens, and most woodpeckers is insects and spiders and their eggs. Thrushes like robins, waxwings, bluebirds, and solitaires are fruit eaters that depend on the fruit of native plants like elderberry, raspberry, madrone, and toyon, though all of these species also eat flying and terrestrial insects and even mollusks and slugs. Hummingbirds also eat insects but feed mainly on nectar from flowers.

Birds will be attracted to feeding stations because they offer food in concentrated doses and require little expenditure of energy. To attract a range of species, you need to supply a range of the above foods, or their nearest equivalents.

BLACK-OIL SUNFLOWER SEEDS
Expensive, but highly nutritious and popular with most birds—the best all-round seed

I value my garden more for being full of blackbirds than of cherries, and very frankly give them fruit for their songs.

JOSEPH ADDISON (1672–1719), English writer

HULLED SUNFLOWER SEEDS *Enjoyed by most seed eaters and some insectivores, such as chickadees*

HIDDEN DANGERS

Be wary of the dangers lurking in some foods you may think suitable for birds.

What may be considered low-level pesticides by farmers using them on human food can turn out to be poisonous for small wildlife. All seeds and fruit left out for birds should thus be purchased from suppliers of pesticide-free produce.

Sticky stuff like peanut butter can be a danger as it clogs the nostrils of messy eaters like chickadees and Yellow-rumped Warblers. Serve this and other butters sparingly, or mix them into suet cakes (see p. 49).

STRIPED SUNFLOWER SEEDS *The next best thing to the more costly black-oil sunflower seeds*

Kitchen scraps will attract birds, but it is questionable as to whether these are good for them, and scraps give you little control over which species you attract. It is better to select foods that correspond to birds' natural preferences. That means seeds for seed eaters; suet for insect eaters; fruit for fruit eaters; and sugar water for hummingbirds.

The foods illustrated here are among the most effective and widely available.

SHELLED PEANUTS
Favored by jays, titmice, and some woodpeckers

THISTLE SEED *The best way to attract goldfinches and siskins*

WHITE PROSO MILLET
A favorite with finches and sparrows

FRUIT *Treats for fruit eaters include raspberries, grapes, and bananas, and dried fruit such as raisins.*

MILO (SORGHUM) *Commercial seed mixes with a strong orange color probably have too high a level of milo. Such mixes are unpalatable to most birds and should therefore be avoided.*

SUET *Ideal food for chickadees, nuthatches, and woodpeckers. Ready-made suet cakes that fit suet feeders are available. Suet is primarily a cold-weather food. In warm weather, it can melt and transfer to a bird's feathers, causing loss of insulation and flight form, and possibly loss of feathers.*

SCRATCH
racked corn is inexpensive and will be by most sparrows. Quail and doves love it.

MAKING SUET CAKES

There are a number of advantages in making your own suet cakes. First of all, it's a fun activity that even the children can become involved in (under close supervision of course!). Secondly, it means you can control exactly what is going into your "cakes" and add extra ingredients to increase the variety of birds that will feed on them. And finally, making your own cakes adds a personal touch to what you offer your feathered friends.

Rendering suet can be done on a stovetop or in a microwave. Suet is available in large chunks from butchers and supermarkets. Usually it is free but some outlets may charge a small fee.

Cut the suet block into one-inch (2.5-cm) squares (or ask the butcher to do it) and heat, stirring occasionally, until it has melted. Drain off the liquid into a container. Discard any crispy chunks or leave them out in your garden for nocturnal mammals. Repeat the process until you have 2 quarts (2.5 l) of liquid.

Then stir in a pound (500 g) of chunky peanut butter and a couple of cups of corn meal or flour. These dry materials will help keep your suet cakes from melting in the sun or during a hot spell. Also add some raisins or other dried fruit. It is better not to add seeds as these will entice jays and sparrows, which will crowd out the insectivores that the suet is intended for.

You can use the warm suet mixture for log or cone feeders (see p. 51). Otherwise spoon the mixture into pie tins (½–¾" [1–2 cm] deep) and refrigerate. When firm, cut it into chunks that will fit your suet holder, serve some immediately, and freeze the rest for future use.

BIRDFEEDERS

*Most birds will come to a handful of food thrown
onto the ground, but birdfeeders offer the birds protection and comfort,
and give the birder a clearer view of the bird.*

Birdfeeders offer a number of advantages over ground feeding. They let you choose where you view the birds, and at the same time keep your yard tidier by holding all the food in one place. They also allow you some degree of control over which species you attract. You can use a variety of foods and feeders if you want to draw in as many birds as possible, or you can select from a wide range of specialized feeders in order to target individual species.

Some species—many sparrows, for example—like to feed on the ground, but most prefer feeders because they simulate their natural foraging conditions. For finches, tube feeders are just like the stalks of thistle they feed on. To hummingbirds, a well-maintained feeder is a wonderful, perpetual flower. Other birds find feeders attractive because they allow them to feed at a safe distance from predators (see p. 52).

The following types of feeders are the best known and most effective. Each is available in a variety of styles.

Platform feeders These simple wooden platforms with raised sides are suitable for all types of food, will hold large quantities, and are easy to clean. A canopy to keep the seeds dry and shelter the birds, and a mesh base to allow water to drain away are desirable features. Platforms are good for attracting feeding flocks and larger birds.

Hopper feeders These can be hung up or mounted on a pole. Look for models with even-flow seed distributors that ration seeds—thus avoiding the need for frequent refilling—and a canopy.

Tube feeders The best of these have dividers below each portal so that only one section at a time is emptied and you can fill each compartment with a different type of seed.

Tube feeders are usually hung but can also be pole-mounted. Often they feature a tray under the bottom portal to catch any seeds that are spilled.

Some tube feeders are made specifically to hold thistle seeds.

Bowl feeders These normally consist of a clear plastic bowl and an adjustable dome that will keep out larger, more aggressive birds and squirrels. They are easy to clean and hold a considerable amount of seeds. Most have perches for small birds.

Tube

PLATFORM FEEDERS *hold large quantities of food and will accommodate larger birds such as jays and doves. They also allow whole flocks, like these Evening Grosbeaks, to feed together in one place.*

Hopper feeder

Window feeders These clear plastic seed feeders can be attached to your window by means of suction cups, bringing the birds as close to you as possible. To prevent nervous birds flushing every time there is movement inside your house, install one-way glass or hang see-through curtains.

SUET *can be presented in any number of ways.*

Suet feeders Suet can be presented in a ready-made feeder (a variety of models is available), or in a simple net or mesh bag hung from a line or a tree. Another type of suet feeder can be made by drilling ½ to 1 inch (1 to 2.5 cm) holes in a log or a wooden stump and plugging them with homemade suet, or by dipping a pine cone in warm suet.

FEEDING HUMMINGBIRDS

Hummingbirds are among nature's most wonderful creations, and by far the best way to see them is at a feeder in your yard.

Hummingbirds feed on insects and nectar. They are particularly attracted to bright red flowers but will also visit artificial feeders filled with a sugar water solution. They are fearless little birds and will happily feed close to buildings.

Feeders and Food

Most hummingbird feeders are made of plastic, and have a main reservoir linked to a number of outlets. They are often red, as this color attracts hummers. Some ready-made sugar solutions contain red food coloring for the same reason, but this should not be used as it may be harmful.

To make your own "nectar", put 4 cups of water in a pan with 1 cup of granulated white sugar. (Hummingbirds will not eat brown sugar. Nor should you use honey as it can transmit a fungal infection.) Stir while heating almost to the boil, then cool. Any excess can be stored in the refrigerator for several weeks.

Begin by offering small amounts of fluid. It may take time to attract birds, and the mixture will go off and lose its appeal if it remains in the feeder for any length of time.

Maintenance of Feeders

Change the fluid and clean the feeders every week, even if no birds are in attendance. Use bottle brushes, Q-tips, pipe-cleaners, and hot water. To remove black slime from the main reservoir, half fill it with water and drop in a 10 inch (25 cm) bathtub chain or some sand. Shake and swirl the feeder until clean.

Sometimes a single bird will claim your feeder as its own and chase other birds away. To discourage such behavior, hang a second feeder in another area or hang two or three spaced out along a clothesline. The bully will soon tire of trying to keep other birds away from all the feeders.

Preparing for Winter

In colder parts of the country in particular, hummingbirds should be weaned off their food before migration. To do this, weaken the solution to 5 or 6 parts water to 1 part sugar. If a freeze occurs, bring the feeders in at night, but remember to put them back out at first light, as hummers must be able to feed throughout daylight hours.

SUGAR WATER *is an acceptable substitute for the nectar that hummingbirds normally feed on. It should be presented in feeders like this.*

TAKING CARE *of* YOUR GUESTS

While feeders offer birds a concentrated supply of food, they also expose them to a number of risks. A responsible feeder steward makes sure that these risks are minimized.

Like having children or buying a puppy, beginning a bird feeding station requires commitment. Try to have fresh food available at all times (or at least at regular intervals). Birds can tolerate some change in food availability but try to be consistent, especially in cold weather.

Some birds become partly or wholly dependent on a particular feeding station. If their supply of food suddenly stops or is erratic, it can leave them in a precarious position, particularly in winter when millions of feeder visitors move from northerly nesting grounds to temperate winter locations. If you have to be away, make sure you get someone to take your place as feeder steward.

Make sure that all food is fresh and clean. Check suet occasionally to make sure that it is not rotting and change the hummingbird sugar water each week. Scrub containers and thoroughly dry those which will contain dry food like seeds or nuts. Wet seeds are not as nutritious and are likely to be rejected.

PLACEMENT OF FEEDERS

Of course, you will want to place your feeders where you can see them, but bear in mind that the placement of feeders can also affect the well-being of the birds.

Particularly in cold areas, try to place feeders in sheltered parts of your yard where there is a reasonable amount of sun. This will help the birds stay warm and keep the seeds dry.

Coming to the same spot every day makes birds vulnerable to attacks from predators. Careful placement of your feeders can minimize these risks. Most ground-feeding birds like to be near shrubbery so that they can take cover as soon as they perceive a threat. Low platform feeders and ground-feeding areas should therefore be within reach of cover but not so near that predators can creep up on the birds unawares.

Other seed eaters that take flight when disturbed, such as goldfinches, Purple and House finches, and siskins, will only feed in comfort from elevated structures that provide them with a good view of their surroundings. Hopper feeders and tube feeders should therefore be at least 3 feet (1 m) off the ground.

Insect eaters dislike flying through wide open spaces and will feel safer coming to suet feeders on or close to trees.

WINTER FEEDING *Birds often become dependent on winter feeders, bringing responsibilities as well as rewards for their human carers.*

DETERRING PREDATORS

You may need to take certain steps to protect your visitors from a range of predators.

Cats are the most common threat to birds that visit yards. If a cat enters your refuge, you should chase it away. Squirting cats with water may keep them away and of course a dog—particularly a small one that barks a lot—

PREDATORS WITH PURR *Finding effective ways of discouraging feline hunters is a challenging aspect of backyard bird-feeding.*

can be effective. You may have to talk to cat-owning neighbors and ask them to keep their pets away. The Humane Society may be able to help you deal with intruders that no-one claims.

Hawks—usually Cooper's, Sharp-shinned, or American Kestrels—can be a problem too. Birdfeeders provide them with a concentrated source of prey.

While it may be painful to watch a hawk take a finch or a junco, these native birds are protected by law and need nourishment as much as your local goldfinches. Remember that the hawk is going to get its meals somewhere. If it happens to be at your feeder it can be a spectacular sight to witness, and a reminder that birds face a constant struggle for survival.

If, however, you find the prospect of one of your visitors being taken too distressing, try scaring the hawk away by making a loud noise when it appears. If that does not work, consider downgrading the amount of food offered so that the abundance of prey is thereby reduced.

SQUIRRELS

Squirrels are cute and fun to watch, but where they occur (mainly in the east) even one can terrorize the entire bird population of a backyard.

Keeping them away from feeders and nestboxes is an eternal problem as squirrels are remarkably adept at overcoming obstacles and outwitting all attempts to thwart their activities.

In particular, platform and suet feeders that aren't protected are constantly in danger of being ambushed. Squirrel-proof feeders, special squirrel baffles (impassable cones that attach to the pole

or post supporting feeders and nestboxes), and unclimbable poles are all available.

One diplomatic solution is to give your squirrel its own feeding station, positioned well away from the birdfeeders, and stocked with favorites like cracked corn, corn-on-the-cob, pine nuts, walnuts, and whole peanuts. In exchange, it should keep its distance from the birds. The drawback is that when the squirrel realizes what a good deal this is, it is likely to return with its friends and family!

WINDOW KILLS

Estimates suggest that over 100 million songbirds are killed each year as a result of collisions with windows. In descending order of frequency, the species most often involved are: Pine Siskin, American Goldfinch, Dark-eyed Junco, Northern Cardinal, Mourning Dove, and House Finch.

Most strikes happen during panic flights caused by the appearance of a predator. The birds are either confused by the reflection or decide that what they see through the window would be a good place to lie low for a while until the danger has passed.

To reduce the chance of birds colliding with your windows, consider placing some attractive and prominent decals on windows that are near feeders, or hang nylon netting in front of them.

NESTBOXES

Attracting birds to nest in your yard will help species that are struggling to find suitable nesting sites, and give you an insight into the fascinating events that take place during breeding.

Whether it be as a result of habitat destruction or competition with introduced species, many birds have trouble finding places to nest. One way to help birds in this predicament and entice more species to your yard is to provide nestboxes.

CHOOSING A NESTBOX
Three main types of nestbox are available.

A basic shelf suits birds like robins that, in the wild, place their mud-based, grass-cupped nests in the fork of a tree or on a stout limb.

An enclosed box is favored by most species. Preferred dimensions vary (see the table below) but the basic shape is the same. Some birds, such as chickadees and nuthatches, like to pause before entering the nest and therefore prefer boxes that have a front porch perch. Others—wrens and woodpeckers, for example—dive directly into the nest.

Large condominium-style birdhouses suit birds that nest colonially, particularly Purple Martins.

SITING A NESTBOX
Finding the right spot for a nestbox is to some extent a matter of trial and error. Generally, it should be hung at least 6 feet (2 m) off the ground in a sheltered and secluded part of your yard. Try to find a place that will receive enough sunshine to keep the box dry but not so much that the birds will suffer from the heat. Give some thought to protecting the box from predators (see p. 53).

Open-shelf boxes should be placed on the trunk of a tree, and will be all the more attractive to the birds if overhanging leaves provide extra cover.

To discourage House Sparrows, hang nestboxes away from buildings—their favored habitat. If introduced species like starlings or House Sparrows do take up residence and you do not welcome them, you can evict them at the nestbuilding stage without causing them any great harm.

TYPES OF NESTBOXES *Open shelf (above left); enclosed box (above and top left); martin house (below left)*

SPECIES PREFERENCES

Species	Entrance hole	Floor	Depth	Height of hole above floor	Height above ground or water
House Wren	1⅛"	4" × 4"	6–10"	4–7"	4–10'
Chickadees	1⅛"	4" × 4"	8–10"	6–8"	4–15'
Titmice	1¼"	4" × 4"	8–10"	6–8"	5–15'
Bluebirds	1½"	5" × 5"	8"	6"	3–6'
House Finch	2"	5½" × 5½"	6–7"	4–5"	5–7'
Robin	open sides	6" × 8"	6–8"	open sides	5–20'
Purple Martin	2¼"	6" × 6"	6"	1"	10–20'
Downy Woodpecker	1¼"	4" × 4"	7–10"	5–8"	5–15'
Hairy Woodpecker	1½"	6" × 6"	12–14"	8–12"	12–20'
Flickers	2½"	7" × 7"	16–20"	14–18"	6–30'

BUILDING A BASIC NESTBOX

Anyone who can saw, turn screws, drill, and hammer nails can build a basic nestbox. If the end result is less than perfect, don't worry—the birds won't notice!

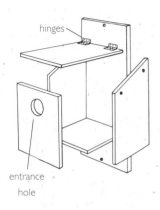

hinges

entrance hole

First of all, decide what kind of birds you want to attract and refer to the chart opposite for the appropriate dimensions.

Use insect and rot resistant wood like cedar or pine from ½ to 1 inch (1 to 2.5 cm) thick. Cut the wood to the required lengths. Drill ventilation and drainage holes, and partly screw in the hinges.

Use galvanized box nails to hammer the pieces together as shown in the diagram (left) and screw in the hinge to the top.

Be sure any rough areas are sanded smooth—especially the entrance hole. Do not use

chemical finishes or paint. Leave the wood untreated. Weathering and aging will give the birdbox a natural look.

Attach the backboard firmly to your chosen tree or post.

Put nestboxes out only when you know your preferred species will be looking for a nesting site (see The Habitat Birdfinder). Don't be discouraged if your nestbox isn't occupied straight away. Try moving it, and carefully consider the needs of the species you are targeting. If birds do take up residence, do not approach the nest as this may cause the birds to abandon it or direct predators to the nest.

Leave the nestbox in place until the nesting season is over, as many pairs will try to raise two or even three broods a season, or another species might move in. Once the season is over, however, take the nestbox down and clean it for the next year.

OBSERVING NESTING

The presence of a single bird or a pair near a nestbox may be the first sign of future occupancy. After a few hours

or days of inspection of the area and the box, one or both parents may start lining the box with sticks, and grasses. Most hole-nesters build a cup-shaped nest in the cavity.

Things will then slow down and you may only see the male bringing food to the incubating female. Once the eggs have hatched, the female will reappear and both parents will make trips to find food for the chicks, increasing in frequency as the chicks grow.

Often, after entering the box with food, the adult will leave with a white ball in its beak. This is a fecal sac containing nestling feces. To keep the nest clean, clear of parasites, and free from smells that may attract predators, the adult will dispose of the sac well away from the nest.

After fledging, some family groups will remain in the yard, so you can observe parent birds caring for their young.

HOUSE WRENS *(above) are not too fussy about design and are easily lured to any nesting opportunity. Nestboxes* *have helped the Eastern Bluebird (above right) cope with competition from introduced species for nesting sites.*

55

PLANNING *a* GARDEN *for* BIRDS

Creating a haven for birds can entail more than providing feeders and nestboxes. A little extra effort can turn your garden into an attractive wildlife habitat.

Exactly how you plan your birding garden will, of course, depend on what kind of yard you have and your geographical location. There are, however, three elements that are crucial in attracting birds: cover, in the form of trees and shrubs; food, in the form of native plants; and water for the birds to drink and bathe in.

COVER
Dense vegetation will attract birds as it is likely to provide shelter, nesting sites, and protection from predators. Coniferous trees and denser deciduous species will attract many species.

Cover should include both live and dead vegetation. Planting a dead tree or hanging up some attractive leafless branch can add stark beauty to the garden and provide perches for birds.

In most areas, trees will be the main features in a garden, but remember that many seed-eating birds live near or on the ground and will therefore prefer brush piles, bushes, and flowers.

PLANTS AS FOOD
Food in the form of native plants should be the mainstay of a bird's diet, and, as far as possible, the food you place in feeders should only supplement natural forage.

Most coniferous trees are attractive to insects and these, in turn, provide food for many birds. Fruit-bearing trees and berry-bearing shrubs provide food for mocking-birds, robins, and waxwings.

Use only native plants in your garden. Native deciduous trees like maples, alders, some oaks, and dogwood provide much better general forage for birds than do exotics. Birds tend to avoid non-native species like acacias because they fail to attract native insects.

The chickadee and the nuthatch are more inspiring society than statesmen and philosophers.

A Winter Walk,
HENRY DAVID THOREAU (1817–62),
American writer and naturalist

PLANTING FOR BIRDS

Plant	Provides	Favored by
Shrubs and Vines		
Elderberry (*Sambucus*)	Fruit, insects, shelter	Warblers, vireos, robins, Hermit Thrush
Honeysuckle (*Lonicera*)	Flowers, insects	Warblers, wrens, hummingbirds
Blackberry/raspberry (*Rubus*)	Fruit, dense cover, insects	Wrens, thrushes, sparrows, thrashers
Gooseberry/currant (*Ribes*)	Fruit, nectar	Kinglets, thrushes, hummingbirds
Trees		
Oak (*Quercus*)*	Acorns, insects, cover	Titmice, chickadees, woodpeckers
Pine (*Pinus*)*	Nuts, insects, cover	Crossbills, creepers, woodpeckers
Maple (*Acer*)*	Seeds, insects	Finches, warblers, vireos, tanagers
Plum/cherry (*Prunus*)*	Fruit, insects, nectar	Warblers, thrushes, orioles, sapsuckers
Mulberry (*Morus*)*	Fruit, insects, cover	Warblers, woodpeckers, thrushes, grosbeaks

* Make sure you use the right species for your area.

Eucalyptus trees can even be dangerous, as native birds have not evolved the subtle adaptations required to forage from this source. Many short-beaked nectar feeders, such as Yellow-rumped Warblers and Ruby-crowned Kinglets, have trouble removing the pitch of eucalypts from their bills and may even suffocate as a result.

Try to avoid using pesticides. These may have little effect on humans, but they can be extremely harmful to birds.

BIRDBATHS AND PONDS

Water is an important factor in attracting birds to your garden. On larger properties, a pond may attract ducks, geese, herons, and even some migrating shorebirds in late summer and fall.

In more restricted areas, a small pond with a recirculating stream will bring migrant tanagers, orioles, warblers, and vireos, as well as the resident jays, towhees,

A GARDEN HAVEN *for birds involves water, food, shelter, and safety from predators. A mixture of carefully chosen ornamental shrubs can fill several of these roles.*

MAIN ATTRACTIONS *A homemade birdbath like this one (above) will be almost irresistible to small birds. Feeders (left) are all the more attractive if positioned close to cover.*

and thrashers to bathe and drink. Overhanging branches and thick cover nearby will keep them coming back.

Birdbaths are an attractive addition to almost any backyard. Those which recirculate

MAKING A BIRDBATH

A simple birdbath can be made out of almost anything that is non-toxic and can hold shallow water. To accommodate several birds at one time, a surface diameter of at least 20 inches (50 cm) is best. Nearly any garbage can lid will do and the dark-colored plastic ones are best.

Place the lid on the ground or on a solid foundation above ground level. To avoid puncturing it with nails, use rocks or branches to weigh the lid down. If placed in the water, these objects will be used as perches by the birds.

Since birds find moving water particularly attractive, something like a dripping garden hose supported above the edge of the bath on a forked stake will be very effective. Overflow can easily be channeled so that it irrigates nearby plants. You can even create a waterfall effect by placing another lid at a lower level below the first and increasing the water supply. However, it may then be necessary to recycle the water.

dripping water are much more appealing to birds than those with still water.

Many commercial ponds, pond and stream liners, recirculating pumps, pond and bath heaters, and even waterfalls are available, but it can be much more fun to design and build your own.

57

I never for a day gave up listening to the songs of our birds, or watching their peculiar habits, or delineating them in the best way that I could.

JOHN JAMES AUDUBON (1785–1851),
American artist and ornithologist

CHAPTER THREE
GOING BIRDING

PREPARATIONS

Good preparation and some thorough groundwork
will help you make the most of your birding trips.

Most of us are birders of a kind, in that we are bound to notice the birds around us from time to time. It is unusual to find a person who cannot tell the difference between a pelican and a hawk, for instance, or who has trouble identifying a sparrow. Really, we are all just a step away from the great enjoyment birding can bring.

And what an array of birds there is to become acquainted with! In North America there are two kinds of pelicans, six types of wild geese, twenty-five "hawks", four crows, twenty-two woodpeckers, seven chickadees and over thirty sparrows. In total, almost 900 species of birds have been recorded north of Mexico. This is a daunting number for a beginning birder.

But, of course, many species have only small populations, and are found in remote places, so you are hardly likely to encounter more than a small proportion of all North American species in a single outing. On the other hand—and this is one of the joys of birding—you never know what you are going to find. In some northern states in winter you may struggle to see 10 species in an entire day, while a summer visit to the same spot may yield over 100. The key to getting the most from any outing is to be well prepared.

FIRST STEPS

It's best to begin slowly. Start by browsing through The Habitat Birdfinder (p. 84) at home to become familiar with the various groups and species you are likely to come across. Don't be discouraged by the great diversity. Think about the kind of environment you live in, select a corresponding habitat in The Habitat Birdfinder, and read the entries that relate to the birds you are most likely to see.

FIELD GUIDES *The prime purpose of a field guide (left) is to help you through the vital first step in birding: to identify your bird.*

A BIRDER'S VEST *(above) is a useful item of clothing. Its many pockets are ideal for field guides and other birding paraphernalia, such as pocket knives, notebooks, and magnifying glasses (top).*

The next step is to study an area in your neighborhood, such as a park, using the information in this chapter to help you develop your identification skills. Parks with lakes are particularly rewarding as most waterbirds are large, easily observed, and distinctively marked—three desirable attributes. You are also likely to find exotic visitors in such parks, which might be a little confusing, but don't be put off.

Once you have mastered some basic skills you will be ready to go further afield. Be thorough, but don't get frustrated when birds disappear before you have clinched their ID! Another new bird will be nearby.

O to mount again where

erst I haunted;

Where the old red hills

are bird-enchanted…

Robert Louis Stevenson
(1850–94), Scottish novelist
and poet

Field Guides

The Habitat Birdfinder introduces you to over 200 of the most commonly encountered North American species and is a great place to start your birding. Fairly soon, however, you are likely to want to acquire a complete field guide to North American birds. After binoculars, a good field guide will be your most important birding tool. A wide range is available (see p. 274).

BIRDING GEAR *As in any other out-door activity, staying warm and comfortable is an important consideration. A wide range of clothing and accessories is readily available for birding, from rain-proof jackets, back-packs, and sturdy boots (far right) to field bags and carry-pouches (right) for your field guide.*

At first the organization of a field guide may seem odd, as the birds will not be presented in any obviously logical order, such as alphabetically or large-to-small. This is because birds (and other vertebrate animals) are classified by scientists in taxonomic order (see p. 20).

Out in the field you will become aware of the usefulness of this in at least one respect: physically similar birds are grouped together,

A STARTING POINT *A good place to start birding is at a local pond or lake, as waterbirds are often fairly easy to identify. However, particularly if you are in a park, watch out for exotic species that may mislead you.*

and these, of course, are the ones that you are most likely to confuse.

Once you identify a bird and know its name, you will find that more information is available in your guide.

GETTING EQUIPPED

In addition to a field guide, the only other essential piece of equipment for a birder is a good pair of binoculars (see p. 62). Otherwise, use the clothing and provisions that you would take on any hike or field trip.

Bear in mind, however, that birding may involve sitting or standing in one spot for long periods. Warm clothing will therefore be important in colder areas. If it's hot, be wary of the sun's rays: brimmed hats and sunscreen will protect you but if you are at sea, remember that the sun may be twice as intense as it is on land.

If you are likely to be out in the rain, remember to take something along to dry the lenses of your binoculars, spotting scope, or spectacles. A baby diaper is extremely effective—after all, they were invented to soak up moisture. Avoid rainwear that squeaks, as it will alert the birds to your presence.

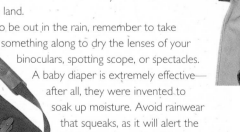

CHOOSING BINOCULARS

*As your most important piece of birding equipment,
binoculars should be chosen with
a good deal of care.*

Many people have an old pair of binoculars at home, but if they have been lying around for some time they may well have been knocked out of alignment. Unless they are particularly valuable, you may be better off investing in a new pair rather than paying for expensive repairs.

When buying binoculars, the following features should be considered carefully.

MAGNIFICATION

All binoculars feature a set of numbers such as 7 x 40. The first number denotes the power of the binoculars: a 7x pair of binoculars will make a bird look seven times larger than it appears to the naked eye; a 10x pair will make the bird look 10 times larger, and so on.

Anything less than 7x is of little benefit. 10x binoculars will give you a great view, but you may have trouble keeping the image steady— the greater the magnification, the more any hand tremor is accentuated. So, depending on how steady a hand you have, you should select a pair between 7x and 10x.

BRIGHTNESS AND WEIGHT

The second number that appears on your binoculars— 40 in the above example— denotes the diameter of the objective (front) lenses. The larger these are, the more light will enter the binoculars and the brighter the image will be. However, the larger the objective lenses are, the heavier the binoculars will be.

SIZE AND WEIGHT *are important considerations in choosing binoculars, but the pair you buy must also deliver a bright, crisp image at both short and long ranges.*

CONSTRUCTION AND WEIGHT

There are two types of binoculars—porro prisms and roof prisms (see below)—and their designs have a bearing on their weight and price.

Until the 1980s, the best binoculars were porro prisms. Porro designs are still popular and, in general, dominate the lower end of the price range ($40 to $400). Many provide bright, clear viewing and, in some cases, good close focus.

Recently, however, new technology has allowed manufacturers to create roof prisms that provide the same power and clarity in a more compact design. Roof prisms are therefore lighter but tend to be more expensive.

DURABILITY

Porro designs tend to be frailer than roof prisms. Even with average usage, some part

IN CLOSE-UP *A 7x pair of binoculars will magnify the image you see seven times (top inset). A 10x pair will give you a larger image (bottom inset), but at this magnification you may have trouble keeping the image steady.*

of the frame may eventually break or a prism may slip out of alignment.

Many binoculars now feature rubber armoring for protection. However, there is a tendency for some rubber eyecups to crack and break, and for bubbles to form in armored panels.

CLOSE FOCUS

A good pair of birding binoculars should focus on objects that are as close as 14 feet (4.2 m), and the closer they can focus, the better. Some roof prism models, designed for birding, will focus to 12 feet (3.7 m) but some binoculars have a minimum viewing distance of 23 feet (7 m) or more, which is totally impractical.

PRICE

There are good, robust binoculars available at the lower end of the price range, but, as with most equipment of this kind, you get what you pay for and top-quality binoculars are a joy to use. On the other hand, as binoculars are easily damaged, you should buy only what you can afford to replace.

COMFORT

Before buying binoculars, talk to someone who owns the model you have in mind, or

USING BINOCULARS

When aiming binoculars, it is important to find an object (or at least a specific area) first with the naked eye and to keep watching it while bringing the binoculars up to the appropriate line-of-sight. Practice aligning your binoculars to what you are looking at. You will take longer to find what you want if you search the landscape aimlessly.

If you turn your binoculars round, they can function as a microscope for making monsters out of ladybugs or examining flowers.

try to find a salesperson who is a binocular specialist and ask them for guidance.

In the shop, hang the binoculars around your neck to check their weight: if they feel heavy, they'll feel a good deal heavier at the end of a day in the field. Look through them and roll the focus wheel to be sure all parts are running smoothly. Check how well they focus on objects close by.

How well do the eyepieces fit your eyes? If you wear glasses, can you use them with your glasses? Comfort and ease of use are as important as power. Last but not least, check what kind of warranty the manufacturer will provide.

MAINTENANCE

Binoculars must be properly aligned and kept clean. Use a soft cloth to wipe oily dust and lunch crumbs from the lenses. Q-tips are good for small, hard-to-reach crannies.

ROOF PRISMS

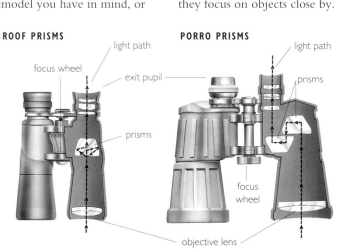

focus wheel
light path
exit pupil
prisms

PORRO PRISMS

light path
prisms
focus wheel
objective lens

ROOF AND PORRO PRISM *binoculars both use prisms to fold the light path passing through them. However, the roof prism design (far left) achieves a slimmer style and reduced weight by means of a more complex prism configuration than that found in the somewhat simpler (and consequently less expensive) porro prism design (near left).*

CHOOSING *a* SPOTTING SCOPE

If you plan to do a good deal of long-range viewing in open areas, such as in grasslands or at the seashore, you may find it worthwhile to invest in a spotting scope.

Having used binoculars in the field for a while, you may decide you would like to buy a spotting scope. A spotting scope will complement your binoculars, rather than replace them, as only in certain environments and for particular activities will a spotting scope prove more effective.

In particular, spotting scopes are excellent for identifying distant, perched raptors or for scanning flocks of shorebirds. They are also useful for close scrutiny of nesting activity and birds at feeders. They are less effective for observing small, fast-moving forest birds.

A wide range of brands and models of spotting scopes is available and, as a general rule, you get what you pay for— the more expensive ones give brighter, sharper images and their optics and construction are more rugged. Given the expense, it's a good idea to

THE RIGHT FIT *You may find that scopes with offset eyepieces (below) are more comfortable to use as you don't have to stoop so low to see through them. On the other hand, straight scopes (below left) are generally easier to aim.*

talk to other birders about the spotting scopes they like to use and even try looking through them.

After settling on a make and model, you still need to consider configuration and eyepiece power.

CONFIGURATION

Spotting scopes are available in two forms: either with an eyepiece aligned with the barrel or one that is offset by 45 degrees.

You may find straight scopes easier to aim, but, on the other hand, offset scopes are often more

TRIPODS

Choosing a tripod is a matter of finding just the right compromise between stability and weight. The heavier your tripod is, the more stable it will be, but, on the other hand, the heavier it is, the less convenient it will be to take on birding outings. There are also a number of other features that may have a bearing on your decision.

Probably the most important single element is the head. Tripods are mostly made for cameras and have all sorts of knobs and screws for adjusting the head to various positions. Birders need rapid-action controls, and the fewer there are the better. A single handle with a grip-tightener for locking, and vertical and horizontal lock screws are all you need. The handle should be on the opposite side of the head from the eye you normally look through.

The fixtures at the junction of each telescoping section of the legs of your tripod must be sturdy. Screw locks are usually stronger and last longer than flip-locks, but flip-locks allow quick set-up and collapse. Tubular legs are normally steadier than square ones and you may appreciate the difference when birding on windy days.

SMALL FRY *Setting the tripod low is not merely a convenience for younger birders (left), it also makes the spotting scope more stable, improving the view for all concerned.*

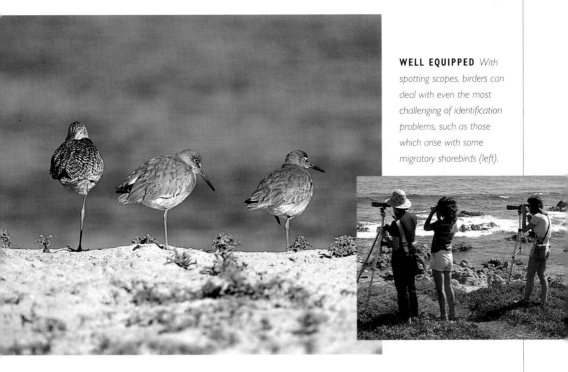

WELL EQUIPPED *With spotting scopes, birders can deal with even the most challenging of identification problems, such as those which arise with some migratory shorebirds (left).*

comfortable to use as you may not have to stoop so low to look through them. Try the different types out and think about how you will be using your scope. Weigh carefully the pros and cons of the two types before you buy.

EYEPIECE POWER

The most common magnifications are: 15x; 22x wide angle; 30x; 40x; and 20x to 60x zoom.

A spotting scope at lowest power (15x) is hardly worth the expense if you are proficient with 10x binoculars. A 40x eyepiece may give a nice view of a hawk ¼ mile away, for instance, but will not be particularly effective for scanning shorebird flocks.

A zoom lens may seem a good compromise, and there are many worthwhile models available, but some cheaper zoom eyepieces are optically incorrect, giving fuzzy images, and most of them lose their light-gathering ability quickly as the power increases.

All things considered, the best all-round magnification is in the region of 25x to 30x.

USING YOUR SPOTTING SCOPE

Spotting scopes have a smaller field of view than binoculars and are, therefore, even more difficult to master. Once you have your scope, it's a good idea to practice using it at home before you go on a birding trip.

Aim at a stationary object like a telephone pole or your neighbor's fuchsia, trying to locate the object and focus on it as quickly as you can.

ON THE ROAD *Car window clamps for spotting scopes (below) facilitate birding on the move, allowing you to stop and take a close look at birds such as this Yellow-headed Blackbird (below right). If you don't have a clamp, a plump beanbag flopped over the open window will do much the same job.*

I find it hard to see anything about a bird that it does not want seen. It demands my full attention.

ANNIE DILLARD (b. 1945), American poet and essayist

GOING AFIELD

An effective birder is one who has a good idea of when and where to go looking, and who causes the birds a minimum of disturbance.

From the beginner's viewpoint in particular, birds can seem very difficult to even get close to. However, providing you go looking for them within their range and at the right time of year, and keep in mind the following information, you will find that a large number of birds can be located with just a little careful planning.

Birds are always more conspicuous first thing in the morning, for then they are at their most active, and are generally in full song, often singing from prominent perches. This is particularly the case in spring, when most male (and some female) landbirds sing from perches or perform showy displays.

In winter, swimming birds gather together on oceans, bays, lakes, and rivers where various species may be studied side-by-side. During spring and fall migration, shorebirds, hawks, seabirds, and many small songbirds become gregarious and may be observed in single-species and mixed flocks.

BIRDING ETHICS

It is important that all birders are aware of their responsibilities in relation to birds and to the natural environment in general. The members of the American Birding Association pledge to adhere to the following "general guidelines of good birding behavior".

Birders must always act in ways that do not endanger the welfare of birds or other wildlife.
- Observe and photograph birds without knowingly disturbing them in any significant way.
- Avoid chasing or repeatedly flushing birds.
- Only sparingly use recordings and similar methods of attracting birds and do not use these methods in heavily birded areas.
- Keep an appropriate distance from nests and nesting colonies so as not to disturb them or expose them to danger.
- Refrain from handling birds or eggs unless engaged in recognized research activities.

A complete version of this code can be obtained from the ABA (see p. 278 for the address).

GONE BIRDING *The father of the modern outdoor movement, John Muir (right), pictured on a field trip with Theodore Roosevelt, another keen birder.*

Fields, meadows, and particularly forests may seem birdless until you find a flock. To locate flocks, scan open ground near brushy areas or weedy fields, or listen for the calls of the birds—as they forage they remain in constant vocal communication.

HABITATS

The best first step to take in a search for a particular bird is to find out what kind of habitat and niche it favors (see pp. 30 and 86). Within habitats, often the best places to look for birds are what could be termed "boundary areas" (known as ecotones), such as forest edges, the fringes of meadows, and reed beds on lakes, as many species prefer to remain constantly within reach of cover.

APPROACHING BIRDS

While some birds may be approached openly, many are timid and will flee at the first hint of danger. To many, such a hint is the sense of some-

WATCHING *treetop birds in level wood-land (left) is often uncomfortable. Look for a slope or similar vantage point from which to watch with greater comfort. Always keep your distance from nests or hatchlings like these Least Bitterns (above left).*

FIELD TACTICS *An experienced birder will look first along the edges of habitats, where visibility is least obstructed and the greatest variety of birds is to be found. In grasslands (above left), this tactic may reveal birds such as the Scissor-tailed Flycatcher (above), while the edges of wetlands (left) are the haunt of birds like the Great Blue Heron (below left).*

Your first observations of birds and their behavior can be done by simply learning to drift gently through a wood: a naturalist in a hurry never learns anything of value.

GERALD DURRELL (b. 1925)
English naturalist and writer

thing unusual happening in their environment. A sudden movement, an unfamiliar sound, a flash of light, or the shape of a predator (you) outlined against the sky can all alarm the birds and result in their departure.

When arriving at a birding spot by car, shut off the motor at once. If possible, remain in the car. Birds are much less fearful of a car that does not move than they are of people running around and aiming things at them. If you get out, try not to slam the doors.

In a new habitat, look around and plan your approach before advancing. Avoid walking into the sun as this will make it hard for you to see clearly. Move slowly and avoid talking loudly or snapping twigs. Look into a clearing before you step into it. Standing still in one spot for some time is often the most effective tactic, particularly in woodlands.

Try to avoid breaking the horizon line with the outline of your body. Earth-toned clothes may camouflage you to some extent. Use cover wherever possible: hide behind vegetation, a rock, or even a car. Remember, however, that the bird's observation skills are far better than yours and it will almost always know you are there. The key is to move around in a way that will not alarm it. If you can assure the bird that you pose no threat, it will usually tolerate your presence.

Once you have obtained a good view, back off and leave quietly. Birds have a hard enough time finding places to rest and forage in peace without birders putting them under more pressure.

HUNTERS

Be very careful during the hunting season as each year people are killed or wounded by hunters mistaking them for quarry. If you do hear hunters, try to head away from them. If they are already close to you, shout to them to warn them of your presence. Do not try to hide—if you do, you are far more likely to be shot at.

IDENTIFYING BIRDS:
the BASICS

By learning to focus on particular features of the birds you see, you can become proficient in identifying all but the most difficult species.

Frequently, novice birders are dismayed by the huge number of species listed in field guides. But of the total checklist of any given locality, less than half the species of regularly occurring birds are likely to be present at any given time.

FAMILY TRAITS *Most people are able to recognize an owl and a duck (above) when they see them. Once you have established which family a bird belongs to, you are well on your way to making a positive identification.*

When you are trying to identify a bird, always start by considering what you see in front of you. Don't reach immediately for your guide to see what you ought to be seeing or whether the bird looks like any others in your book. Describe the bird to yourself and try to draw on information you already have in your head. Consider the following questions.

FAMILY TRAITS
What family or group does the bird belong to?
Most families of birds share certain physical characteristics and if you can be sure what group a bird belongs to you are well on your way to making a positive identification. Familiarizing yourself with the information on pp. 88–93 will assist you greatly in this respect.

What size is the bird?
The size of a lone bird may be hard to deduce, but try matching it to one you know. Is it bigger or smaller than a robin? Is it similar to the size of a crow? Size comparisons are, of course, easiest when the mystery bird is with something you know.

BEHAVIOR
What is the bird doing?
Because different groups of

BEHAVIOR *Only nuthatches (above) move down tree trunks head first, a behavior so distinctive that the family can be identified by this feature alone.*

birds demonstrate different behaviors, what a bird is doing may help to identify it. Is it pecking at the ground, leaf-gleaning in a tree, or making short flights to and from an exposed perch? Is it swimming and surface diving? Drilling in mud at the edge of a pond or flying in a V-formation?

Is the bird alone or in a group?
During fall and winter, most small sandpipers join huge flocks of their own and similar species. Insect-eaters such as chickadees, kinglets, nuthatches, creepers, and vireos come together to increase foraging efficiency and predator avoidance. Other birds are solitary, except during the breeding season.

How much it enhances the richness of the forest to see in it some beautiful bird which you never detected before!

HENRY DAVID THOREAU (1817–62), American naturalist and writer

PHYSICAL FEATURES

What distinguishing features does the bird have?

To really pin down a species you have to learn to recognize its field marks.

Field marks are those characteristics of a species that, taken together, distinguish that bird from others. Usually they are plumage features. Pay particular attention to the following parts of the bird:

- eyebrow (supercilium)
- rump
- outer tail feathers
- wingbars

Make sure you are familiar with the names used for the different parts of a bird's body and the tracts of feathers that make up its plumage (see p. 24). In The Habitat Birdfinder, the identifying marks are highlighted in the Field Notes boxes. Always bear in mind that patterns are more significant than colors.

TIME AND PLACE

Where are you and what time of year is it? What kind of habitat are you in?

Always make a note of where you are, what time of year and day it is, and what kind of habitat the bird is in. It is important that you have noted these details as they may help you confirm a sighting. Many birds are common only within a particular range at particular times of year and favor a specific habitat. Most field guides indicate the distributions of species and their habitat preferences.

ROGER TORY PETERSON *Author of the first compact field guides, Roger Tory Peterson (right) has probably done more to introduce people to birding than any other single person.*

EYE MARKINGS *The pattern of the eyebrow (supercilium) or eye-ring often distinguishes a species, as with the Black-capped Vireo (left), the Northern Wheatear (center), and the White-throated Sparrow (right).*

WINGBARS *are often important field marks. For example, they help to distinguish this Black-throated Green Warbler (right) from the Wilson's Warbler (left).*

OUTER TAIL FEATHERS *are field marks in many species. Frequently the distinguishing mark is a lighter tip or sides.*

ROGER TORY PETERSON

The first compact, mass-market field guides were written and illustrated by Roger Tory Peterson, and were first published in 1934. These guides introduced the innovative and influential system of "field marks".

A bird's field marks are those physical features that distinguish it from all other species. In Peterson's guides, these marks are highlighted both in the text and in the accompanying illustrations.

Peterson's system was so successful that its principles were adopted during the Second World War to assist allied troops in identifying aircraft. Almost all contemporary field guides use field marks to assist in identification.

IDENTIFYING BIRDS: CASES

The following cases—one from each of the six habitats in The Habitat Birdfinder—show how to put the advice on the previous pages into practice.

DOWNY WOODPECKER

We hear a weak tapping noise and a black-and-white head peeks out from behind a tree trunk. Sidestepping around, we see that the bird is clinging to the trunk with its claws and using its tail to provide further support. As we watch, we see that it is drumming its narrow, sharp beak against the bark. This is unquestionably a woodpecker, but which one?

What stands out in the bird's generally black-and-white patterned plumage is an obvious, solid white line down the middle of its back. This alone indicates that it is either a Hairy or a Downy woodpecker.

Looking more closely, we note that our bird has black spots on its tail. These mean that it can only be a Downy.

YELLOW-RUMPED WARBLER

During a winter walk in a wood beside a river, a sharp chip note followed quickly by another attracts our attention to a group of small birds flitting through the trees. From a distance, these birds seem plain and colorless. Sparrows and finches are common in woods but they would appear brownish, not gray like these birds. The habitat, color, and call suggest that these are warblers.

Only a few warblers remain in North America in winter, so we don't have too many birds to consider. On closer inspection our generally nondescript birds show a flash of color: a small, bright yellow mark on the rump. Few warblers have a yellow rump, so that is a help. Any other features? A small fleck of yellow on the crown. That clinches it: the only bird with both these features is the Yellow-rumped Warbler.

KILLDEER

Driving along a country road through prairie, we spot a couple of brownish, long-legged, robin-sized birds standing in the middle of a field. As we watch, the birds suddenly sprint along the ground, their legs a blur, and then, even more abruptly, stop dead. This action, repeated over and over as we watch, is characteristic of plovers.

Not many plovers feed in dry open areas such as grasslands. As we sight the birds from the front, we are able to identify them positively. Both birds display two distinctive black bands across their white chests— a feature that distinguishes them as Killdeers.

BLUE-WINGED TEAL

As we pass a marshy pond in the countryside, we note a group of birds swimming and splashing in the water. About half of the group are brown and mottled. The shape of their bills instantly identifies them as ducks of some kind. (All other birds found on open water have pointed bills.) This should be easy!

The birds we are observing are tipping up or "dabbling". As they tip forward, we can see that they are kicking at the surface to keep themselves submerged. This is significant

as ducks can generally be divided into two groups—those that dabble and those that dive. Among the dabblers, the males are usually more distinct than the females. The brown birds must therefore be the females. The rest have slaty blue faces which bear prominent bold white crescents. The combination of dabbling behavior and the white crescent on the face confirms beyond doubt that these are Blue-winged Teals.

HERRING GULL

On a walk along the seashore on a pleasant winter afternoon, we notice several crow-sized birds squabbling over scraps of fish thrown to them by fishermen on the pier. The birds have a white head and body, and a yellow bill. The seashore environment, the plumage features, the scavenging behavior of the birds, and their tolerance of humans all imply that these are gulls.

Juvenile and immature gulls are tricky to identify (see p. 232), but adults are more straight-forward. The pale gray back and white head of these birds indicate that they are adults. The next things to check when looking at gulls are the bill, the legs, and the wingtips. Looking through our binoculars, we see that these gulls have a red spot on their yellow bills, pink legs, and white-spotted black wingtips. These features identify the birds as Herring Gulls.

CURVE-BILLED THRASHER

On an early morning walk in the desert, our attention is drawn to a bird singing on top of a saguaro cactus. The song is a long, rich, scratchy, warbling song, and some phrases are repeated before the sequence starts again. The bird is slender, with a long bill, and has a strikingly long tail. These features suggest a member of the Mimidae family (Mockingbirds and Thrashers) but which one?

The bird's plumage seems to lack distinct markings. So what other features can we use to identify it? The bill quite obviously curves downwards. And although they are faint, there are some dusky spots on the bird's chest. After a while, the bird flies off. As it does so, we note pale tips to its tail feathers. These clinch it: the combination of decurved bill, mottling on the chest, and pale tail feathers is found only on the Curve-billed Thrasher.

BIRDING *by* EAR

If you are able to learn the vocalizations of the birds

in your area, you will be able to identify many more of them than

if you were relying on your eyes alone.

Birding by ear is a learned discipline. Because each bird species has its own range of vocalizations and because birds frequently vocalize in areas of thick vegetation, a person who can identify each voice will be able to record many more birds in a given area than one birding only by sight.

During spring, each territorial male sings persistently from several perches, seldom leaving his area. At such times, an experienced birder can estimate the number of territories in an area simply by counting singers.

LEARNING
People gifted with a musical memory and perfect pitch can remember a bird's song or call after hearing it only once. The rest of us have to work at it! Listening to tapes may be helpful—many commercial cassettes are available at bird stores—but listen to only a few songs at a time. If you try to learn too many in a session, they tend to sound very much the same.

The best method for learning bird sounds is to go where the birds are and to watch them vocalize. You will probably find that you are able to retain the visual and audible connection—at least for a while.

REMEMBERING
The easiest way to remember a song or call is to compare it with one you already know. For example: "This song sounds like a robin's but is more abrupt and rolls along through shorter phrases," or "This call note is like the Song Sparrow's but is louder and more metallic." Occasionally, when you hear an unfamiliar bird voice, you may find it useful to record it in the field for later identification at home, by comparing it with tapes of known species.

Some field guides (notably those published by Golden Press) contain sonograms—graphs representing bird calls—(see p. 37), which some people find very helpful.

It is truly wonderful how love-telling the small voices of these birds are, and how far they reach through the woods into one another's hearts and into ours.

JOHN MUIR (1838–1914), Scottish-born American naturalist and writer

PARABOLIC REFLECTORS *are often used in the field to obtain high-quality recordings (above). An Eastern Meadowlark in full song (top).*

TED PARKER

Far-and-away the world's expert on the birdlife of South America, the late Ted Parker was able to identify over 3,000 species of birds by ear.

Many tropical birds live in thick vegetation (either beneath ground cover or within the dense canopy of tall forest) and are very hard to see, so visual censusing simply does not work. Identifying the little voices in the jungle is the only way to know what's there.

Ted could be dropped into a rainforest containing hundreds of birds and emerge an hour or two later with a thorough analysis of the avifauna.

A chief scientist for Conservation International, Ted was working on a program assessing the faunal and floral qualities of tropical rainforests when, in August 1993, the plane that had been leased for aerial surveys hit a fog-veiled mountain, killing Ted and a number of other team members. With his death, a large part of our knowledge of South American birds was lost.

RECORDING BIRDS

As recently as twenty years ago, to record a bird song or call one needed an umbrella-sized cone called a parabolic reflector, a microphone, and a cumbersome reel-to-reel recorder. Nowadays, of course, small, lightweight directional microphones and digital recorders do the same job far more effectively.

For best results when recording bird sounds, try to find a bird that is vocalizing where there are no other sounds. Running water, other birds, wind, airplanes, whispering humans, and rustling leaves will all cause interference. Indeed, it's only when you try to record a bird singing that you fully appreciate just what a noisy world we live in!

It is a good idea to find a quiet spot in advance and then, on recording day, have your equipment set up and ready to go before dawn.

ATTRACTING BIRDS WITH SOUNDS

Many birders play tapes of bird calls in the field in order to attract birds, and this is often very effective. However, as birds will assume that the recording is the call of a territorial rival, repeated playing can place them under extra strain. You should therefore use tapes sparingly.

Another way of attracting birds with sounds is by using techniques known as spishing—making a *spssh, spssh* sound with your lips—and squeaking—kissing the back of your hand to produce crude but effective imitations of calls. Small birds, such as warblers, sparrows, wrens and chickadees, will gather round apparently fascinated by these sounds.

For a similar effect you can also use a "squeaker", a gadget, available from birding stores, consisting of a cylinder with a resin-coated wooden plug that squeaks when the plug is rotated.

INSTANT REPLAY *Portable recorders (left and far left) allow you to record the calls of birds—such as this Marsh Wren (above)—in the field and then listen to them at home. One way to learn more about recording is to attend a course like Cornell Laboratory of Ornithology's annual sound recording workshop (below).*

KEEPING NOTES *and* RECORDS

From short notes on scraps of paper to exhaustive, computerized compendiums, a birder's records can take many forms.

S ome birders become habitual listers. Almost all keep at least one list of all the species that they have seen.

A list may take the form of scribbled notes in the margin of one trusty field guide, or it may be checked off in one of the many printed lists available from birding organizations. It may record all the birds you have seen on your travels or only the birds you have seen in your region, local park, or even just your backyard—a local list can be every bit as challenging as a national or world list.

Many active birders start a new list each year, month, or even week. Breaking out a clean, unmarked checklist on January First can instill a good deal of vigor in even the most jaded birder!

Nowadays a respectable life list might cover 300 to 400 species, though many avid, well-traveled birders have been able to notch up 700 or more. At the top end of the scale, a few listers have managed to see over 7000 species!

JOURNALS

One way to get more out of your adventures in birding is to keep a journal recording the details of places visited and wildlife observed.

Use a robust and, if possible, waterproof notebook. Write in it in pencil rather than pen. Pencil is more appropriate for sketching and won't run if the journal gets wet.

Use your journal to record not just the species seen but an estimate of the numbers present, the time and weather when you saw them, and any other relevant observations

A VISUAL REFERENCE *When you are out birding and see a bird that you are unable to identify, it's a good idea to make notes and even do a quick sketch of the bird in your notebook. Note the time and the place, what kind of habitat you are in, and any distinctive plumage or behavioral features of the bird (right). With this information at hand, you can then take time at home to consult field guides and other reference works in order to positively identify the bird—and add another species to your life list!*

(see p. 68). Such notes will help you if you wish to do further research on a bird's identity at home or if you intend to report a rare sighting to your local birding organization.

Many people choose to enliven their birding notes with sketches, pressed flowers, and other jottings. All of this will make your journal a valuable reference source and something to treasure throughout your birding career.

OTHER TYPES OF RECORDS

In addition to maintaining a running narrative on trips afield, many birders also keep a computer file, loose-leaf

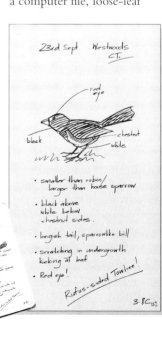

23rd Sept.   Westwoods CT.

red eye

black — chestnut / white

- smaller than robin / larger than house sparrow
- black above white below chestnut sides.
- longish tail, sparrowlike bill
- scratching in undergrowth kicking at leaf
- Red eye!

Rufous-sided Towhee!

3.8C

BIRDER'S LISTS *Printed "tick" lists (below) are now available for most regions, but many birders still prefer a traditional notebook (left).*

binder or card index arranged according to species. Looking, for example, under Red-necked Grebe, a well-traveled birder would find several entries detailing encounters with this species.

COMPUTERS
There are many software programs designed for recording

bird sightings. Some incorporate complete world or American species lists. Some feature information on the abundance of species in different areas at different times of year.

Many field guides, birding reference books, and encyclopedias of birds are now also available on CD-ROM.

GREAT AMERICAN BIRD ARTISTS

The first serious American ornithological work and one of the great works of bird art was the *Natural History of Carolina, Florida and the Bahamas* by the English artist and naturalist Mark Catesby (1683–1749). Catesby undertook two extended journeys to the Americas between 1712 and 1726, and ultimately succeeded in illustrating around one quarter of all species found in the eastern United States. His two sumptuously illustrated folios were published in London in 1731 and 1743.

Not until the beginning of the nineteenth century was Catesby's work bettered. Alexander Wilson (1766–1813), a weaver, school master, and poet, arrived in America from Scotland in 1794. He was so overwhelmed by the beauty and variety of the birdlife that, despite little training in either art or ornithology, he began work on a large-scale guide to American birds. The first volume of Wilson's superb *American Ornithology* was published in 1808, with eight other volumes appearing subsequently.

To finance his work, Wilson sought sponsors by displaying published volumes wherever he went. On one of his trips he approached a storekeeper by the name of John James Audubon (1785–1851). Audubon had arrived in America from France in 1803 and, unknown to Wilson, was at work on a similar project. Initially dismayed, Audubon was subsequently inspired by the meeting to work even harder at his plan to paint every bird in America.

Published serially from 1827 to 1838, to great acclaim, the four volumes of *Birds of America* were a landmark in bird art and are now among the most valuable books in the world.

PORTRAIT PAINTERS TO THE BIRDS
An illustration of a Bald Eagle by the English artist Mark Catesby (top). America's first great ornithologists, Alexander Wilson (above right) and John James Audubon (right), alongside a more recent successor, Louis Aggassiz Fuertes (above).

Like Audubon, Louis Aggassiz Fuertes (1874–1927) was not only an exceptional artist but an avid and observant naturalist. One ability that set him apart from his peers was his acute memory. After studying his subjects closely in the wild, he would draw them hours later with astounding accuracy. Fuertes' publications are now among the most highly regarded of all bird books.

PHOTOGRAPHING BIRDS

Bird photography can be immensely satisfying, but for beginners it can also be frustrating. Good results require a significant investment of time, money, and patience.

The sense of satisfaction achieved by taking a good color slide or print of a bird—perfectly composed, accurately exposed, crackling sharp, and with good saturated colors— is enormous, and most birders want to try their hand at capturing their quarry on film at some time or other.

Bird photography is, however, harder than it might seem. Suitable equipment is quite expensive, and outstanding results need technical commitment. Perhaps the best single piece of advice is: choose your equipment with great care.

CAMERAS
Cameras come in two basic styles, usually referred to as rangefinders and single lens reflexes (SLR). Rangefinder cameras are unsuitable for bird photography for several reasons, but especially because you cannot normally change lenses with this type of camera, so you cannot use a telephoto lens.

The recommended style and format is therefore an SLR that uses 35mm film, preferably one with automatic exposure control and focusing capability.

FOCAL LENGTH
The most important variable to consider when choosing a lens for bird photography is its focal length. Usually expressed in millimeters, this is what governs the size of the image of the bird on the film. With a 35 mm camera, you can roughly equate this with the magnification of your binoculars by dividing the focal length of the lens by 50: a 400 mm lens, for example, is roughly the equivalent of 8x binoculars. (This only applies to 35 mm cameras; for other formats the formula is different.)

In a simple lens, the focal length is roughly the same as

the length of the barrel, which means that a 1,000 mm simple telephoto lens would be about 3 feet (1 m) long. Sophisticated design in modern lenses has resulted in substantial improvement in this respect, but lenses suitable for bird photography are nevertheless long and heavy.

The greater the focal length, the harder it is to maintain focus and to "target" your bird in the finder. Beyond about 400 mm you will need a tripod (see p. 64), as you will find that you simply cannot hold the lens steady enough by hand to get worthwhile results.

A QUESTION OF BALANCE
A Night Heron (above right) perches on some high-quality camera equipment. Experienced bird photographers use a tripod whenever possible, even with birds as tame and cooperative as this Brown Pelican (left).

THE F-STOP

The second critical parameter is the f-stop, which measures the light-gathering capability of the lens. The smaller the number, the wider the lens opens, the more light is let into the camera, and the quicker the image will be processed. An f4 lens is therefore better (that is, faster) than an f5.6. On the other hand, the smaller the number, the bigger, heavier, and more expensive the lens.

ZOOM AND MIRROR LENSES

Zoom lenses are those in which the focal length is variable (75 to 125 mm is a typical range). Mirror lenses (so-called because the wizardry inside is done with mirrors, not lenses), are much smaller, lighter, and more compact than normal tele-photo lenses, but their f-stop is fixed. Such consider-ations are not that important in bird photography, however, as you will usually find yourself operating the lens at maximum zoom, in order to get as close as possible to the bird, and with the aperture wide open (that is, at its lowest f-setting), in

MIRROR LENSES *(top) are more compact than other lenses, whereas zoom lenses (center) provide increased flexibility. If you can afford it, this 600mm lens (right) will provide the ultimate in power and image clarity.*

order to record the image as quickly as possible.

You can extend the focal length of your lens by using a telextender, a small lens that attaches to the back of your telephoto before you mount it on the camera. These are convenient, but you pay for the increased range with some reduction in image quality and speed. You can also buy a mounting collar that allows you to mount your camera onto a spotting scope.

FILM

The most important difference in film types is in speed. High speed films (indicated by higher numbers) allow you to use a faster shutter speed and are there-fore better for catching birds in motion, but they tend to give you grainier pictures.

Store film in the coolest place you can find (the refri-gerator is fine), and protect it from marked temperature changes when you use it.

If you want the very best results, get it processed by a custom lab (check the Yellow Pages for one near you) rather than by the corner drugstore.

VIDEO

Something to consider carefully before investing in photographic equipment is whether you wish to opt for a video camera instead. The latest video cameras are small and easy to use, and you may feel that capturing a bird's appearance, sound, and motion outweighs consider-ations of image quality.

You may well find yourself getting much more enjoyment out of your video tapes of birds than from still photographs. With a few video cameras (the more expensive models) you can even interchange lenses with your still camera, thus getting the best of both worlds.

FIELD OF VIEW *A group of budding bird photographers (above) sets its sights on a Great Egret (right).*

Beyond Basic Birding

The best way to broaden your birding experience is to get to know other birders through clubs, birding tours, and other group activities.

In most areas of North America there are local birding organizations, ranging from chapters of the National Audubon Society to university ornithological societies and small birding clubs. Most of these groups organize meetings and field trips, and they may help you to become involved in other aspects of birding such as censuses and research projects.

MOVING ON *Joining a club (above) is the first move to make if you are serious about birding. Organized tours will take you to a wide range of places, from mountain-top hawk watches (below) to tropical wetlands (bottom).*

National and state parks, too, offer a range of naturalist-led walks, some specializing in birds. Some city museums, colleges, and universities offer classes in ornithology or birding (field ornithology). There is even a college level correspondence course run by the Cornell Laboratory of Ornithology, which is highly recommended, especially for people living in isolated areas.

The principal organization for birders in North America is the American Birding Association (see p. 278 for their address). Joining the ABA will put you in touch with thousands of other like-minded birders and provide you with a variety of useful resources in the form of journals and newsletters.

Travel

A continent filled with superb and diverse birding areas awaits you. For a selection of top sites, see p. 82. If you want to explore these and other areas on your own, our Resources Directory lists details of birdfinding guides and birding groups for almost every state in the US and every province in Canada.

If you prefer to go on an organized tour, there is a huge range of companies and trips from which to choose. Most are inclusive, with similar travel arrangements. The big difference will probably be in the leader or tour guide—some are excellent, some can be a disappointment. Ask other birders for recommendations.

Specialty Birding

Some people focus their birding activities on one kind of bird. For example, hawk-watching is a popular form of specialized birding. Diurnal raptors (hawks, eagles, ospreys, kites, and so on) follow well-established migration routes (often over mountains where these birds ride the rising air currents), and along these routes there are localities, known as hawk watches, where hundreds, even thousands, of raptors may be seen in a single day.

Pelagic (open sea) trips to watch seabirds are also popular. Many species of seabirds which cannot normally be seen from land may be observed from ocean-

COUNTING BIRDS *Researchers often welcome the help of volunteers in the routine work of censusing (above).*

going boats on one- or two-day trips. Again, a wide range of trips is on offer, but if you are planning your first pelagic birding trip, be sure the organizer tells you exactly what is involved and how to prepare for it.

BIRDING AS SPORT
One fun activity undertaken by many birders is known as a "big day". The aim is to record as many species as possible between one mid-night and the next within a clearly defined area and following strict rules.

This can be done as a competition between members of a group or as a group effort aimed at improving on previous tallies. Frequently, it is done to raise money for a birding group or for conservation efforts, with each species recorded bringing in a small sum from sponsors.

RESEARCH
A number of national censuses and feeder-watch programs are organized each year and all birders can participate. Perhaps the best known of these censuses are the Audubon Society's CBCs (Christmas Bird Counts).

Each CBC takes place on one day between mid-December and the first week of January and covers one of nearly 1,700 circles around North America, each of them 15 miles (24 km) in diameter. Participants record all the species they see that day within their circle.

The information gathered during the CBCs has given rise to a database that is one of the most important birding resources in the world. To take part in a CBC, contact the National Audubon Society (see p. 278).

Other important censuses include the Breeding Bird Surveys, run by the US and Canadian Fish and Wildlife services, and the Breeding Bird Atlas Projects that take

BIRD AID *Many regions have organizations dedicated to nursing back to health injured and abandoned birds (below). One way of monitoring the movements of birds is by banding (right). A metal leg-ring bearing an address and a number (above right) will identify a bird if it should be found again.*

Birds are Nature's most vital and potent expressions.

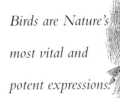

FRANK M. CHAPMAN
(1864–1945), American ornithologist

FRANK M. CHAPMAN *(above) organized the first Christmas Bird Count on Christmas Day 1900, as a protest against traditional Christmas bird shoots. As curator of ornithology at the American Museum of Natural History and editor of various journals, Chapman did as much as any ornithologist to encourage members of the public to take up birding.*

place from time to time in many states and provinces.

Observatories and banding stations also conduct research which requires volunteer participation. Each year, the American Birding Association lists volunteer opportunities available through government agencies such as the US Forest Service and the US Bureau of Land Management.

BIRDS *in* DANGER

Although public attitudes to conservation have changed radically in the past one hundred years, many bird species are still in grave danger of extinction.

For early ornithologists the gun was as important a tool as writing and sketching materials, as most of their studies were based on dead specimens. Early in his career, John James Audubon (see p. 75) said "I consider birds few if I can shoot less than a hundred a day".

Even in the nineteenth century the wholesale slaughter of America's birds continued in the name of sport and fashion, but the attitude of the ornithological community began to change.

OVERHUNTING *exterminated the Passenger Pigeon, a species once so numerous that flocks of millions (below right) were a common sight. At the height of this destruction, in the 1880s, Frank Chapman (see p. 79) undertook a survey of headwear in New York and found that of the 700 hats that he counted, 542 sported mounted birds. Of these, he recognized at least 20 species.*

CONSERVATION GROUPS

These changing attitudes led to the foundation of the first American conservation groups. The most significant of these was the Audubon Society, founded in 1886 in New York City by George Bird Grinnell. Similar groups throughout North America adopted its name and were amalgamated in 1905 under the banner of the National Association of Audubon Societies (it was renamed the National Audubon Society in 1935).

During the early 1900s, Audubon Society members fought vigorously for the protection of endangered species. Some campaigners were prepared to put their own lives on the line and, tragically, three wardens lost their lives in disputes with hunters.

Ultimately, however, the campaigns led to the establish-

HABITAT DESTRUCTION *today threatens many birds, such as the Burrowing Owl (left).*

ment of wildlife sanctuaries throughout the country, and saved a number of species including the Great and Snowy egrets. They also gave rise to the first bird protection laws, introduced in New York City in 1895 and adopted by 32 states during the next ten years.

Unfortunately, legislation came too late for some birds. The last Carolina Parakeet and the last Passenger Pigeon both died in September 1914 at the Cincinnati Zoo.

A NEW THREAT

In the early 1960s it became clear that we were poisoning our continental wildlife through widespread use of pesticides such as DDT. These "miracle" sprays were great for growing insect-free

EXTINCT SPECIES

Labrador Duck, Great Auk, Passenger Pigeon, Carolina Parakeet

SOME ENDANGERED SPECIES

Species	Range	Status	Causes
Wood Stork	Southern US	Faltering	Habitat destruction
Whooping Crane	Alberta to Texas	Recovering	Habitat destruction; shooting
Piping Plover	East	Faltering	Forced out of habitat by humans
Eskimo Curlew	North America	May be extinct	Overhunting
California Condor	California	Extinct in the wild	Pesticides; displaced by humans
Ivory-billed Woodpecker	Southeastern US	Probably extinct	Habitat destruction
Black-capped Vireo	Oklahoma to Mexico	In danger	Nest parasitism; habitat destruction
Bachman's Warbler	Southeastern US	Probably extinct	Habitat destruction
Kirtland's Warbler	Michigan to Bahamas	Faltering	Habitat destruction; nest parasitism

produce but were devastating to apex predators (animals and birds at the top of the food chain). For birds such as Brown Pelicans, Ospreys and Peregrine Falcons, the absorption of DDT caused them to lay eggs with shells too thin to incubate or eggs with no shells at all. As a result, populations of all three species plummeted.

By the time Rachel Carson's prophetic *Silent Spring* (see p. 36) alerted politicians and public to the danger, much damage had already been done.

CONTEMPORARY THREATS

There is no question that the most serious contemporary threat to birds is the continuing destruction of habitat. Numbers of many migratory species have dropped dramatically as their habitats in their summer homes in the US and Canada and their winter residences in Latin America have been cleared for agriculture and urban development.

Other threats to the survival of native species are also a result of human intervention. Clearance of native vegetation has allowed nest parasites like the Brown-

headed Cowbird to thrive (see pp. 41 and 191), and some populations have been wiped out by cats. Human structures too have taken their toll: huge numbers of birds die annually as a result of collisions with plate-glass windows (see p. 53).

ON THE BRIGHT SIDE

Illegal shooting and trapping is now rare in North America, and legislation prohibits misuse of pesticides. Many wildlife agencies have implemented cowbird control programs, and many private organizations are buying property to protect habitats and care for animals and birds.

Organizations such as The National Audubon Society,

UNDER SIEGE *The California Condor (above) is now extinct in the wild, while the number of free-living Whooping Cranes (above left) remains dangerously low even after decades of support. The Kirtland's Warbler (top) is in a precarious position as a result of habitat loss.*

The Nature Conservancy, BirdLife International, and Partners in Flight continue to campaign effectively for endangered species and habitats. To counterbalance continuing habitat destruction, it is imperative that these efforts are not only continued but stepped up. If you want to help, you can start by contacting one of these groups or joining a local birding organization. See page 278 for a list of addresses.

TOP BIRDING SITES

North America offers an extraordinary range of habitat types, a superb system of national parks, and some of the world's top birding areas.

It is not easy to make a selection of top birding sites because there are so many of them scattered around the continent. Here, however, are ten of our favorites. More information on all of these destinations and many others can be found in the birdfinding guides listed in the Resources Directory on p. 275.

❶ SAINT PAUL ISLAND, ▶ PRIBILOF ISLANDS, ALASKA
Reached by biweekly flights from Anchorage. Nesting seabirds (fulmars, kittiwakes, murres, auklets, and puffins) may be viewed and photographed at close range and, during migration, Asiatic strays may show up. Lapland Longspurs, Arctic Foxes, reindeer, fascinating local history, and amazing wildflowers (above right) are all part of the package.

❷ MANNING PROVINCIAL PARK, BRITISH COLUMBIA *Excellent for mountain species including Ruffed, Blue, and Spruce grouse; Black Swifts; and Calliope Hummingbirds (below). Many warblers and flycatchers also occur in summer. A beautiful park with quite stunning mountain scenery. Summer is really the only time to visit. ▼*

◀ ❸ MONTEREY BAY, CALIFORNIA
A diversity of habitats makes this a great year-round birding spot. The shoreline (left) is frequented by Black Turnstones, Wandering Tattlers, and oystercatchers, and you will hear Pygmy Nuthatches and Chestnut-backed Chickadees calling from the nearby cypresses. Also the departure point for some great pelagic trips.

LOCAL LISTS

The following list will give you some idea of the number of species you can expect to find in different regions of North America.

Texas	600
California	580
Arizona	500
British Columbia	450
Alaska	445
Ontario	430
Nova Scotia	410
Saskatchewan	375
South Dakota	370
Prince Edward Island	280

◀ ❹ PAWNEE NATIONAL GRASSLANDS, COLORADO *One of the last remaining areas of shortgrass prairie left in North America. In summer, specialties include Chestnut-collared and McCown's Longspurs and Lark Buntings. Keep an eye out too for nesting Swainson's and Ferruginous (left) hawks, and herds of American Pronghorns.*

❺ SANTA ANA NATIONAL ▶ WILDLIFE REFUGE, TEXAS *This refuge features a remarkably high concentration of wildlife and is home to a number of East Mexican birds found nowhere else in the US, including the Hook-billed Kite, Altamira Oriole, Great Kiskadee, Parauque, Green Jay (right), Groove-billed Ani, Plain Chachalaca, and Tropical Parula.*

❻ CHURCHILL, MANITOBA

Located where boreal forest merges with tundra, Churchill attracts astonishing numbers of migrating (late May to early June), then nesting (late June through August), waterbirds. The chance of spotting a Polar Bear keeps visitors on their toes.

❼ POINT PELEE, ONTARIO

Arguably the best place in North America to observe northbound landbird migration in spring (mid-May is best). If the weather is right, warblers, thrushes, vireos, buntings, orioles, and tanagers amass here, sometimes in astounding numbers.

❽ CAPE MAY, NEW JERSEY

If Point Pelee is the best place to witness northbound migration in the spring, Cape May is the place to be for southbound migration in the fall. Nowhere will you see more passing waterbirds, songbirds, and birds of prey. Hawkwatching here can be exhilarating.

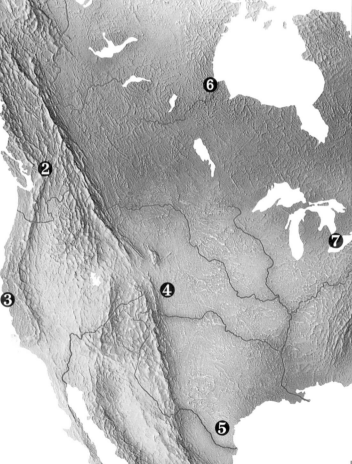

❾ EVERGLADES NATIONAL PARK, FLORIDA

Even under the siege of habitat loss, the Everglades is a wetlands showcase. An attractive system of trails, boardwalks, and roads allows close observation of some fascinating wildlife, including numerous ibis, herons, and egrets, and alligators and turtles.

❿ THE DRY TORTUGAS, FLORIDA

These low coralline islands support large numbers of nesting Sooty Terns and Brown Noddies. Other visitors include Masked and Brown boobies, White-tailed Tropicbirds, and Magnificent Frigatebirds. In spring, a wide variety of landbird migrants break their northward journey here, and they are usually easy to approach and photograph.

O quick quick quick, quick hear the song-sparrow,

Swamp-sparrow, fox-sparrow, vesper-sparrow

At dawn and dusk. Follow the dance

Of the goldfinch at noon. Leave to chance

The Blackburnian warbler, the shy one. Hail

With shrill whistle the note of the quail, the bob-white…

All are delectable. Sweet sweet sweet…

Landscapes, T.S. ELIOT (1888–1965),
British poet and critic

CHAPTER FOUR
The HABITAT
BIRDFINDER

INTRODUCTION

In North America there are over 850 species of birds. How does a beginning birder start getting to know them? Our Habitat Birdfinder offers you the perfect introduction—to all the main bird groups and to over 200 of the most commonly encountered species.

Getting to grips with the large number of species that may be encountered in North America can be a daunting task. A good way to start is to learn something about the general characteristics that distinguish groups of related birds.

THE TAXONOMIC APPROACH

On the following pages you will find concise but informative descriptions of the main bird groups in North America. These include information on shared physical features; behavioral characteristics; differences in plumage between males and females, and from season to season; and the number of species in that group found in North America compared with the world as a whole.

It may be a little hard to digest all of this information at once, but it is worth persevering as it will give you a good foundation on which you can build.

You will probably be surprised at how much you already know. For example, you probably recognize a duck or an owl when you see one. You may not be able to say exactly what species it is, but you at least know it right away as a duck or an owl.

Greater familiarity with the shared characteristics of bird groups will help you narrow down the identity of an unknown bird in the field. Knowing how many species there are in a group will mean that you are aware just how many similar birds there are. And an awareness of plumage cycles and differences will mean you are better placed to make a more precise identification. For all these reasons, it makes sense to read this section carefully and return to it again and again.

THE HABITAT APPROACH

Learning about families and other groups will give you a good grounding in American birds, but groups can be large and widespread. Furthermore, you will quickly want to start naming the individual species that you see around you. So how can you predict what species you are likely to see in your area? One answer is to consider birds in relation to their habitats.

FAMILY TRAITS *Most of us recognize an owl—like this Burrowing Owl (top)— immediately, even though we may not know the exact species. It takes only a little more practice to learn to recognize the family traits of many less familiar birds, such as the Marsh Wren (right).*

Birds do not occur at random across the landscape. Instead, each species has its own set of environmental requirements and preferences, based on what it eats and where it nests (see p. 30). Most of the species that you find in grasslands, for instance, do not normally occur in woodlands, and vice versa.

This concept sometimes holds good for entire groups of birds: if you want to look for a duck, for example, you go to a lake or marsh, not to a dry grassland or a wooded park. But it is generally true at

START WITH THE HABITAT

Many birds are restricted to an easily recognizable habitat, offering a useful aid to identification. You will normally find Pied-billed Grebes, for example, only in a lake or marsh.

the species level as well: the Short-eared Owl, for example, lives in grasslands, while its close relative the Long-eared Owl lives in forests and woodlands.

We have therefore arranged our selection of the most commonly encountered North American birds into six habitat categories: urban areas, woodlands, grasslands, wetlands, seashores, and deserts. These are broad, widespread, familiar environments, and it should be easy for you to relate them to the kind of area you live in. This in turn will help you familiarize yourself with the birds you are most likely to see around you.

PITFALLS

The habitat approach is ideal for the beginner; however, it does have its limitations, and to use the approach to best effect it is important to be aware of them.

In the first place, birds don't always relate to their environment in ways that make sense to humans. Some occur in many habitats, while others are found only in very restricted environments. Some dwell in different habitats at different times of the year.

Moreover, the concept of habitat alone may give us an incomplete notion of how the bird relates to its environment, and we need the concept of niche to complete it. For example, both vireos and towhees occur in woodlands (often the very same patch of woodland), but towhees are seen on the ground and in bushes whereas vireos are usually seen only in the leafy crowns of trees.

To help you deal with this, preferences for particular niches are described where relevant within the species profiles. Furthermore, each habitat is introduced by two sections, the first of which presents a typical scene from that habitat and highlights commonly used niches. The second recommends strategies and equipment that may assist you within a particular environment.

A TWO-PRONGED APPROACH

Both approaches—the taxonomic and the habitat—have advantages and disadvantages. On the whole, it is best to view them as complementary: by exploiting them both fully you will rapidly improve your birding knowledge and your identification skills.

Family Groups
88

Urban Areas
95

Downtown Areas, Parks, Gardens, Vacant Lots

Woodlands
121

Forests, Clearings, Riparian Groves, Edges, Thickets

Grasslands
163

Prairies, Open Fields, Farmland

Wetlands
193

Lakes, Marshes, Reservoirs, Rivers, Swamps

Seashores
229

Beaches, Sand Dunes, Coastal Cliffs, Estuaries, Mangroves

Deserts
255

Scrublands, Chaparral, Mesas, Sagebrush Plains

FAMILY GROUPS

All North American bird species belong to broad family groups. A sound knowledge of these groups and their shared characteristics is a real boon to any birder.

In taxonomy, bird species are organized into groups at different levels: order, family, subfamily, genus, and so on (see p. 20). To most birders, groups of certain species will be better known at one level than another.

For example, we tend to think of thrushes as one group and wood-warblers as another, even though the thrushes constitute a family while the wood-warblers are only a subfamily; we think of owls as one group even though there are two distinct families. It is simply more straightforward and more useful for us to think of the birds in these groups, even if they are not at the same taxonomic level.

We have therefore arranged the birds of North America into the groups that we feel will be most familiar to birders and most easily grasped by beginners. These groups are listed in traditional taxonomic order.

Each group name in our list is highlighted in bold. Scientific names of families and subfamilies are given. These names can prove useful when consulting other publications.

A useful starting point when considering groups is to think of birds as either passerines (songbirds) or non-passerines, as passerines make up over half of all species.

Familiarizing yourself with the traditional taxonomic sequence will also help you to navigate through other sources of information on birds, as most field guides (including this one), handbooks, and bird lists use similar sequences.

NON-PASSERINES

Loons (Gaviidae) are strongly aquatic birds that dive beneath the surface for their food and come ashore only to nest. To some extent, they resemble ducks and cormorants, but they ride low in the water and their bill is pointed and often quite stout.
♂♀ 🖊 4/5 ➤ 234

Grebes (Podicipedidae) resemble small loons and, like them, are strongly aquatic, inhabiting wetlands generally. One distinctive feature is their apparent lack of a tail—their bodies end in a powder-puff effect of loose feathers.
♂♀ 🖊 7/20 ➤ 198–99

The three families of seabirds—**albatrosses** (Diomedeidae), **shearwaters and petrels** (Procellariidae), and **storm-petrels** (Hydrobatidae)—are often known as tubenoses because their nostrils are set in tubes on top of the bill. Strictly pelagic, they seldom come within sight of land except when breeding.
♂♀ 🖊 30/105 ➤ 235

KEY TO SYMBOLS

♂♀	No difference in plumage between males and females	🖊	No seasonal variation in plumage
♂♀	Males and females have different plumage	🖊	Seasonal variation in plumage
♂♀	Plumage difference between sexes in some species but not in others	🖊	Seasonal variation in plumage in some species but not in others
7/20	Number of species in the group in North America/the world	➤23	Page references for species in the group that feature in The Habitat Birdfinder

Cormorants (Phalacrocoracidae) are mainly black in plumage and their longish bills are distinctly hooked at the tip. They swim low in the water, dive for their food, and inhabit fresh and salt water alike. There are several related groups with few species and widely differing appearance: **anhingas** (Anhingidae) resemble cormorants but have longer tails and pointed, spear-like bills; **pelicans** (Pelecanidae) have huge, pouch-like bills; **gannets and boobies** (Sulidae) inhabit coastal waters and dive for fish in spectacular plunges from high above the sea.
♀♂ **18/62** ➤ 200, 236–37

Herons, egrets, and bitterns (Ardeidae); **storks** (Ciconiidae); and **ibises and spoonbills** (Threskiornithidae) are all long-legged, long-necked, long-billed, and short-tailed birds that wade in shallow water in search of much of their food. Many egrets are entirely white but dull reds and grays are common among herons. Bitterns may be brown and streaked. Ibises have downward-curving bills; spoonbills have the bill shape their name suggests; and the only American stork has a naked, featherless head and upper neck.
♀♂ **35/117** ➤ 168, 201–5, 238

Ducks, geese, and swans (Anatidae) all have some recognizable variation of the familiar duck bill, which is difficult to describe concisely but is instantly recognizable. Most lose their flight feathers all at once, so are flightless for a few weeks every year while the new feathers grow.

Male ducks often have a striking courtship plumage.
♀♂ **55/150** ➤ 206–16, 239

The diurnal **birds of prey** are often known collectively as raptors. It is convenient to include the New World vultures and condors (Cathartidae) in this group although they are not related. Key subgroups are the hawks, kites, and eagles (Accipitridae) and falcons (Falconidae). Raptors are extremely variable in plumage, and in identification subtle details of flight silhouette (length of tail, breadth of wing, and so on) are often far more important than color pattern.
♀♂ **35/292** ➤ 126–28, 169–73, 217–18

Of the **gamebirds** (Phasianidae) only the Wild Turkey, grouse, and quail are native to the North American continent; partridges and pheasants have been introduced. All are chicken-like birds that feed almost exclusively on the ground.
♀♂ **24/257** ➤ 129, 174, 260

In body form, **crakes, rails, and coots** (Rallidae) look faintly chicken-like but for the most part inhabit swamps and marshes. Shy and elusive, most are seldom seen by the casual observer. Their tails are frequently cocked high, and persistently flicked. Allied to the crakes and rails are the single species of Limpkin (Aramidae) and the two American cranes (Gruidae), the Sandhill Crane and Whooping Crane.
♀♂ **12/158** ➤ 219

Top to bottom: Green Heron (Ardeidae); Purple Gallinule (Rallidae); Sage Grouse (Phasianidae); Cinnamon Teal (Anatidae)

Anyone familiar with the Killdeer should have little difficulty recognizing any of the other **plovers** (Charadriidae). These are birds of coasts and open country, with long, pointed wings, rather large dark eyes and a pigeon-like bill. Plovers have a characteristic habit of dashing over the sand or mud on twinkling feet, with head held low, then periodically coming to an abrupt halt, as though called smartly to attention.

♂♀ **10/64** ➤ 175, 240

The **sandpipers** and their relatives (Scolopacidae) mostly inhabit seashores, especially tidal mudflats. Many are strongly migratory, nesting in the High Arctic and traveling south in fall. Most are gregarious and habitually congregate in large mixed roosting flocks at high tide, scattering to feed over exposed mudflats as the tide recedes. Plumage is mainly dull brown or gray, and many species are extremely difficult to identify. The slender bill ranges from very long to quite short, and may be straight, strongly down-curved, or even slightly upcurved. An important first step in identifying shorebirds is to carefully note length and shape

Right: Black-necked Stilt (Recurvirostridae); below: Sanderlings (Scolopacidae); bottom left: Common Murre (Alcidae).

of bill; whether there is a white rump or not; and whether there is a white stripe down the length of the upper wing (wingbar) or not.

♂♀ **52/87** ➤ 221–22, 241–46

Closely related are two other small but distinctive groups: **stilts and avocets** (Recurvirostridae) and **oystercatchers** (Haematopodidae). The former are common on prairie sloughs and similar wetlands, especially in the west and south; they are mainly black-and-white in plumage, and have very long legs. The latter live along coastlines and have long, stout, chisel-like beaks.

♂♀ **4/23** ➤ 220

Almost everyone knows what **seagulls** (Laridae) look like but there are many different species (and quite a few live nowhere near the sea). Furthermore, most take several years to reach maturity, going through a series of different immature plumages, which make species identification a matter of considerable intricacy. A typical adult gull is white below and gray above, and some have black heads.

Terns are similar to gulls but usually smaller and slimmer, with long, slender,

pointed wings, and a black cap. The bill is sharply pointed and the tail is often forked. Generally, gulls are scavengers but most terns feed on small fish captured by splash-diving from a few feet above the surface.

There are two smaller groups closely related to gulls but very distinctive in appearance: one **skimmer** (Rynchopinae) occurs in the southern US and looks a bit like a large tern, but the lower mandible is much longer than the upper. **Skuas and jaegers** (Stercorariinae) look rather like dark brown gulls but specialize in piracy, bullying and harassing other seabirds until they abandon their catch.

♂♀ **46/99** ➤ 247–53

The family Alcidae includes **murres, guillemots, and puffins**. Alcids are exclusively marine birds that catch their food underwater. Their small wings lend their flight a distinctively buzzy appearance, low to the water. Many species congregate in large colonies on seacliffs to nest. They are well represented in the Arctic, but several species extend southward, especially along the Pacific coast to Mexico.

♂♀ **20/23** ➤ 254

Left: White-winged Dove (Columbidae); above: Anna's Hummingbird (Trochilidae); below left: Great Horned Owl (Strigidae); below right: Gila Woodpecker (Picidae)

Pigeons and doves (Columbidae) come in a range of colors and sizes, but all resemble the ordinary street pigeon closely enough to make confusion unlikely at the group level.
♂♀ **15/302** ➤ 100, 176, 261

The **cuckoos** (Cuculidae) are a worldwide group with relatively few species in North America; the group includes the anis and the Greater Roadrunner. These are all generally slender, long-tailed birds with somewhat curved bills.
♂♀ **6/130** ➤ 262

There are, in fact, two distinct groups of **owls**— barn owls (Tytonidae) and

"typical" owls (Strigidae)— but they are so similar in most respects that the distinction is more or less academic. A typical owl is a nocturnal bird of prey with remarkably well-developed night-vision and acute hearing; and strong,

curved talons. Their eyes are forward-facing, like those of humans and unlike most other birds.
♂♀ **19/149** ➤ 130–31, 177

Nightjars (Caprimulgidae) are for most people disembodied voices in the night. They catch flying insects at night but spend the rest of the day on the forest or woodland floor, trusting entirely to their extra-ordinarily cryptic coloration to avoid detection.
♂♀ **8/79** ➤ 178

Swifts (Apodidae) quite closely resemble swallows in general appearance and behavior, though they are not related. They spend almost all of their time in the air, feeding on small flying insects. They have compact, cigar-shaped bodies and long, narrow, scythe-like wings. They typically fly much higher than swallows and martins.
♂♀ **4/94** ➤ 101

Hummingbirds (Trochilidae) are unmistakable. No other bird beats its wings so rapidly (up to 200 beats per second) that they are visible only as a blur. The hummingbird hovers and flies in all directions with equal facility,

in much the same way as a helicopter.
♂♀ **18/353** ➤ 102, 263

The only common and widespread **kingfisher** (Alcedinidae) in North America is the Belted Kingfisher. Kingfishers perch in trees overhanging rivers and streams and catch fish by splash-diving.
♂♀ **3/92** ➤ 223

A typical **woodpecker** (Picidae) clasps a tree trunk with strong-clawed feet, leans back to throw much of its weight onto its stiffened, spine-tipped tail feathers, and uses this tripod stance as a fulcrum from which to batter away at the bark with its rather heavy, chisel-like bill. Males often have some small patch of red on the head.
♂♀ **21/221** ➤ 103, 132–33

91

PASSERINES

The **tyrant flycatchers** (Tyrannidae) are an exclusively American family with a distinctive habit of perching bolt upright on some vantage point and sallying forth to catch flying insects with an audible snap of the bill. Most are drab and inconspicuous in plumage, and lack complex songs—though it is often easier to identify a tyrant flycatcher by its call than by its plumage.
♀♂ **35/390** ➤ 134, 179–80, 224

Larks (Alaudidae) are small, inconspicuous, brownish birds of open country. Most occur in Eurasia and Africa, and only the Horned Lark is common in North America.
♀♂ **2/79** ➤ 181

Swallows and martins (Hirundinidae) are small, slender birds that catch insects in midair, more or less sucking them up as they fly in graceful swoops, flurries, and glides usually at no great height over open ground. When not feeding they may perch in twittering flocks along telephone lines.
♀♂ **9/81** ➤ 104–5, 225

Jays, magpies, crows, nutcrackers, and ravens all belong to the group

Corvidae. Jays are often brightly colored, but crows and ravens are black. Most are big, bold, conspicuous, and versatile songbirds, and they appear in most habitats.
♀♂ **17/126** ➤ 106, 182–83, 264

The **chickadees and titmice** (Paridae) are sometimes the most obvious small songbirds in the winter woods across North America. Small, intensely active, acrobatic birds, many share a similar color pattern consisting of a dark cap, white cheeks, and a small black bib across the lower throat. Similar to these but plainer are the **bushtits** (Aetithalidae).
♀♂ **10/47** ➤ 107–8, 265

Both **nuthatches** (Sittidae) and **creepers** (Certhiidae) are usually instantly recognizable by their behavior alone: nuthatches are the only birds to creep headfirst down tree trunks, and treecreepers are the only small birds that creep up the trunks of trees.
♀♂ **5/30** ➤ 135

Wrens (Troglodytidae) are small, drab, brown birds that usually inhabit undergrowth or very low vegetation. They are active, have high-pitched, vigorous songs. Many species habitually

carry the tail cocked above the back.
♀♂ **9/61** ➤ 109, 266–67

The few North American members of the enormous, essentially Old World assemblage of **warblers** (Sylviidae) are very small, energetic birds of forests and woodlands. This group includes kinglets and gnatcatchers. Kinglets are birds of coniferous forest, given to dangling and fluttering acrobatically at the very tips of branches, nervously flicking their wings. The gnatcatchers are equally small but bluish above, with long slender tails that are often held cocked.
♀♂ **6/384** ➤ 136–37

Thrushes (Turdidae) are medium-sized songbirds that spend much of their time in the middle levels of woodlands. They are soberly colored, and often have strikingly beautiful, evocative songs. They include the bluebirds and the Townsend's Solitaire, as well as the familiar American Robin.
♀♂ **17/316** ➤ 110, 138

The **mockingbirds and thrashers** (Mimidae) somewhat resemble thrushes except they have curved bills and long tails. Many

Left to right: Steller's Jay (Corvidae); Cedar Waxwing (Bombycillidae); Eastern Kingbird (Tyrannidae)

*Left: Red-winged Blackbird (Icterinae);
below: Evening Grosbeak (Cardinalinae)*

frequent undergrowth, and their songs often include mimicry of other birds.
♂♀ **10/32** ➤ 111, 268

Across North America there are only two resident species of **pipits** (Motacillidae), a group otherwise widespread in Eurasia and Africa. These are small, drab, streaked birds resembling larks, except that they have slender bills and frequently wag their tails.
♂♀ **5/54**

Waxwings (Bombycillidae) are slender, elegant, crested birds with soft silky plumage and yellow tail-tips. They are gregarious, and feed largely on fruit. Allied to them is the Phainopepla (Ptilogonatidae) of the southwest.
♂♀ **3/8** ➤ 112, 269

The most characteristic feature of the **shrikes** (Laniidae) is that they seem like a songbird version of a hawk: they select the highest perches available in open country as a vantage point from which to look for large insects, mice, or small birds.
♂♀ **2/74**

Vireos (Vireonidae) often sing persistently, even through the heat of a summer's day when other birds are silent. Though common and widespread, they are seldom noticed, as they spend most of their time high in the canopy of trees.
♂♀ **11/44** ➤ 139–40

Strongly migratory, **wood-warblers** (Parulinae) of one species or another (and often several together) are common in summer in all kinds of woodlands and forests across North America. Spring males often have bright colors and distinctive patterns, and spring females—though duller—look similar enough not to present identification difficulties. In fall, however, many molt into a drab plumage that makes most look much alike. The fall warblers are a challenge to the identification skills of any birder.
♂♀ **53/126** ➤ 141–52, 226

One of the largest groups, **New World sparrows** (Emberizinae) are present in virtually all habitats from suburban gardens to arctic tundra and southern salt marshes. A group of similar birds is Cardinalinae, including the **grosbeaks and buntings**. Most are small, brown and streaked, and have short, conical bills.
♂♀ **60/319** ➤ 114–17, 154–60, 184–87, 270–71

Male **tanagers** (Thraupinae) are among the most brilliant and intensely colored of all American songbirds. Females are plain and duller in color. All spend much of their time in the canopy of trees. In contrast to the orioles, the bill is moderately long, fairly stout, and usually yellowish rather than black.
♂♀ **4/242** ➤ 153

The **cowbirds, blackbirds, grackles, and orioles** all belong to an exclusively American group, the Icterinae. Many are birds of open country (though orioles are strongly arboreal), and a number are familiar in suburban and rural areas.
♂♀ **20/95** ➤ 118, 161–62, 188–91, 227–28, 272

The **finches** (Fringillidae) are very like the weavers and sparrows in size and appearance but are, on the whole, more brightly colored, and have stout, seed-cracking bills.
♂♀ **16/124** ➤ 119, 192

The **weavers** (Ploceidae), **starlings** (Sturnidae), **Old World sparrows** (Passeridae) are Old World groups with no native members in North America. Several, however, have been introduced, notably the House Sparrow and the European Starling.
♂♀ **4/261** ➤ 113, 120

93

USING *the* HABITAT BIRDFINDER

The following pages present 148 of the most commonly encountered species, arranged according to the habitat that they favor. In many cases, similar or related species are also discussed, bringing the total number of birds featured to over 200. Each page incorporates the features shown here.

A clear photograph of the species in typical plumage and attitude. Captions indicate, where relevant, the sex, age, seasonal plumage, and subspecies.

The habitat code indicates which type of environment the bird most often frequents. See the key on page 87.

The name of the group of birds— family or subfamily—that the species belongs to.

The common and scientific names of the species. Within each habitat, the species are arranged in taxonomic order.

The map shows the bird's breeding distribution in yellow and its winter range in blue. Green indicates that the species is resident.

The calendar bar highlights the period during which the eggs are normally in the nest.

The text provides important information on where and how you are likely to encounter the bird; its behavioral characteristics, life cycle, and migration patterns; and how to identify the species in the field, including how to distinguish it from any similar species.

Accurate, full-color illustrations show field marks; plumage variations; similar species and subspecies; and behavioral characteristics.

Quick-reference Field Notes include:
- *The size of the bird from the bill tip to the end of the tail*
- *Distinctive plumage and behavioral features*
- ▲ *Information on similar species that may confuse you*
- *Form and location of nest*
- *Number and color of eggs in a clutch*

Gaviidae: Loons

Adult (breeding plumage)

Common Loon
Gavia immer

In the north, Common Loons are often seen nesting on large freshwater lakes, where their loud, yodeling calls are a sign of summer. Some of these birds also spend the winter on inland waters, especially the Great Lakes. For most people, however, loons are birds of the coasts.

All loons in winter are dark above and white below, and it is important to note the shape of the head and a stout, straightish bill. These features, along with a distinct whitish area around its eyes in winter, distinguish it from the smaller Pacific Loon (*Gavia pacifica*; 22–26" [56–66 cm]), which nests in the far northwest and is common along the Pacific coast in winter. The Pacific Loon has a puffier, more rounded head, and a slighter bill than the Common.

In summer the adult Pacific has a pale gray head and hindneck, and a blackish foreneck bordered by white stripes, while the Common Loon has a black head and neck with two striped white cross-bands.

Pacific Loons tend to fly low over the ocean and, unlike Commons, often occur in fair-sized flocks. Common Loons can also be distinguished in flight by their large feet that stick out behind them like paddles.

FIELD NOTES
- 26–33" (66–84 cm)
- Pointed bill
- Large, angular head
- Rides low in water
- Darker than most other loons
- ▲ Difficult to distinguish from several other loon species in winter
- Bowl of grass and twigs, on land or anchored to vegetation
- 1–3; olive-brown with fine dark flecks

Common (winter)

Common (breeding)

Pacific (breeding)

234

Urban Areas

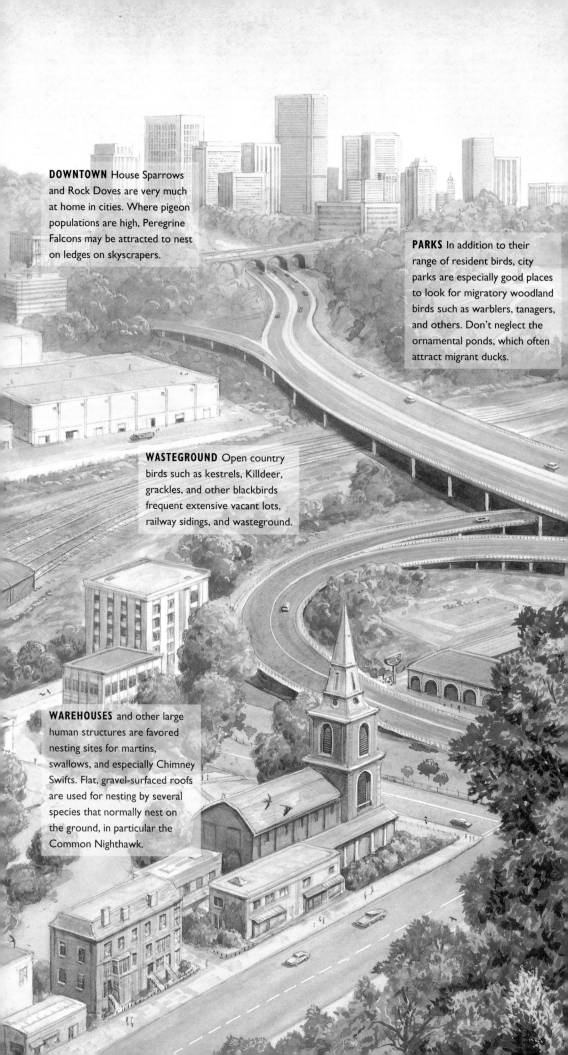

DOWNTOWN House Sparrows and Rock Doves are very much at home in cities. Where pigeon populations are high, Peregrine Falcons may be attracted to nest on ledges on skyscrapers.

PARKS In addition to their range of resident birds, city parks are especially good places to look for migratory woodland birds such as warblers, tanagers, and others. Don't neglect the ornamental ponds, which often attract migrant ducks.

WASTEGROUND Open country birds such as kestrels, Killdeer, grackles, and other blackbirds frequent extensive vacant lots, railway sidings, and wasteground.

WAREHOUSES and other large human structures are favored nesting sites for martins, swallows, and especially Chimney Swifts. Flat, gravel-surfaced roofs are used for nesting by several species that normally nest on the ground, in particular the Common Nighthawk.

URBAN AREAS
Downtown Areas, Parks, Gardens, Vacant Lots

All urban and suburban areas, by their very nature, are characterized by the presence of humans and major alterations to the natural environment. These factors affect bird populations in a variety of ways.

The loss of natural habitat inevitably leads to the elimination of certain species, and many birds are unable to live where they are constantly disturbed and where the air and water are polluted.

On the other hand, some species thrive in urban environments. Birds such as the Rock Dove and the House Sparrow have made themselves entirely at home in cities, to such an extent that they are seldom seen in places that have *not* been disturbed by human activities.

Many woodland birds too, such as mockingbirds and cardinals, have adapted quite well to the parks and gardens of urban America. Gulls scavenging along waterfronts and at garbage dumps, and ducks bobbing on the waters of local ponds are further examples of birds that co-exist happily with humans.

For a number of birds the change to an urban habitat makes little difference to their behavior or feeding tactics. In many cities around the world, for example, Peregrine Falcons live and breed on skyscrapers very much as they have always lived around sea cliffs, hunting pigeons. (Indeed, there are hopes that the Peregrine, almost wiped out in North America a few decades ago, will come to flourish in our cities.) From the Peregrine's perspective, of course, city skyscrapers and sea cliffs are much alike.

GARBAGE DUMPS attract large numbers of gulls and other scavengers such as crows and ravens. Gulls often use such areas for roosting.

GARDENS Birdfeeders and nestboxes will tempt a variety of birds to gardens. Depending on place and season, frequent visitors include wrens, jays, chickadees, and finches.

BIRDING *in* URBAN AREAS

From the relatively sterile concrete and glass environment of downtown business districts to the suburbs with their gardens and shade trees, opportunities for urban birding abound.

It is a mistake to think that if you live in a city there will be few opportunities to observe birds. Urban birding can be extremely rewarding. Even if you live in an apartment block you will normally not be too far from a park, a formal garden, a reservoir, or even some wasteground, all of which attract their share of birdlife.

If you have your own garden then chances are that you are already aware of various bird residents and visitors, and the information and suggestions in Chapter Two will add to the pleasure of your backyard birding.

YOUR LOCAL PATCH
Learning to recognize and appreciate the variations in common local birds is the first step to becoming a good birder, and building up a degree of familiarity with one area is the best way to form a reference base to build upon when you visit other habitats and regions. Even in urban areas, if you look carefully around your neighborhood you will find a surprising range of habitats. Corners of your town or city that you may pay little attention to from day to day—a piece of open wasteground, a small ornamental garden—may prove very interesting from a birding point of view.

Once an area becomes your "local patch", you will soon learn when certain species of migrants arrive in the spring and fall, which birds are most common in winter, which species start to sing when, and so on. With time and patience, you can learn a great deal about bird behavior and nesting biology right on your own doorstep.

URBAN SPECIALISTS *Herring Gulls (above left), Common Grackles (above), and Canada Geese (left) are all among the birds that have thrived in urban areas across much of North America.*

IN THE CITY *New York's Central Park (left) attracts a host of migrant birds. High on a city skyscraper (below), a researcher checks a Peregrine Falcon chick. Hummingbirds (right) are easily attracted to almost any suburban garden.*

RARE VISITORS

While relatively few species of birds live permanently in cities, or are regular visitors, a quite remarkable number of different species have been recorded in towns and cities at one time or another.

This is in part due to the fact that all urban areas are fragmented environments that can contain a broad range of habitat types, and these habitats attract a correspondingly varied range of species. In particular, many migrating and vagrant birds (birds that are lost or off course) will make temporary use of any small pocket of suitable habitat that they can find, even in the center of a city.

These migrants and vagrants are far more likely to be detected in urban areas than in more remote regions. In cities and suburbs there are often hundreds or thousands of birdwatchers, and there is a good chance of any visiting rarity being noted. Indeed, a number of birding groups in North America have

well-organized "hotlines" (see p. 277) that you can telephone to receive a recorded and regularly up-dated summary of the rarities "in town tonight".

Many a birder has accumulated a very respectable life list based solely on the species seen over the years in his or her own home town.

LOCAL RESOURCES

For birders, one great advantage of living in an urban area is that you will almost certainly have access to local resources such as birding clubs and educational institutions that may hold classes relating to birding.

Most of these clubs have the equivalent of an activities officer, who organizes birding trips and excursions, typically ranging from half-day walks in a local park to two-week expeditions to somewhere as remote as the Pribilof Islands. Many trips are

designed as outings for beginners, and some are bound to fit your own particular circumstances.

With a guidebook such as this one you can identify many species on your own, but nothing equals having an experienced birder explain to you—on the spot, while the bird is in view—just what you should be looking for.

For details of organizations in your area, see p. 278.

99

Rock Dove

Columba livia

Rock Doves, also known as Feral Pigeons, are among the birds most familiar to city dwellers throughout North America. They are native to Eurasia, where they inhabit rocky seacoasts and desert canyons. An outstanding example of a bird that was domesticated for showing and racing purposes, this species has "gone wild" in the New World, with the result that there are healthy populations in most towns and cities in North America.

Many city dwellers enjoy feeding these birds, so they have become extremely tame and are sometimes quite a nuisance, large numbers of them nesting on window sills and in enclosed areas. However, the Rock Dove's tameness provides many opportunities for observing interesting aspects of bird behavior (often difficult and time-consuming when watching wild birds). These include social hierarchy in feeding groups (individual recognition is made easy by the pigeons' varied plumages), courtship, and even drinking. Pigeons are among the very few birds that drink by sucking up water.

J F M A M J J A S O N D

plumage variations

FIELD NOTES

- 12–14" (30.5–35.5 cm)
- White rump
- Double black wingbar
- Plumage very varied
- ▲ Band-tailed Pigeon (western forests) is bigger, has gray rump, plain upperwings, yellow bill and white collar
- Shallow saucer of sticks on a ledge
- 1–2; white

100

Chimney Swift

Chaetura pelagica

Each summer, after wintering in South America, the Chimney Swift returns to eastern North America. Look for it over towns, open country, woodlands, and lakes, and listen for its high-pitched twittering calls. These often draw attention to it high overhead, where it might otherwise be missed.

Swifts are supreme aerialists, well adapted for a life on the wing. In this way they resemble swallows, but although the two families look alike and are often seen together, they are not closely related. The Chimney Swift can be distinguished from swallows by its more rapid, stiff wingbeats; faster and more direct flight; and overall blackish plumage.

The Chimney Swift originally nested in hollow trees but, as its name implies, it has readily adapted to nesting on walls of chimneys and other buildings.

The slightly smaller Vaux's (rhymes with "corks" or "corks's") Swift (*Chaetura vauxi*; 4½" [11.5 cm]), the Chimney Swift's counterpart in the west, favors open conifer woods and canyons.

J F M A M J J A S O N D

going to roost

Vaux's

Chimney

FIELD NOTES

■ 4¾–5" (12–12.5 cm)
■ Aerial; dark and featureless overall
■ Squared-off tail
▲ Vaux's Swift (west) almost identical
🪹 Half saucer of twigs glued together with saliva, on a building
● 3–6; white

101

Ruby-throated Hummingbird

Archilochus colubris

The Ruby-throated is the only hummingbird in eastern North America, and it occurs in woodlands, parks, and gardens. Seeing hummingbirds in the field can be difficult since they are small and fly at great speed. Your best chance of seeing one is at a hummingbird feeder. You will then be able to see how tiny they are and admire their iridescent plumage and remarkable flight.

Like most hummers in North America, the Ruby-throated migrates south in winter to Mexico and Central America for the warm climate and ready supply of nectar-rich flowers.

The female Ruby-throated is green above and whitish below, with white corners to her tail, and lacks the male's ruby red throat patch (or gorget). During the breeding season, males display in front of females with a rocking, pendulum-like flight.

The very similar Black-chinned Hummingbird (*Archilochus alexandri*; 3¼–3½" [8–9 cm]) is the western counterpart of the Ruby-throated. It tends to occur in drier areas but also visits hummingbird feeders in gardens. Females of the two species are almost impossible to tell apart in the field.

J F M A M J J A S O N D

Ruby-throated ♂

Black-chinned ♂

FIELD NOTES

■ 3¼–3½" (8–9 cm)

■ Male: Green flanks and ruby-red throat patch

■ Female: No throat patch; white corners to tail

▲ Male Black-chinned (west) has black and violet gorget

Cup of lichens, spider's silk, plant down

● 2; white

Ruby ♀ on nest

Downy Woodpecker

Picoides pubescens

This small woodpecker is common and widespread in deciduous and mixed woodlands, parks, and gardens. In winter, it regularly visits bird feeders, where it is partial to suet, and joins feeding flocks (known as guilds) of small woodland birds such as chickadees and titmice. Equally widespread, but less often seen in gardens, is the Hairy Woodpecker (*Picoides villosus*; 7½–9½" [19–24 cm]), a larger version of the Downy.

J F M A M J J A S O N D

Telling these two species apart can be quite difficult. Basically, if you can see the bill it's a Hairy, and if you can't it's a Downy. Note also that the Downy has black bars on its white outer tail feathers (which the Hairy lacks), and that the Hairy shouts rather than speaks its sharp call.

Occasionally, you may be rewarded by views of a Hairy and a Downy side by side—the difference in bill size is then obvious. Note that western birds of both species generally have less white on their wings than eastern birds.

Hairy ♂

Hairy & Downy (from above)

Downy ♀

FIELD NOTES
- 6–6½" (15–16.5 cm)
- White back stripe
  Hairy Woodpecker has larger bill and lacks black bars on outer tail feathers
- Hole in tree lined with wood chips
- 3–6; white

103

Purple Martin

Progne subis

The male Purple Martin, in his glossy blue-black plumage, is one of the most handsome birds in North America. In the east this large swallow is a familiar sight during summer in urban areas, especially around "martin houses"—condominium-style nestboxes erected on poles. In the west, the species occurs more locally and favors natural nest sites such as holes in dead tree limbs.

The best way to find Purple Martins in the west is to check dead trees along ridges or to visit ponds and lakes where swallows gather to drink, swooping down to dip their bills into the water. Purple Martins stand out as they are significantly larger than other swallows.

Purple Martins spend the winter in South America, return to Florida in February, and reach Canada in May. By October, this fine bird has once again departed from North America.

J F M A M J J A S O N D

FIELD NOTES

- 7½–8" (19–20.5 cm)—noticeably larger than other swallows
- Male: Overall glossy blue-black plumage
- Female: Brownish, pale-bellied
- Cavity in dead tree or nestbox lined with grass, mud, and feathers
- 3–8; white

martin house

Barn Swallow

Hirundo rustica

A familiar summer visitor to urban and rural areas across North America, the Barn Swallow is often welcomed as a herald of spring. This graceful bird, identified by its long tail streamers (short or lacking in the juvenile), nests singly or in small colonies on buildings, where it builds a cup-like nest of mud.

Also widespread and common in summer is the closely related Cliff Swallow (*Hirundo pyrrhonota*; 5–5½" [12.5–14 cm]), identified by its chunkier build, squared-off tail and pale rump. The Cliff Swallow's nest is a gourd-shaped mud structure built under eaves or bridges, and colonies sometimes number up to a thousand pairs.

Like all swallows, these two species are masters of the air, where they swoop and glide, apparently effortlessly, for hours on end. As they fly, they dip down to the surface of lakes and rivers to drink and bathe. They also feed as they fly, their wide gapes enabling them to catch insects on the wing.

J F M A M J J A S O N D

Barn   Cliff

FIELD NOTES
- 5–5½" (12.5–14 cm)
- Glossy blue above, reddish below
- Deeply forked tail with streamers
- ▲ Cliff Swallow has pale rump, square tail
- Mud cup lined with grass and feathers, on a building
- 4–7; white spotted with browns

Cliff Swallows at nest

Blue Jay

Cyanocitta cristata

The handsome, unmistakable Blue Jay is a common and familiar bird in parks and gardens from the Atlantic coast to the Great Plains, and often visits bird feeders in winter.

Its counterpart in the west is the Steller's Jay (*Cyanocitta stelleri*; 11–12" [28–30.5 cm]), which takes over from the Rockies to the Pacific coast. The Steller's tends to be more of a forest bird although, like most jays, it can be tame at campgrounds and picnic areas. Northwestern Steller's Jays tend to be darker, while southern birds have a white crescent above each eye.

Best known for their loud and raucous calls, both jays are also accomplished vocalists whose repertoires range from convincing imitations of hawk screams to occasional soft, sweet warbling songs. Tracking down a scolding group of jays can frequently lead to a hawk or a roosting owl, as jays often mob these birds.

Both jays (but particularly the Blue Jay) vary their diet in summer by stealing other birds' eggs, while in fall they conceal acorns in the ground for times of hardship during winter.

| J | F | M | A | M | J | J | A | S | O | N | D |

FIELD NOTES

■ 10–11" (25.5–28 cm)

■ Blue and white plumage and crest

▲ Steller's Jay (west) has blackish head

🪺 Cup of twigs and grass at mid to upper levels in tree

⬤ 3–7; greenish to bluish, marked with browns

Blue Jay

southern form

northern form

Steller's Jay

Black-capped Chickadee

Parus atricapillus

Chickadees are frequent winter visitors to bird feeders, where they are noted for their acrobatic behavior. The Black-capped Chickadee is a familiar bird in gardens and woodlands across northern North America, where its *chick-a-dee-dee-dee* call can be heard throughout the year. In the southeastern US, the Black-capped is replaced by the slightly smaller but virtually identical (even experts argue about how to tell the two apart!)

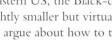

Carolina Chickadee (*Parus carolinensis*; 4¼–4¾" [11–12 cm]).
Tracking down the call of a chickadee can transform a late fall or winter walk through a wooded area into an exciting experience, as it may lead you to woodpeckers, titmice, nuthatches, creepers, kinglets, and warblers, all moving and feeding together, with the chickadees acting as a nucleus species. Following the chickadees' scolding calls may also lead you to an owl on its daytime roost, as chickadees are known to mob these birds.

FIELD NOTES

- 4¾–5¾" (12–14.5 cm)
- Black cap and bib
- Grayish back
- ▲ Carolina Chickadee (southeast) almost identical
- Tree cavity lined with grass, feathers
- 5–10; white dotted with reddish browns

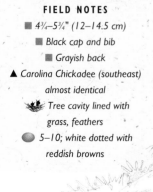

chickadees at feeder (with Evening Grosbeaks)

107

Tufted Titmouse

Parus bicolor

In the New World, titmice are simply crested chickadees. The Tufted Titmouse is a readily identifiable, familiar visitor to bird feeders in the east and its *peter peter peter* song is a common sound in parks and woodlands. Should titmice be regular winter visitors to your garden, you may be able to persuade them to stay all year by erecting a suitable nestbox.

If you live in south Texas or are a visitor there, note that the local Tufted Titmice have a whitish forehead and black crest. At one time they were considered a separate species—the Black-crested Titmouse.

In deciduous and mixed woodlands of the west, especially among oaks, you can find the

Tufted's western counterpart, the well-named Plain Titmouse (*Parus inornatus*; 5½" [14 cm]), which often visits gardens during winter.

Like chickadees, titmice are regular members of mixed-species feeding flocks in woodlands in winter.

J F M A M J J A S O N D

eastern form

south-western form

Plain Titmouse

FIELD NOTES
■ 5–6" (12.5–15 cm)
■ Gray and white with crest
▲ Number of similar species in southwest
🪹 Tree cavity lined with grass, feathers
🥚 4–8; white flecked with browns

House Wren

Troglodytes aedon

A lively, chortling song or an insistent, scolding chatter often attracts attention to this small, fairly drab-looking brown bird with its slender bill, long tail, and the dark barring on the wings that is characteristic of wrens. The House Wren is common and widespread in North America, and different populations live all the way to Tierra del Fuego at the southern tip of South America. Like most small wrens, it can be difficult to see as it slips in and out of thickets and brush piles.

House Wrens nest in cavities, and the male builds several dummy nests of sticks from which the female chooses one, lines it with fine grass, and makes it home. Sometimes a pair will destroy the eggs of other wrens nesting nearby. This species can be attracted to nestboxes in gardens, but the entrance hole must be small enough to keep out starlings and House Sparrows. In winter, most House Wrens migrate to the southern US and Mexico.

J F M A M J J A S O N D

FIELD NOTES

- 4½–5" (11.5–12.5 cm)
- Small, brown; skulking
- Barred wings and tail
- Foundation of sticks lined with fine material, in cavity
- 5–12; white dotted with browns

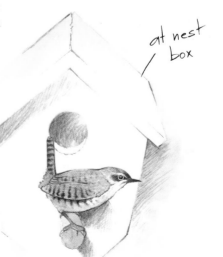

at nest box

109

American Robin

Turdus migratorius

Perhaps the most familiar and widespread North American bird, the American Robin—found in urban and forested areas from coast to coast—needs little introduction. Its melodic, caroling song usually starts before dawn and is considered a harbinger of spring in much of the north.

J F M A M J J A S O N D

The American Robin's brick red chest reminded early European settlers of the small, red-breasted Robin of the Old World. It would be more correct to call the New World species the American Thrush, but few ornithologists would have the nerve to suggest that its name be changed!

This is the only widespread large thrush in North America and although the sexes are similar in appearance, by looking carefully you may note that the male has a blacker head and brighter plumage. The juvenile is paler than the adult and has dark brown spotting on its chest; its bill is dark, changing to yellow in winter.

FIELD NOTES

- 9–10" (23–25.5 cm)
- Brick red breast
- Juvenile: Paler with spotting on chest
- ▲ Varied Thrush (western forests) has dark breast band
- Cup of grass, mud, low to high in bush or tree
- 3–7; unmarked pale blue

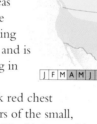

adult feeding fledglings

110

Northern Mockingbird

Mimus polyglottos

The English translation of the Northern Mockingbird's scientific name—"many-tongued mimic"—sums up well the best-known quality of this slender, long-tailed, gray and white bird. Its remarkable song, characterized by frequent three- to six-times repetition of phrases, is heard all over rural regions in the southern US, and in recent years the species' range has expanded into much of New England. As well as imitating other birds, mockingbirds incorporate a variety of sounds, such as barking dogs, into their repertoire, which they give day or night, from a perch or in flight.

J F M A M J J A S O N D

If you watch a Northern Mockingbird running around on a lawn, you may see it flash its white wing patches. This is apparently a way to flush out insect prey and is also useful in distracting predators from the nest.

As with all members of the family Mimidae, the sexes are alike in appearance. The juvenile Northern Mockingbird can be identified by the dusky spotting on its chest and by its dusky eyes.

← white wing patches

Mockingbird attacking cat!

FIELD NOTES

- 9–10" (23–25.5 cm)
- Active and noisy
- Slender, long-tailed
- Bold, white wing patches
- Cup of twigs, grass, wool at low to mid levels in bush or tree
- 2–6; pale bluish, heavily marked with browns

Cedar Waxwing

Bombycilla cedrorum

The first sign of Cedar Waxwings is often high-pitched, sibilant calls overhead. On looking up, you may then see a tightly packed group of pointed-winged, short-tailed birds wheeling around in the sky. (In flight they resemble the European Starling.) With luck, the flock will then land to reveal one of the most beautiful of all birds, with its sleek plumage in soft pastel shades and a tufted crest above its narrow, black mask. The name "waxwing" comes from the waxy red tips on its inner wing feathers. Juvenile Cedar Waxwings have streaked underparts.

While they nest in northern North America, Cedar Waxwings move south in winter (some reaching as far as Panama) and frequently visit parks and gardens to feed at berry-bearing trees and shrubs.

A good way to attract these birds to your garden is to plant cedars (*Cedrus*), and rowans (*Sorbus aucuparia*), as the berries of these plants are their favored food. In summer, Cedar Waxwings often eat insects, caught as the birds fly.

J F M A M J J A S O N D

juvenile

Cedar

Bohemian

FIELD NOTES

- ■ 6–7" (15–18 cm)
- ■ Smooth, elegant, crested
- ■ Yellow-tipped tail
- ■ White undertail coverts
- ▲ Bohemian Waxwing (northern forests) is larger and has brick red undertail coverts
- Cup of twigs, grass, moss at mid to upper levels in tree
- 2–6; pale blue with dark markings

European Starling

Sturnus vulgaris

Whether feeding and squabbling in city parks, or flying in vast swarms to roost in the urban warmth of downtown areas, starlings are a familiar sight in cities across North America. Sixty European Starlings, natives of the Old World, were introduced into New York's Central Park in 1890, and their offspring has multiplied to the 200-million-plus starlings we see today.

These birds are easy to watch and provide a good opportunity to observe how summer and winter plumages can vary. Most songbirds molt twice a year, but the starling has a single molt in late summer (after breeding), when the glossy adult and the dull gray juvenile acquire new blackish feathers marked profusely with pale spots. The spots then wear off through the winter, to be replaced by the purple and green sheens of breeding starlings. The bird's bill is darker in winter and changes to bright yellow in breeding birds.

J F M A M J J A S O N D

FIELD NOTES

- 8–9" (20.5–23 cm)
- Stocky, stub-tailed bird
- Glossy black plumage
- Winter: Speckled plumage, dark bill
- Summer: Yellow bill
- Cup of grass and twigs in cavity
- 4–8; pale blue

winter plumage

juvenile

113

Northern Cardinal

Cardinalis cardinalis

The Northern Cardinal is characteristic of eastern North America, and the male, with his stout red bill, black face, and tufted crest, is unmistakable. In spring and summer, he sings his loud song of bright whistles from a prominent perch, and in winter he adds a splash of color to many a snow-covered bird feeder.

juvenile ♂

The female and juvenile are pale grayish brown overall with some red in their wings and tail; the female has a reddish pink bill, and the juvenile's bill is dark gray. In late summer, the young male molts into his all-red plumage and his bill turns red.

There is a separate population of Northern Cardinals in the brushy washes of the south-western deserts, where the closely related Pyrrhuloxia (p. 270) also occurs. The Northern Cardinal can be seen, too, in Hawaii, where it was introduced by homesick Americans from the eastern US.

winter ♂
(on holly)

| J | F | M | A | M | J | J | A | S | O | N | D |

FIELD NOTES

- 8–9" (20.5–23 cm)
- Male: Stout red bill, black face and tufted crest—unmistakable
- Female: Paler brownish color; reddish pink bill
- Bowl of twigs, grass at low to mid levels in thicket or bush
- 2–5; whitish marked with browns and grays

♀

114

California Towhee

Pipilo crissalis

This large, plain brown sparrow is common in urban and rural California where you may see it hopping on the ground, often with its long, dark tail held cocked; the cinnamon undertail coverts are a distinctive field mark. California Towhees often feed in areas of open ground but quickly run for cover—under a bush or a parked car—when disturbed.

Until a few years ago, this bird was considered to be the same species as the Canyon Towhee (*Pipilo fuscus*; 7½–9" [19–23 cm]) of the interior southwest, and the species was at that time known as the Brown Towhee. It has been shown, however, that the two types look and sound different, and ornithologists now recognize two distinct species whose ranges do not overlap.

The California Towhee gives a loud metallic *chink* call, while the Canyon Towhee's call is a two-syllable, complaining *ch-eh*. The Canyon Towhee, less often found in urban gardens than the Californian species, is further distinguished by its rustier cap and a dark spot on the center of its chest.

J F M A M J J A S O N D

FIELD NOTES

- 7½–9" (19–23 cm)
- Plain, brownish
- ▲ Canyon Towhee (southwest interior) has rustier cap and dark spot on chest
- Bulky bowl of twigs, grass at low to mid levels in bush or tree
- 2–6; pale bluish marked with browns, grays, and black

California

Canyon

115

Song Sparrow

Melospiza melodia

In spring and summer, the Song Sparrow sings a varied arrangement of chips and trills from a low perch on a bush or post. During other seasons, although common and widespread, the Song Sparrow does not draw attention to itself. Look for it in and near brushy thickets, especially in damp areas.

JFMAMJJASOND

This is one of the most variable birds in North America, and some 31 subspecies have been identified, from the huge (7" [18 cm]) birds of the Aleutian Islands in Alaska to the pale birds of the southwestern deserts, which have sparse, rusty spots on their chest.

The "typical" Song Sparrow is gray and brown above (its broad gray supercilium, or eyebrow, is a good field mark) and its underparts are white marked with blackish streaks which often form a dark spot in the center of its chest. The juvenile has a pale yellowish, or buffy, wash to its face and underparts, which are less distinctly streaked than those of the adult.

FIELD NOTES
- 5½–7" (14–18 cm)
- Broad gray supercilium (eyebrow)
- Blackish streaks on chest—often form spot in center of chest
- ▲ Similar to many other sparrows
- Cup of grass, weeds on or near ground in grass or thicket
- 2–6; pale bluish to greenish white, marked with reddish browns

in full song!

Song Sparrow

Aleutian

White-throated Sparrow

Zonotrichia albicollis

The sweet, whistled *Old Sam Peabody, Peabody, Peabody* song of the White-throated Sparrow is a characteristic sound in the bird's summer home in Canada's coniferous forests. In winter, this common species migrates southward, mainly to the eastern US, although small numbers also spend the winter in the south and west.

| J | F | M | A | M | J | J | A | S | O | N | D |

If you live in the east, following up a rustling sound in the bushes of your local park or woodland in winter may well reveal a flock of White-throated Sparrows. You may also be able to find them if you can recognize and follow their high-pitched, lisping *tseet* call.

The adult has a brightly marked head with a clean-cut, white throat patch and a yellow spot forward of the eyes; the supercilium (eyebrow) varies from white to buff. The immature has dark streaking on its chest; its throat may be pale gray; and its head pattern, while similar to the adult, is more subdued.

buff-striped adult

white-striped adult

FIELD NOTES

- ◼ 6–7" (15–18 cm)
- ◼ Clean-cut, white throat patch
- ◼ Yellow spot in front of eye
- ▲ White-crowned Sparrow— see p. 159
- 🐦 Cup of grass, pine needles on or near ground in thicket
- 🥚 3–6; pale bluish marked with browns and black

immature

Common Grackle

Quiscalus quiscula

The Common Grackle is a familiar and common blackbird in the east, where it lives in urban areas, farmland, and open woodlands. As with other blackbirds, males are slightly larger and brighter than females, although at a distance the sexes appear similar. Seen close up, the males have particularly glossy plumage. This varies from an overall bronze color in birds of New England and west of the Appalachian Mountains, to purplish in birds east and south of the Appalachians. Adults have pale yellow eyes but these are dusky in the sooty brown plumaged juveniles. The birds have long slender tails that are broader toward the tip.

The Common Grackle could be confused with the Rusty Blackbird (*Euphagus carolinus*; 8" [21 cm]), common in the east, and Brewer's Black-bird (*E. cyanocephalus*; 8½–9½" [21.5–24 cm]), common in the west, but both are shorter-tailed than the Common Grackle.

shear-tooth

FIELD NOTES

- 10–12" (25.5–30.5 cm)
- Black, glossy blue-green and bronze
- Long slender tail, broader toward tip, carried folded lengthwise
- ▲ Rusty Blackbird (east) and Brewer's Blackbird (west) similar but shorter-tailed
- Cup of sticks and grass in tree or building
- 4–5; pale green or brown with dark markings

purple form

bronzed form

House Finch

Carpodacus mexicanus

Native to the semi-arid lands of western North America and Mexico, House Finches were released on Long Island, New York, in the 1940s. They have since spread into much of the eastern US and southeastern Canada, and their range apparently continues to expand in the east, where they compete with another introduced species, the House Sparrow (p. 120), for nest sites and food.

J F M A M J J A S O N D

The House Finch is a common visitor to birdfeeders, where the drab female may be overlooked among House Sparrows. Note her plain face and wings and the extensive dusky streaking on her underparts. The male is more conspicuous by virtue of his red brow, bib, and rump. On some males this red tends to orange or yellow. The juvenile resembles the female, and the young male attains adult-like plumage by fall. The House Finch's song is a prolonged warble, ranging from a scratchy to a fairly melodic sound.

House Finch ♂

House Sparrows

FIELD NOTES

- 5½–6" (14–15 cm)
- Male: Red brow, bib, and rump
- Female and juvenile: Paler; dusky streaking on underparts
- ▲ Purple Finch (north and west) similar, but male lacks streaked flanks and female has white streak above eye
- Cup of grass, twigs in cavity or dense foliage
- 2–6; bluish white flecked with browns

119

House Sparrow

Passer domesticus

Introduced to New York in the middle of the nineteenth century, the House Sparrow, also known as the English Sparrow, has spread through most of the Americas. It likes to live near humans and, with the Rock Dove (Feral Pigeon), is perhaps the bird most familiar to city dwellers. Its chirps and chatters may be heard all over town, from wooded parks and gardens to ledges high on skyscrapers.

The male is quite handsome, with his chestnut-colored head stripes and black bib. In winter his bill is dusky pale brownish but in summer it becomes black. If you would like to practice taking notes and sketching birds in the field, the female House Sparrow is a good subject to start with, providing an excellent introduction to bird anatomy and the subtleties of bird behavior. This superficially nondescript bird can puzzle even experienced birders when they encounter it out of context.

J F M A M J J A S O N D

dustbathing ♀

FIELD NOTES

- 5½–6" (14–15 cm)
- Male: Gray crown, gray rump
- Female and juvenile: Dingy gray
- ▲ In St Louis and Illinois beware of confusion with the Eurasian Tree Sparrow
- Bulky dome of grass and straw in a cavity or dense foliage
- 2–6; whitish with brown spots

120

Woodlands

WOODLANDS
Forests, Clearings, Riparian Groves, Edges, Thickets

Before European settlement, much of North America was heavily forested. The forests differed widely in character across the land, reflecting profound differences in climate and landform as did the bird communities that depended upon them.

Dense fir and spruce forest characterized the cold north, while at the extreme tip of Florida the forests were tropical in character. The eastern half of the continent was covered in broadleaf deciduous forests of various species of oak, elm, maple, hickory, magnolia, beech, and dogwood, while the cool, humid forests of the Pacific northwest were dominated by huge Douglas firs and redwoods. Riparian groves of cottonwoods and similar trees were characteristic of much of the arid southwest.

In the west, some of the original tree cover remains intact, but most old-growth forests in the eastern United States were cut down by the 1920s, either for lumber or to create farmland, and much of what remains is second-growth woodland. This term refers to those forests that are at an intermediate stage of regrowth after felling or some disaster such as fire.

During regrowth, forests go through a series of distinct stages, each with its own plant community and therefore its own bird community. Many birds are characteristic of a specific stage in this process, rather than of a particular area.

Without further setbacks, second-growth woodland will grow to maturity and return to its original state. Forests that have reached equilibrium with their environment are described as climax forests.

In general, deciduous trees lose their leaves in winter, while conifers do not. A forest canopy is described as closed if the trees' foliage overlaps; if it does not, it is said to be open.

While the terms "forest" and "woodland" are generally interchangeable, the former is often used to imply a closed canopy, whereas the latter often suggests an open canopy.

CONIFEROUS FOREST is favored by a number of species. In spruce and fir, look for Black-throated Green and Blackburnian warblers.

CLEARINGS and DAMAGED AREAS are attractive to many birds that use woodland for nesting and roosting but prefer to feed in the open. Birds such as Chestnut-sided Warblers are more common in damaged areas than in undisturbed forest.

RIPARIAN GROVES Magpies, flycatchers, and warblers are typical of many species that are common in riverside vegetation.

CANOPY Vireos and tanagers are typical of a number of songbirds that spend most of their time high in the canopy.

MIDDLE LEVEL Thrushes, nuthatches, chickadees, and most woodpeckers are among those birds most commonly seen in the middle foliage layers of the forest.

FOREST EDGE Birds along forest edges may be of the same species as those within the forest, but are much easier to locate and observe.

UNDERSTORY Some woodland birds, such as towhees and most wrens, spend almost all of their time on or very near the ground. Depending on locality, grouse, woodcock, and nightjars may also be found at this level.

BIRDING in WOODLANDS

North American woodlands contain a wealth of birdlife. However, dense foliage can make it difficult to locate many species, so you may be able to identify some only by their calls. Moreover, what you hear and see will depend very much on the time of year.

In winter, the northern woods are home only to those birds that eat foods which last through cold weather, such as seeds, and insects that shelter under tree bark. These birds often congregate in wandering, mixed feeding parties of several species—woodpeckers, nuthatches, creepers, chickadees, and others—all moving through the woods together in search of food. You might walk for an hour or more through a forest that seems to be entirely empty of birdlife, then suddenly

encounter such a flock. For a few moments the trees will be crowded with birds, but the encounter will usually be brief because the birds keep moving along. Soon their soft calls will die away in the distance and the woods will become silent again.

In the warmer climates of the south and west, you'll find a greater diversity of species in winter, including a few warblers and flycatchers.

In spring and summer there is food for many more birds, and flycatchers, thrushes, vireos, warblers, and

a host of other birds return from their winter homes in the New World tropics (the Neotropics) to nest. The spring and fall migration periods (mainly April to May and August to October) are therefore the best times to see the most species, particularly if you live in the south.

WOODLAND WATCHERS *A group of birders takes a close look at a woodland bird. Stiff necks are an occupational hazard of forest birding, as so many of the birds are situated directly above you!*

HABITAT PREFERENCES *Some species frequent only one type of forest—either deciduous or coniferous. White-breasted Nuthatches (above right) prefer deciduous woods; Gray Jays (right) favor conifers.*

KNOWING THE HABITAT

In woodlands, perhaps more than in other habitats, it pays to learn something about the details of the environment, in particular the names of the trees and other plants that you will see around you.

Many bird species are closely associated with specific trees and bushes. If you take time to learn the names of these plants and note which birds you see on or near them, you will soon be able to predict, just by studying the surrounding flora, which birds are likely to inhabit a particular area of forest.

In the text of The Habitat Birdfinder we indicate, where relevant, which trees and plants each species is most closely associated with.

TRACKING BY EAR

Unlike marshlands and open country, where birds can be readily seen, woodlands may at first seem less rich in birdlife, since birds can easily remain out of sight in the foliage. In these conditions, your hearing becomes an important aspect of birding.

It takes practice to learn the songs and calls of different species (see p. 72). A useful way to start is to listen to recordings of songs and calls at home.

When in your local woods, try tracking down the sources of songs and calls for yourself. At first, identifying the bird by sight will be easier than by its call, but as you match the most common songs and calls

WOODLAND BIRDS *may live mostly on the ground, as the American Woodcock (above) does, in the middle layers of foliage, as the Black-capped Chickadee (left) does, or high in the canopy, as the Red-eyed Vireo (below left) does.*

with the species that make them you will soon be able to identify those birds as soon as you hear them. In turn, you will be able to distinguish the songs of species that are new to you.

Learning something of the meaning or context of bird calls in woods can also be useful. For example, small woodland birds have a characteristic alarm note they use if a hawk is in the area, and the scolding notes they make on discovering an owl at its daytime roost can often lead you to the owl itself.

STEALTH AND STRATEGY

You need to move quietly in woodlands, not so much for fear of scaring birds away as for your own ability to concentrate on what you can hear. Look for a trail or some little-used country track to wander along, because then you don't need to keep watching where you put your feet, and you make less noise than when you go crashing through the woods.

Remember to keep scanning all levels of the forest. Some species are birds of the treetops

and seldom come low. Others prefer the middle levels, and quite a few species are almost always found in the understory or on the ground.

Woodland birds vary widely in their response to a human observer. Some are extremely wary, while a few are inquisitive, and may even follow you as you go. If you are patient and move carefully, or, better yet, sit still for a while, many woodland birds will accept your presence. The trick is not to crowd the

bird, or trigger its "startle" response. Once startled into flight, the bird is unlikely to allow you within range again.

Sharp-shinned Hawk

Accipiter striatus

The Sharp-shin, or "Sharpie" as it is often known, is the most common small woodland hawk across much of North America. Like other accipiters (from the genus name), it preys mainly on small birds, and may visit gardens to take birds from feeders—a spectacular sight to witness.

To tell the Sharp-shin from small falcons such as the American Kestrel (p. 173), note its broad, rounded wings and its flight style—bursts of quick flapping followed by a glide. Adults are blue-gray above, barred with orange-red below, while juveniles are brown above and streaked reddish below.

The larger Cooper's Hawk (*Accipiter cooperii*; 15–20" [38–51 cm]), of the US and southern Canada, is generally less common than the Sharpie, and favors more open woodlands and, in winter, semi-open country. Many papers have been written on how to tell these two species apart, but experts still disagree at times. The Sharpie has a proportionately smaller head and a shorter, squarer tail than the Cooper's, but you may find it easier to simply write "accipiter species" in your notebook.

J F M A M J J A S O N D

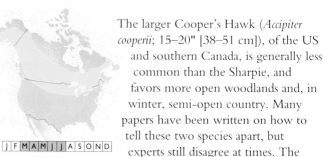

Sharp-shinned ♂

Cooper's ♂

immatur

FIELD NOTES

11–14" (28–35.5 cm)

■ Squared or slightly notched tail tip

■ Females: Clearly larger than males

▲ Cooper's Hawk has more rounded tail and larger head

❀ Stick platform at mid to upper levels in tree

⬤ 3–6; whitish marked with browns

126

Red-shouldered Hawk

Buteo lineatus

A medium-sized buteo, the Red-shouldered Hawk is common in eastern woodlands and hunts mainly from perches such as roadside wires, from where it drops on small mammals and reptiles. Its persistent screaming *kyaah kyaah kyaah* call often draws attention to it. A brighter-marked race occurs in the west.

The other medium-sized buteo widespread in the east is the Broad-winged Hawk (*Buteo platypterus*; 15–17" [38–43 cm]) which is present only in summer, as it migrates south to the tropics for the winter. It has broader, more pointed wings and a shorter tail than the Red-shoulder and spends more time soaring; its wingbeats are looser and more measured. The Red-shoulder is larger and often flies with bursts of quick flapping followed by glides, suggesting an accipiter.

Watching Red-shoulders in winter, when you can be sure there are no Broad-wings around, is a good way to start learning the field marks of these two similar species.

| J | F | M | A | M | J | J | A | S | O | N | D |

Broad-winged

Red-shouldered

FIELD NOTES

- ■ *18–22" (45.5–56 cm)*
- ■ *Reddish shoulders*
- ■ *Dark wings, barred white*
- ■ *Reddish wing-linings, dark bars on underside of tail*
- ▲ *Broad-winged Hawk has broader, more pointed wings, shorter tail*
- *Stick platform at mid to upper levels in tree*
- *1–4; whitish marked with browns*

immature

Red-tailed Hawk

Buteo jamaicensis

This buteo, the most widespread and familiar hawk in North America, is found in woodlands, farmlands, deserts, and wooded urban areas. As well as hunting from perches such as roadside phone poles, Red-tails often hunt while flying. At times, the Red-tail hangs, or hovers, in the wind, like a giant kestrel, and then drops down on its prey, usually a rodent.

J F M A M J J A S O N D

The Red-tail is highly variable in plumage. Most birds are dark above and pale below, but some are dark all over. Adults have a rufous, or orange-red, tail, and a V-shaped area of pale mottling on the back is a good field mark on perched birds. The juvenile Red-tail, like many young hawks, is proportionately longer-winged and longer-tailed than the adult, and its tail is brownish above with numerous dark bars.

The Red-tail's silhouette is useful as a yardstick for comparison with less common species.

dark form (Harlan's)

pale form (Krider's)

from below

FIELD NOTES

- ■ 19–23" (48–58.5 cm)
- ■ Most common and widespread buteo
- ■ Reddish tail
- ■ V-shaped pale mottling on back
- ■ Pale underparts, streaked belly
- ▲ Plumage extremely variable
- Stick platform at mid to upper levels in tree
- 1–5; whitish flecked with browns

128

Ruffed Grouse

Bonasa umbellus

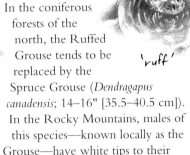

'ruff'

The Ruffed Grouse is typical of deciduous and mixed forests across northern North America, and is often encountered at the side of a quiet road, especially early and late in the day.

Finding one in the woods is really a matter of luck, since this bird's cryptic plumage helps it blend in with leaves on the forest floor. A good way to detect Ruffed Grouse is to listen for the "drumming" of the male's display, which he does from a low perch, in spring. The sound is made by air rushing through his wingtips as he beats them rapidly.

Ruffed Grouse are found in two forms: redder birds are more common in warmer climates, and grayer birds prevail where the climate is cool.

In the coniferous forests of the north, the Ruffed Grouse tends to be replaced by the Spruce Grouse (*Dendragapus canadensis*; 14–16" [35.5–40.5 cm]). In the Rocky Mountains, males of this species—known locally as the Franklin's Grouse—have white tips to their upper tail coverts and lack the orange tail tip of male Spruce Grouse elsewhere.

| J | F | M | A | M | J | J | A | S | O | N | D |

FIELD NOTES

- 16–18" (40.5–45.5 cm)
- Black ruff on side of neck
- Reddish or pale grayish tail with conspicuous dark band near tip
- ▲ Spruce Grouse is darker, looks more compact, and has blackish tail with brownish-red tip
- Hollow in ground, lined with leaves, pine needles
- 8–14; buff, sometimes flecked with browns

Spruce ♂

Ruffed ♂

Great Horned Owl

Bubo virginianus

The low *hoo h-hoo, hoohoo* of this spectacular large owl is a familiar sound in much of North America, where the bird appears equally at home in woods and deserts. The Great Horned Owl is often seen perched at dusk on roadside phone poles, wires, or even television aerials. In open country, these birds often use the perches that Red-tailed Hawks use in the daytime. This owl's cryptic plumage varies in color from the pale, frosty gray birds of the Canadian tundra to the dark, heavily marked birds of the wet Pacific coast forests. All Great Horned Owls can be distinguished from other large owls by their widely spaced ear tufts, their fluffy white throat bib, and the dark cross-barring on their underparts.

If Great Horned Owls are nesting near your house, you will hear the persistent begging shrieks of the juveniles for a month or more in summer, often beginning in late afternoon and continuing till dawn.

J F M A M J J A S O N D

bringing food to young

FIELD NOTES

- 19–24" (48–61 cm)
- Very big and bulky
- Yellow eyes
- Conspicuous, widely spaced ear tufts
- White throat bib
- Old nest of hawk or crow; cavity in tree or rocks
- 1–6; white

Barred Owl

Strix varia

The large, brown-eyed Barred Owl is common in the deep woods of the east, especially in river valleys, and also occurs across Canada as far as the west coast, from where its range is expanding south into California. Its western counterpart is the Spotted Owl (*Strix occidentalis*; 17–19" [43–48 cm]), famous for its key role in the battle to save the old growth forests of the Pacific northwest.

The Barred Owl has dark barring across its chest, with dark vertical streaks on the rest of its underparts, while the Spotted Owl has spots and bars all down its underparts.

Both species give a varied series of barking hoots: the Barred Owl says *Who cooks for-you? Who cooks for-you-all?*, while the Spotted has a shorter *Who, cooks for, you-OU!* call.

You may hear these birds in the late afternoon and therefore be able to track them down in daylight. If you are fortunate enough to find them roosting during the day, they can be remarkably tame, and usually allow you to come quite close.

J F M A M J J A S O N D

Spotted Owl

FIELD NOTES
- 18–22" (45.5–56 cm)
- Chunky build
- Dark eyes
- Barring on chest; streaked belly
- ▲ Spotted Owl (west) is darker with marbled and spotted underparts
- Tree cavity or stump; old nest of hawk or squirrel
- 1–4; white

Barred Owl nestlings

Acorn Woodpecker

Melanerpes formicivorus

One of the most handsome woodpeckers in North America, the unmistakable, "clown-faced" Acorn Woodpecker is common in oak woods of the west and southwest. It is a notably social woodpecker, and often the first clues to its presence are its burry chattering and rhythmic laughing calls. It lives in groups of up to 15 birds centered around their famous "granaries", where acorns are wedged into holes in trunks. Up to 50,000 acorns have been counted in a single hiding place! Studies have shown that these communities of Acorn Woodpeckers are composed largely of siblings, their cousins, and parents.

J F M A M J J A S O N D

Up to four males may mate with one female, and all eggs are laid in a single nest. All members of the community are involved in incubating and feeding the young. As well as feeding on insects on trunks, Acorn Woodpeckers may be seen flycatching in lazy, soaring flights.

FIELD NOTES

- 8¼–9¼" (21–23.5 cm)
- Unmistakable
- White eye contrasts with black cheek
- White rump and white flash near each wingtip
- Female: Black patch at front of red crown
- Hole excavated in tree
- 4–6; white

♂ (flying)

Northern Flicker

Colaptes auratus

The Flicker is the most common and conspicuous large woodpecker over much of the continent, and has three distinct subspecies that were once considered to be separate species: the Yellow-shafted Flicker of the east ("shafted" refers to the wing- and tail-feather shafts), the Red-shafted Flicker of the west, and the Gilded Flicker (with golden yellow shafts) of the southwestern deserts. Hybridization of these forms is now common.

Flickers live in open woodlands and can often be seen feeding on lawns, where they search with their long tongues for ants. Males can be identified by their "mustache" marks: black in the Yellow-shafted, and red in the Red-shafted and the Gilded.

In all of these forms, the white rump is conspicuous in flight.

The Flicker's strident call, a loud *wick wick wick*, is a common sound in woodlands during spring.

Yellow-shafted in flight

| J | F | M | A | M | J | J | A | S | O | N | D |

Gilded

Yellow-shafted

Red-shafted

FIELD NOTES
- ◼ 10–12" (25.5–30.5 cm)
- ◼ Barred, brownish back
- ◼ Red or yellow "shafts"
- ◼ Bold black crescent across chest
- ▲ Three different populations with variations in color of crown, nape, and "mustache" marks
- Hole excavated in tree
- ⬤ 3–10; white

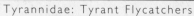

Great Crested Flycatcher

Myiarchus crinitus

Like almost all flycatchers in North America, this fairly large species is present here only in summer. It is common in woods and residential areas in the east but often stays out of sight in the canopy where it can be detected by its call—loud bickering chatters and an ascending, emphatic whistled *wheeep!*

In the west you'll find the closely related and similar-looking Ash-throated Flycatcher (*Myiarchus cinarascens*; 7½–8" [19–20.5 cm]) which inhabits drier, more open habitats, especially riparian

groves, and is seen more easily. Its calls include a bright *ka-brick* and a quiet *pic*. Where both species occur, note the darker upperparts of the Great Crested, and its darker gray throat and chest which contrast strongly with the yellow belly. By comparison, the Ash-throated appears washed-out overall. Both species have bright orange-red in their wings and tail.

FIELD NOTES

■ 8–8¾" (20.5–22 cm)
■ Dark gray throat and chest
■ Yellow belly
■ Orange-red in wings and tail
▲ Ash-throated Flycatcher more washed-out overall with smaller, all-black bill
✹ Cavity in tree or post
⬭ 3–8; cream scrawled with browns

Great Crested

White-breasted Nuthatch

Sitta carolinensis

A nasal note, repeated steadily—*neh-neh-neh*—is often the first clue that a White-breasted Nuthatch is close by. These small birds creep along trunks and branches, both head-up and head-down, as they forage under loose bark and in tree crevices. Often they accompany mixed-species flocks of chickadees and titmice in the winter woods, and they will visit bird feeders.

The White-breasted Nuthatch occurs in most woodland and forest habitats, and in the west it is found in dry oak and pine-oak woods.

J F M A M J J A S O N D

The smaller Red-breasted Nuthatch (*Sitta canadensis*; 4¼–4½" [11–11.5 cm]), also widespread across North America, prefers conifers, and therefore nests mainly in the north and west. It moves into the south in winter where it is noted as an irruptive migrant; that is, one whose winter abundance varies greatly from year to year. The Red-breasted is identified by its mostly orangey underparts. In both species, the male's cap is glossy black while the female's is dark gray to blackish.

White-breasted ♀

Red-breasted ♂

FIELD NOTES

- 5¼–5½" (13–14 cm)
- White face surrounds black eye
- Forages up and down tree trunks
- ▲ Red-breasted Nuthatch has orangey chest, and black line through eye
- Bed of grass and bark in cavity at mid to upper levels in tree
- 4–8; whitish, speckled with reddish browns

Ruby-crowned Kinglet

Regulus calendula

Kinglets, among the smallest of North American birds, are olive above and pale below, with two white wingbars. The Ruby-crowned Kinglet has a plain face with a broken white eye-ring. The male has a red crown-patch which can only be seen when the crown feathers are raised.

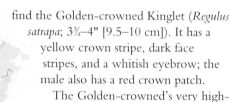

crest exposed

This kinglet frequents northern and western forests in summer, while in winter it often joins mixed-species feeding flocks of chickadees and warblers. Listen for the Ruby-crowned's dry chattering *ch-cht* call and look for a tiny, active bird that often hovers briefly while picking at twigs and leaves for food. In the same habitats you may also

Golden-crowned

find the Golden-crowned Kinglet (*Regulus satrapa*; 3¾–4" [9.5–10 cm]). It has a yellow crown stripe, dark face stripes, and a whitish eyebrow; the male also has a red crown patch.

The Golden-crowned's very high-pitched *see-see-see* call will help you locate it, particularly in summer, high amid the dense foliage of the firs and spruces it favors for nesting. Some of these birds remain as far north as southern Canada through the winter—much farther north than the Ruby-crowned.

J F M A M J J A S O N D

Golden-crowned ♂

Golden-crowned

Ruby-crowned ♂

FIELD NOTES

- 4–4¼" (10–11 cm)
- Tiny, active
- Plain with two white wingbars
- Broken white eye-ring
- ▲ Golden-crowned Kinglet has striped face
- Pouch of moss, lichen, spider's silk at mid to upper levels in tree
- 5–10; whitish finely marked with browns

Blue-gray Gnatcatcher

Polioptila caerulea

The tiny Blue-gray Gnatcatcher nests in open woodland, chaparral, and pinyon-juniper woods. In winter it favors mixed woodland and brushy thickets. It is an active bird that cocks and flicks its long, white-sided tail as it moves through the trees, and it often hovers like a kinglet to pick at the undersides of leaves or twigs. It joins mixed-species feeding flocks in the south in winter when, as in summer, it can be detected by following up its nasal, mewing *meehr* call.

J F M A M J J A S O N D

Its song is a high-pitched, squeaky and scratchy warble.

In summer the male can be distinguished by his narrow black brow, but in winter he has a plain blue-gray face with a white eye-ring, like the female.

Along with many small songbirds in the east, the Blue-gray Gnatcatcher is often host to the Brown-headed Cowbird, which lays its eggs in the nests of other species. The nest of the Blue-gray Gnatcatcher is remarkable: a tiny cup of lichens and other fine materials slung between twigs.

underside of tail

FIELD NOTES

- 4–5½" (10–14 cm)
- Long black tail with white edge
- Blue-gray above, white below
- Summer male: Narrow black brow
- Cup of lichen and fine grasses slung in a fork
- 3–6; pale bluish speckled with reddish brown

Eastern Bluebird

Sialia sialis

Bluebirds are among the most colorful birds in North America. In summer, look for them in open woods, especially where there are pines. In fall and winter, they occur in family groups or small flocks in open farmland and grassland where they often perch on roadside wires and fences. Bluebirds hunt from a perch or while hovering, then drop to the ground to pick up insects.

J F M A M J J A S O N D

West of the Great Plains, the Eastern Bluebird is replaced by the closely related and very similar Western Bluebird (*Sialia mexicana*; 6½–7" [16.5–18 cm]).

The male Eastern has an orange-red throat and chest (paler in the southern Arizona race), and an all-blue back. The male Western is identified by his blue throat, and he often shows some orange-red on his back. The females of both species are similar to one another, but if you look carefully you will see hints of the male plumage features: a pale orangey throat in the Eastern, and a grayish throat in the Western.

Bluebird populations have declined in recent decades, apparently largely because of competition with starlings for nest holes, but specially designed bluebird nestboxes have helped populations recover in some areas.

Eastern ♀

Eastern ♂

FIELD NOTES

- 6½–7" (16.5–18 cm)
- Familiar and unmistakable
- Bright blue above, reddish below
- ▲ Western Bluebird (west of Great Plains) is similar but has blue throat and some red on back
- Cavity in tree; nestbox
- 2–6; pale blue to white

Western ♂

Red-eyed Vireo

Vireo olivaceus

The mellow, repetitive song of the Red-eyed Vireo is often heard on long summer days in eastern woodlands and among suburban shade trees. If you track down the persistent singer (the song may suggest an American Robin but tends to be weaker and more continuous), you will find a small, fairly drab bird, a little chunkier than a warbler.

The Red-eyed Vireo's upperparts are olive and its underparts silky whitish, but the red eyes and the dark lines above and below the whitish eyebrow are its distinctive features (though in fall young birds have brownish eyes). It is a neotropical migrant; that is, it migrates north to breed and raise its young among the rich insect life of the North American summer, then moves south to the Neotropics (the New World tropics) for the winter. Red-eyed Vireos in fact fly all the way to the Amazon Basin.

Like all vireos, the Red-eyed Vireo weaves its deep, cup-shaped nest from fine grass, spider's silk and strips of bark, and suspends it from a fork in a tree.

| J | F | M | A | M | J | J | A | S | O | N | D |

Red-eyed Vireo

FIELD NOTES
- 5½–6" (14–15 cm)
- Red eye
- Black line through eye and along edge of gray crown
- No wingbars
- Cup of grass and bark suspended in fork in mid to upper levels of tree
- 3–5; white with brown flecks

139

Warbling Vireo

Vireo gilvus

A scratchy, fairly rapid warbling song is often the first indication that Warbling Vireos have arrived back from their wintering grounds in Mexico and northern Central America. The first migrants reach California in March, and arrive in Canada by May. Most have departed again from North America by the beginning of October.

These rather nondescript vireos nest in open deciduous woods and riparian groves where, like many vireos, their persistent songs give them away. The Warbling Vireo's head and upperparts are plain grayish, and its underparts are dirty whitish. A broad whitish brow is its best field mark. Fresh-plumaged birds in fall can be washed with olive above and yellow below, looking surprisingly bright if you are used to breeding birds in their dull summer colors. Juveniles have two pale cinnamon wingbars.

The Warbling Vireo, like many small songbirds, often plays unsuspecting host to the Brown-headed Cowbird, which lays its eggs in the nests of other species.

J F M A M J J A S O N D

Warbling Vireo

Philadelphia Vireo

FIELD NOTES

■ 4¾–5¼" (12–13 cm)

■ Broad whitish brow

■ Plain grayish head

■ Smaller, paler and grayer than Red-eyed Vireo

▲ Philadelphia Vireo (east) has yellowish throat and breast, and dull buffy wingbar

✺ Cup of fine grass, spider's silk, bark strips suspended in fork in mid to upper levels of tree

● 3–5; white with brown flecks

140

Orange-crowned Warbler

Vermivora celata

This fairly plain warbler is a common breeding species in the west and north, but is common only as a winter migrant in the east and south. It favors brushy woodland, forest edges, and chaparral.

As is typical of most species in the genus *Vermivora*, the Orange-crowned has a sharply pointed bill and lacks bold wing and tail markings. Its orange crown patch is usually concealed. The Orange-crowned's song is a rapid trill that fades abruptly.

Like many species with a widespread range in North America, the Orange-crowned shows marked regional variation in its plumage: western birds are brightest, and can be quite a strong yellow overall, while eastern birds tend to be a duller, grayish olive overall and have a gray hood. Two useful field marks for all subspecies are the face pattern (narrow pale eyebrows and pale eye-crescents), and the bright yellow undertail coverts.

The Orange-crowned is often confused with the Yellow Warbler and the Wilson's Warbler (pp. 144 and 152).

J F M A M J J A S O N D

FIELD NOTES

- ■ 4½–5" (11.5–12.5 cm)
- ■ Dullest of all the wood-warblers
- ■ Narrow pale eyebrows and pale eye-crescents
- ■ Bright yellow undertail coverts
- ▲ Yellow and Wilson's warblers—see pp.144 and 152
- Cup of grass and bark on or near ground
- 3–6; white marked with reddish browns

eastern form

western form

141

Nashville Warbler

Vermivora ruficapilla

The Nashville Warbler is one of a pair of birds that replace each other geographically as breeding species and which some ornithologists consider to be races of a single species. The other bird is the Virginia's Warbler (*Vermivora virginae*; 4–4½" [10–11.5 cm]), and both are plain warblers in the genus *Vermivora*.

The Nashville nests in open mixed woodlands, often in boggy areas, while the Virginia's favors pinyon-juniper woods with a brushy understory. Experienced birders can find both of these birds by their songs, but, unless you have a well-trained ear, learning any more than the most distinctive songs of the many warbler species that nest in North America is a real challenge. Both of these species give a metallic *pink* note that may help you locate them as they feed low in bushes, wagging their tails as they hop about.

The Nashville has a gray hood and white eye-ring, and is otherwise olive above and yellow below. Males tend to be brighter than females. The Virginia's Warbler is distinguished by its overall gray plumage, and lacks olive on the back. Some males have a yellow chest. Like the Nashville, the Virginia's has a white eye-ring and yellow tail coverts.

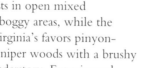

FIELD NOTES

- 4¼–4¾" (11–12 cm)
- Bright yellow below, olive above
- Gray head with white eye-ring
- Virginia's Warbler gray overall, lacks olive on back
- Cup of grass and bark strips well hidden on or near ground
- 3–5; white speckled with reddish browns

Virginia's Warbler ♂

Nashville at nest

Northern Parula

Parula americana

O ne of the smallest North American warblers, and one of the most attractive, the Northern Parula is common in summer in deciduous and coniferous woodlands of the east, especially near water. An important feature of its nesting habitat is the hanging moss or lichens (especially old-man's beard in the north and Spanish moss in the south) in which the nest is hollowed out.

The Parula's song—a high-pitched, wiry buzz that rises and ends abruptly—

J F M A M J J A S O N D

is fairly easy to learn, as warbler songs go. Tracking down the song will lead you to the handsome male, with his slate- and rust-colored chest bands. The female appears duller overall and lacks the chest bands, but she shares with the male the distinctive olive back patch, white eye-crescents, and bright yellowish underside to the bill.

The Parula is an early migrant, moving into the southeast in March and starting to head south in early August.

FIELD NOTES

- 4–4¼" (10–11 cm)
- Bluish above with two white wingbars
- Olive patch on back
- White eye-crescents
- Male: Rusty chest bands
- Deep pocket hollowed out of moss, in tree
- 3–7; white flecked with browns

143

Yellow Warbler

Dendroica petechia

One of the most widespread warblers in North America in summer, the Yellow Warbler nests in second-growth woodlands, groves of willows and alders, and orchards, often near water. It is a well-named bird, the male's face and underparts being bright yellow. The reddish streaks on the male's chest are a good field mark. The female is duller than the male but is still yellowish overall, her head and upperparts washed with olive.

In fall, some immatures are notably dull and can easily be confused with the Orange-crowned and Wilson's warblers (pp. 141 and 152).

J F M A M J J A S O N D

The Yellow Warbler has a blank-looking face with a yellowish eye-ring and lacks the Orange-crowned's distinctive pale eyebrow and sharply pointed bill. It also lacks the Wilson's capped effect and longer, cocked tail.

The Yellow Warbler's bright song has been phrased as *sweet sweet sweet, I'm so sweet* but is variable and sounds similar to the songs of several other warblers.

FIELD NOTES

- 4½–5" (11.5–12.5 cm)
- Almost entirely yellow
- Prominent black eye
- Male: Reddish streaks on chest
- ▲ Orange-crowned and Wilson's warblers (see p. 141 and 152)
- Cup of grass and lichens at mid to upper levels in tree
- 3–6; whitish marked with browns and grays

Wilson's ♂

Yellow ♂

Orange-crowned ♂

Chestnut-sided Warbler

Dendroica pensylvanica

I n summer, the handsome Chestnut-sided Warbler inhabits second-growth woodlands and overgrown brushy fields in eastern North America, where the male sings his loud clear song, sometimes written as *so pleased, so pleased, so pleased to MEETCHA*. Although fairly common today, the Chestnut-sided was apparently quite rare 200 years ago, when the heavily forested eastern US offered little suitable habitat.

In spring and summer, the Chestnut-sided is readily identified by its yellow crown, black eyestripe and mustache, and chestnut sides. After molting in late summer, however, this bird looks quite different and can surprise even experienced birders with its pale gray face and underparts, a white eye-ring, a bright greenish cap and back, and two pale yellow wingbars. Adults in fall may show some chestnut on their sides.

J F M A M J J A S O N D

fall ♂

FIELD NOTES
■ 4½–5" (11.5–12.5 cm)
■ Breeding plumage: Yellow crown; black eyestripe and mustache; chestnut sides
■ Fall plumage: Greenish above with two yellow wingbars; grayish face and underparts; white eye-ring
🪺 Cup of weed stems, grass, and bark strips low in shrub or sapling
● 3–5; whitish marked with browns

breeding plumage ♀

145

Yellow-rumped Warbler

Dendroica coronata

Sometimes known as the "butterbutt", the Yellow-rumped Warbler is one of only a few warblers that remain in North America during winter. It is abundant on both coasts of the US and in winter frequents woodlands, gardens, and overgrown fields. A flock of Yellow-rumps flying up from a field is a common winter sight. In summer, Yellow-rumps are found mainly in coniferous forests.

The two distinct subspecies of Yellow-rumped Warbler—the Myrtle Warbler, nesting in the north and east, and the Audubon's Warbler, nesting in the west—were formerly considered separate species, but they interbreed freely where their ranges meet in southwestern Canada. In summer, the males

J F M A M J J A S O N D

of the white-throated Myrtle and the yellow-throated Audubon's look quite different from one another. Females and winter birds show more subdued features than the summer males: note the pale brow of the Myrtle versus the broken whitish eye-ring of the Audubon's.

The often heard *chip* note of the Yellow-rump is useful to learn as a base for comparison with other warbler calls.

Myrtle breeding ♂

Audubon's ♀

Audubon's breeding ♂

FIELD NOTES

■ 5–5½" (12.5–14 cm)

■ Bright yellow rump

■ Breeding plumage: Bright yellow patch on crown and sides of chest; yellow (western birds) or white (eastern birds) throat

❉ Cup of fine twigs, grass, rootlets low to high in tree

● 3–5; whitish marked with browns

Townsend's Warbler

Dendroica townsendi

The attractive Townsend's Warbler nests in coniferous forests of the west. Its closely related counterpart, the Black-throated Green Warbler (*Dendroica virens*; 4½–5" [11.5–12.5 cm]), nests in mixed and coniferous forests of the north and east. Some Townsend's winter in coastal California, but others, and the Black-throated Green, spend the winter in Mexico and Central America.

Both species spend much time high in trees and may be easily missed if you don't know their songs—varied series of about five hoarse or buzzy notes. Look for these birds feeding down low at forest edges, drinking at pools or creeks, or in mixed-species flocks in late summer and fall.

The males have an extensive black bib. This is smaller in females and may be almost lacking in some fall immatures. The dark mask on the yellow face of Townsend's is a field mark among western warblers; the yellow face and green back of the Black-throated Green are distinctive features among eastern warblers.

J F M A M J J A S O N D

Townsend's ♂

Townsend's ♀

Black-throated Green ♂

Black-throated Green ♀

FIELD NOTES
- 4½–5" (11.5–12.5 cm)
- Yellow face with dark mask
- ▲ Black-throated Green Warbler (north and east) has yellow face, green back
- Cup of grass, moss, bark strips at mid to upper levels in tree
- 3–5; white marked with browns

Blackburnian Warbler

Dendroica fusca

Among the jewels that make up the North American wood-warblers, the male Blackburnian Warbler ranks as one of the most striking, with his flame-colored bib, black mask, and bold white wing-panel. The female and immature are duller but show distinctive traces of the male's face pattern, and have two pale "braces" on the back which are good field marks.

Blackburnians nest in coniferous and mixed forests of the northeast but, like many warblers, spend much time high in the canopy where they are easily overlooked unless one knows the male's thin, high-pitched song.

J F M A M J J A S O N D

An easier way to see the Blackburnian, and see it well, along with many other northern forest-nesting warblers, is to be out in the woods and parks from the last week of April through the first half of May.

in full song!

At this time of year, waves of migrants are moving north through eastern North America, often feeding low in bushes and thickets where they can be easily studied.

immature ♂

FIELD NOTES
- 4½–5" (11.5–12.5 cm)
- Male: Flame-colored bib, black mask, and bold white wing panel
- Female: Traces of male pattern and two pale "braces" on back
- Cup of fine twigs and grass at mid to upper levels in conifer
- 4–5; whitish marked with browns

148

Pine Warbler

Dendroica pinus

As its name suggests, the Pine Warbler is common in eastern pine woods, where the fairly open foliage means that you can see it more easily than many other summer warblers. These birds generally feed by creeping about in clumps of pine needles, but they also forage on or around the base of tree trunks.

This is one of a small number of warbler species that stays in the east through the winter. During that time the Pine Warbler also occurs in deciduous and mixed woodlands. Fall and winter flocks of Pine Warblers may number between 10 and 20 birds, which move through the woods along with chickadees and nuthatches.

Features that identify this stout-billed, fairly long-tailed warbler, besides its affinity for pines, are its plain olive head and back, its short, pale brow and a pale crescent below the eye. In addition, the male has a bright yellow throat and chest which are buffy in the female and immature. Unlike many warblers with white wingbars, the Pine lacks distinct dark streaking on its back or underparts.

The male's song is a chipping trill that may be confused with the song of the Chipping Sparrow (p. 157).

| J | F | M | A | M | J | J | A | S | O | N | D |

immature

FIELD NOTES

- 4¾–5¼" (12–13 cm)
- Plain olive head and back
- Pale brow and crescent below eye
- Male: Bright yellow throat and chest
- Cup of grass and pine needles at mid to upper levels in pine tree
- 3–5; white marked with browns

Black-and-white Warbler

Mniotilta varia

The Black-and-white Warbler is readily identifiable, not only because of its striking, black-and-white striped plumage, but also because of its distinctive, nuthatch-like behavior—creeping up and down trunks and along branches, gleaning insects and larvae from the bark.

Black-and-whites nest in deciduous and mixed forests in much of the north and east, where they may be found by tracking down a high-pitched but not particularly fast song of six to eight *wee-see* phrases.

nuthatch-like behavior

The male has a black mask and throat in summer but after breeding he molts and his throat becomes white. Females and immatures have a white face and throat, with a dusky stripe behind the eye.

Black-and-whites are early migrants, moving north in spring, since their feeding style doesn't require the foliage to be leafed out. They arrive back in the southern US in March, with some returning to Mexico as early as the middle of July.

J F M A M J J A S O N D

o' winter

♀

FIELD NOTES

- 4½–5" (11.5–12.5 cm)
- Creeps along branches and trunks like a nuthatch
- Streaked black and white all over
- White throat
- Breeding male: Black throat and mask
- Cup of grass and bark strips on or near ground at base of stump or shrub
- 4–5; whitish speckled with browns

American Redstart

Setophaga ruticilla

Named for the male's red start, an old English word for tail, the Redstart is one of the most common warblers in North America in summer. Redstarts favor deciduous and mixed second-growth woodlands where they set up territories after returning from wintering in Mexico, Central America, or the Caribbean.

These are notably active and restless warblers: they often fan their long tails and droop their wings as they flit about, showing off the male's flame-colored and the female's yellow wing and tail patches. Unlike most warblers, Redstarts have stiff, hair-like feathers (rictal bristles) around their gape, which help them catch flying insects.

Male songbirds usually molt from their immature plumage to an adult-like plumage by the spring, but Redstarts are an exception. In their first summer, male Redstarts resemble females, although they tend to show a few black flecks on the head and chest and have brighter, more orangey, flashes at the sides of their chest. Adult male Redstarts are also unusual in that they look the same in winter as in summer.

J F M A M J J A S O N D

rictal bristles

FIELD NOTES

- 4¾–5¼" (12–13 cm)
- Constantly fans tail and droops wings
- Male: Glossy black and bright orange
- Females and immatures: Same pattern as male in dull olive and primrose yellow
- Cup of grass, lichens, bark strips, low to high in bush or tree
- 2–5; whitish marked with browns

♂

151

Wilson's Warbler

Wilsonia pusilla

The Wilson's Warbler is a small, active bird that nests in riverside thickets of willows and alders in northern and western North America. In much of the east it is an infrequent migrant, but in the west it is quite common.

The first impression of a Wilson's is usually a small, bright yellow bird flitting around the lower parts of a bush or a tree. A closer look reveals its longish tail, often held cocked, and a big, beady, dark eye. The male has a neat, glossy, black cap, while the female has either a smaller blackish cap or an olive head, the same color as her back. Western birds are bright yellow below and have an almost golden yellow face, while eastern birds are duller overall. The Wilson's Warbler is similar to the Orange-crowned and the Yellow Warbler, and telling these species apart is often difficult (see p. 144).

If you live in the west, where there are relatively few species of warblers, the Wilson's song—an intensifying series of chips that fades abruptly—is one you may soon learn.

By the end of September, most Wilson's have left the US for their winter homes in Mexico and Central America.

J F M A M J J A S O N D

western ♀

eastern ♀

FIELD NOTES

- 4¼–4¾" (11–12 cm)
- Bright yellow below, olive above
- Prominent dark eye
- Male: Glossy black cap
- Cup of grass and weed stalks, well hidden on or near ground
- 4–6; whitish speckled with browns

Scarlet Tanager

Piranga olivacea

Scarlet Tanagers are long-distance migrants that spend winter in South America and move north in summer to nest in the deciduous and mixed woodlands of eastern North America. The Western Tanager (*Piranga ludoviciana*; 6½–7¼" [16.5–18.5 cm]) replaces the Scarlet in the deciduous and coniferous woodlands of western North America.

The unmistakable breeding males of these two species are among the most colorful of all North American birds. The females and immatures are duller—olive and yellowish overall, the Western having two distinct pale wingbars. After nesting, the male Scarlet molts into a more somber, female-like plumage but he can still be distinguished by his black wings.

Despite their bright colors, tanagers are sometimes hard to spot, as they perch high in the canopy and move around little. Familiarity with the songs of these two species will help you locate them. The Scarlet has a caroling song that suggests an American Robin, while the Western repeats a leisurely series of three or four burry phrases.

Western Tanager ♂

J F M A M J J A S O N D

FIELD NOTES

- 6½–7" (16.5–18 cm)
- Breeding male: Brilliant red with black wings (all plumages) and tail
- Female: Olive and yellow overall
- ▲ Females difficult to distinguish
- Cup of twigs, grass, rootlets at mid to upper levels in tree
- 3–5; pale bluish speckled with browns

♀ Scarlet

Scarlet Winter ♂

Scarlet ♂ in molt

153

Rose-breasted Grosbeak

Pheucticus ludovicianus

The Rose-breasted Grosbeak and the closely related Black-headed Grosbeak (*Pheucticus melanocephalus*; 6½–7½" [16.5–19 cm]) are east-west counterparts that exhibit a striking example of delayed plumage maturation. In their first summer, young males do not attain their fully adult plumage, as most songbirds do. Instead, the immatures look variably intermediate between the adult

J F M A M J J A S O N D

male and the more somber female, and thus tend to be at a disadvantage when competing for mates against the brilliantly colored adult males.

Both species nest in summer in deciduous woodlands, often along watercourses. The Rose-breasted is found east of the Great Plains, and the Black-headed to the west. In the Plains themselves the planting of trees in an otherwise open region has enabled the two grosbeaks to come into contact and hybridize, bringing into question whether they are really separate species.

Their songs consist of rich warbling phrases that suggest the American Robin, and the males have the unusual habit of singing from the nest while incubating the eggs.

Rose-breasted ♀

FIELD NOTES

■ 7–8" (18–20.5 cm)

■ Boldly patterned— adult male unmistakable

■ Pale, massive, triangular bill

▲ Replaced in west by Black-headed Grosbeak, females and immatures of which more strongly washed with orange and less heavily streaked below

🪺 Cup of twigs, grass, rootlets, low to high in bush or tree

🥚 2–5; pale bluish speckled with browns

Black-headed ♂

Indigo Bunting

Passerina cyanea

On a summer's day, a flash of bright blue across a trail or road may indicate the presence of a male Indigo Bunting. Stopping at such a sight, you may hear his pleasant song of sweet to buzzy couplets, which is given throughout the summer. The handsome Indigo Bunting returns in April from its winter home in Mexico and Central America, to nest in the woodlands and overgrown fields of the east and south. The female is brown overall, paler below, with diffuse dusky streaking on her chest. After nesting, the male's bright blue is molted for an overall brown plumage punctuated with blue patches.

While the Indigo Bunting is widely seen in summer, as with many neotropical migrants (species that spend the winter in the tropics), little is known about its life in winter, and it was discovered only recently that this species has a complex molting strategy. First year birds have two molts in fall—one before and one after migrating—and another in late winter when they attain adult-like plumage.

♂ molting

♂

♀

J F M A M J J A S O N D

FIELD NOTES

■ 4¾–5¼" (12–13 cm)

■ Breeding male: Deep blue, tending to look black in poor or deceptive light

■ Female: Brown overall with dusky streaks on chest

▲ Lazuli Bunting (western counterpart) has two pale wingbars

❀ Cup of grass, bark strips, at low to mid levels in a tangle or shrub

● 3–6; bluish white

155

Rufous-sided Towhee

Pipilo erythropthalmus

Until as recently as the 1950s, there were believed to be two species of "rufous-sided" towhees in North America: the Red-eyed Towhee of the east, and the Spotted Towhee of the west. While these two forms look and even sound quite different, where they meet in the middle of the country they interbreed freely and are now considered to be a single species.

White-eyed Florida form

As the old name suggests, western birds have white spots on their backs and wings. Eastern males, on the other hand, are solidly black above and the females brown above. Another geographical trait in this large and colorful sparrow is that birds in Florida often have whitish, not red, eyes.

Rufous-sided Towhees are common, though often fairly secretive, in open brushy woodlands, thickets, chaparral, and gardens across North America. Listen for them scratching in dry leaf litter, which they do with a distinctive jump-and-kick motion, thrusting both feet back to move leaves and reveal food. Eastern birds call a rising *tow-hee*, while western birds give a mewing *rreeah*.

J F M A M J J A S O N D

western form ♂

eastern form ♂

FIELD NOTES

- ◼ 7½–9" (19–23 cm)
- ◼ White underparts
- ◼ Chestnut flanks
- ◼ Dark back and head
- ▲ Eye color and white spotting on back varies geographically
- Cup of grass, and rootlets, on or near ground in clump of grass or bush
- 2–6; whitish speckled with reddish browns

Chipping Sparrow

Spizella passerina

This slender, long-tailed sparrow is a common summer resident in open woods, forest edges, parks, and mountain meadows throughout much of North America, particularly in and around pines. In winter, after migrating south, it is often found in brushy fields and in scrub.

The Chipping Sparrow forages on the ground in open, grassy areas but takes cover in bushes or trees if disturbed. It sings from a prominent perch in a pine or other tree. Its song—a dry trill on one pitch—may suggest the song of another eastern pine woods bird, the Pine Warbler (p. 149).

Occasionally, a male Chipping Sparrow may mate with two females. After nesting, both male and female lose their distinctive orange-red cap and gray face for a browner, streaky head pattern that is similar to that of several other winter sparrows, and

their bill turns from black (summer) to pinkish (winter). Note, however, the fairly prominent white or pale brow, and the gray rump—good field marks in both summer and winter. Juveniles, like most young sparrows, are streaky and brownish overall but tend to have a trace of the adult face pattern.

| J | F | M | A | M | J | J | A | S | O | N | D |

winter ♂

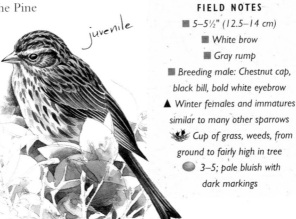

juvenile

FIELD NOTES

- 5–5½" (12.5–14 cm)
- White brow
- Gray rump
- Breeding male: Chestnut cap, black bill, bold white eyebrow
- ▲ Winter females and immatures similar to many other sparrows
- Cup of grass, weeds, from ground to fairly high in tree
- 3–5; pale bluish with dark markings

157

Fox Sparrow

Passerella iliaca

The Fox Sparrow is a good example of how much a widespread songbird can vary in appearance in different parts of North America. Some 18 races of this large sparrow, which nests in dense underbrush of coniferous and mixed woodlands, have been described. In the north (and in the east in winter) you'll see a bird with bright orange-red wings and tail; a broad blue-gray brow; and blue-gray patches on the sides of its neck. In the Rockies, Fox Sparrows tend to have a gray head and back and a reddish tail, and some have very stout bills. Birds nesting in the wet forests of the Pacific northwest have a darker head and upperparts, with the tail only slightly brighter and redder. All forms have a deep-based bill that is paler (gray to orange) below, and coarse, triangular-shaped dark spots on their underparts.

Fox Sparrows are most familiar as winter visitors to the brushy understory of woods and gardens. Although they tend to keep out of sight, they may be detected by their strong, smacking *tssk!* call and the scratching sound they make while kicking in the leaf litter like a towhee.

| J | F | M | A | M | J | J | A | S | O | N | D |

western form

Rocky Mountains

eastern form

FIELD NOTES

- 6½–7½" (16.5–19 cm)
- Dark spots on underparts
- Reddish rump and tail
- Scratches around in leaf litter
- ▲ Wide geographical variation in plumage
- Cup of twigs, moss, grass on or near ground in thicket
- 2–5; pale greenish marked with browns

White-crowned Sparrow

Zonotrichia leucophrys

A familiar winter visitor to parks, open woodlands, and gardens across much of the US, the White-crowned Sparrow nests mostly in the temperate climate of the far north and the mountains of the west. One race, however, shows a remarkable adaptation to a local microclimate on the coast of central California. There, the cool, foggy summers, caused by cold air over the ocean waters meeting hot air from the interior, moderate what would otherwise be too hot a climate. Move a mile or so from the coast, away from the fog's influence, and you won't find a single nesting White-crown!

The closely related Golden-crowned Sparrow (*Zonotrichia atricapilla*; 6½–7¼" [16.5–18.5 cm]) nests in thickets at the timberline in the northwest and is a common winter visitor to the west alongside White-crowns. Adults of the two species are distinctive (compare also the White-crowned with the White-throated Sparrow, p. 117). As with other sparrows, note that the immatures show distinctive traces of the adult head patterns.

| J | F | M | A | M | J | J | A | S | O | N | D |

immature Golden-crowned

immature White-crowned

FIELD NOTES

- 6¼–7" (16–18 cm)
- *Black-and-white striped head*
- ▲ *Immatures difficult—compare carefully with Golden-crowned Sparrow*
- ▲ *White-throated Sparrow (p. 117) has yellow patch in front of eye, and white chin marked off with gray*
- *Cup of twigs, grass, and moss, on or near ground in bush or small tree*
- *3–5; pale bluish to whitish, speckled with browns*

Golden-crowned ♂

159

Dark-eyed Junco

Junco hyemalis

This sparrow shows some of the greatest geographic plumage variations of any bird in North America. At least five types are identifiable: the Slate-colored Junco of the north and east, with its gray hood, upperparts and sides; the Oregon Junco of the west, with blackish hood, orange-red back, and pinkish sides; the Pink-sided Junco of the central Rockies, with gray hood, orange-red back, and pink sides; the White-winged Junco of the Black Hills, with blue-gray hood, upperparts, and sides, and two white wingbars; and the Gray-headed Junco of the southern Rockies, which is gray overall with an orange-red back patch. Juvenile juncos are streaky overall and look quite different from adults.

Dark-eyed Juncos nest in coniferous and mixed woodlands, and in winter also visit parks and gardens where they often occur in flocks and feed on the ground. The junco's song is a ringing trill, and flocks make high-pitched twitters, especially when disturbed. As they fly up, juncos flash their characteristic, bright white outer tail feathers.

white tail feathers

J F M A M J J A S O N D

Slate-colored

Oregon form

juvenile

FIELD NOTES

■ 5½–6" (14–15 cm)

■ Blackish tail with white outer feathers, conspicuous in flight

■ Pinkish bill

▲ Strong regional variations in color

🪺 Cup of grass, twigs, and rootlets, on ground, in bank, under stump, or in brushpile

⬭ 3–6; bluish white speckled with browns

160

Orchard Oriole

Icterus spurius

In spring, in open woodlands, orchards, and among suburban shade trees of the southeast, a loud scratchy warble, sung from a perch or during a display flight over the treetops, may attract your attention to a singing male Orchard Oriole. This is the smallest North American oriole, and the male's deep chestnut plumage is its main distinguishing feature. The female and immature look quite similar to other species of orioles, particularly the Hooded Oriole of the southwest (p. 272). Note, however, the Orchard's small size and relatively shorter, more slender,

J F M A M J J A S O N D

and slightly downward-curved bill. The young male's black bib separates him from the plain-faced female.

This is one of only two species of New World orioles that have been known to nest in colonies. On one 7-acre tract in Louisiana, a total of 114 nests were found!

Orchard Orioles are early fall migrants, and families may begin heading south, to their winter home in Mexico, in July.

immature ♂

FIELD NOTES

■ 6–6¾" (15–17 cm)

■ Male: Black and chestnut—
    unmistakable

▲ Female and immature similar to
other orioles (especially Hooded—see
p. 272) but note shorter bill and tail

Cup of grass suspended
    in fork in tree

3–7; pale bluish marked
    with browns and grays

♀

Northern Oriole

Icterus galbula

Found in summer in deciduous and mixed woodlands, this is the most common and familiar North American oriole. The two very different-looking races of the Northern Oriole—the Baltimore Oriole in the east, and the Bullock's Oriole in the west (their ranges separated by the Great Plains)—were considered separate species for many years. With the planting of trees as shelter belts around homesteads on the plains these two orioles came into contact and ornithologists found that they interbred readily. Thus the two were united as a single species, although most birders still refer to them by their old names.

Males in their first summer look like adult females, with some black in their face and throat. Immatures of the two forms are alike and are not easily told apart.

The Northern Oriole's song is a somewhat disjointed series of rich whistles which may be interspersed with rough chatters, especially in Bullock's Orioles. In fall, these orioles migrate south to spend the winter in Mexico and Central America.

| J | F | M | A | M | J | J | A | S | O | N | D |

Bullock's

Baltimore ♀

FIELD NOTES
- ■ 7–8" (18–20.5 cm)
- ■ Male: Flame orange and black, almost unmistakable
- ▲ Females and immatures nondescript, but with definite hint of orange
- Pouch of grass and bark strips, slung in fork of tree
- 3–6; bluish white marked with dark scrawls

Grasslands

GRASSLANDS
Prairies, Open Fields, Farmland

Once, much of the American interior, stretching from (approximately) the Mississippi and Arkansas rivers westward to the Rockies, south into Texas and north across much of west-central Canada, was covered with native grassland. The eastern part of this area, the tallgrass prairie, was a rich grassland founded on black clay soils, giving way in the west to the more arid, less diverse shortgrass plains, home of the buffalo.

Now, much of the original grassland has vanished, especially the tallgrass prairie, most of which has been converted into a vast grain belt. But grasslands of a sort still cover large expanses of North America. These are mostly croplands and pastures, artificially created over the past two centuries or so through the clearing of forests and woodlands for settlement and agriculture.

Much of this development has taken place in the east, and wherever it has occurred it has had far-reaching consequences on the original grassland bird faunas. Some

TELEGRAPH WIRES and POLES may offer the highest vantage points for miles around and are therefore good places to look for such species as hawks and kingbirds.

NATIVE GRASSLANDS While native grasslands have been much reduced, where they still exist they support Lark Buntings, Lark Sparrows, Burrowing Owls, and such rarities as Baird's Sparrow.

ROADSIDE VEGETATION Some species, including cowbirds, like to forage in these areas, and even bathe in roadside puddles. Quail and some doves also gather grit along verges.

grassland specialists have survived the transition with little overall change in status; a few, such as Baird's Sparrow and McCown's Longspur, have declined drastically; and certain exceptionally adaptable birds have actually prospered. The Brown-headed Cowbird and the Great-tailed Grackle, for example, have greatly expanded their ranges in recent years.

There are open grassland areas of other kinds in North America, such as alpine meadows in the Rockies and the prairies of Florida, but one particular area of open country has an especially profound influence on the continent's birdlife. This is the vast expanse of the remote arctic tundra—the nesting ground for millions of birds, particularly shorebirds and waterfowl, and home in summer to a significant proportion of the birds that inhabit much of the United States in winter.

WINDBREAKS and similar tree plantings allow a wide range of woodland birds to penetrate grasslands. Jays, finches, chickadees, orioles and some woodpeckers are all species to look out for.

PLOUGHED FIELDS attract gulls, Killdeer, blackbirds and grackles. In winter or spring, they also attract flocks of wintering or migrating Snow Buntings and longspurs.

PASTURE Only a few species are common in open pasture and similar grasslands, but these include the Bobolink and the Vesper Sparrow.

FENCES A broad range of birds, from small species such as swallows and sparrows to larger birds such as vultures, will perch on fences and wires to rest, sunbathe, or just look around.

BIRDING *in* GRASSLANDS

The open vistas of grasslands allow easy observation of numerous birds, from hawks perched on overhead wires to larks foraging in farmland. Other species, however, require a more cautious approach.

An excellent way to go birding in open country is by car. Many species are conspicuous along roadsides, and the car acts as a blind, from which you can watch birds more closely than if you were on foot. Driving is also often the best way to spot species that occur in low densities or that have large hunting territories, as is the case with hawks in winter.

However you get around, it is always good birding policy to keep an eye on utility wires, poles, and fences as these all provide perches for many species of birds. For example, in summer, the best place to spot kingbirds is usually on roadside wires, while in winter, poles and pylons are favored roosting and even hunting perches for many hawks. In some areas, particularly the southwest,

ravens nest readily on pylons—tree substitutes in a wide open environment.

It pays to stop and scan any freshly ploughed field you may pass. Ploughing, of course, brings to the surface many insects, grubs, worms, and similar subsurface fauna. These quickly attract birds, ranging from gulls to larks and longspurs. Depending on the season, there are several species of birds

OUT IN THE OPEN *Mist gradually clears over a meadow, home to many grassland species such as the American Goldfinch (above right). This bird is especially attracted to rough pasture and wasteground, where weeds such as thistles abound. Tall grass shelters many birds, like the female Red-winged Blackbird (top). A group of birders (above) explores one of the richest of all grassland habitats—the arctic tundra.*

(some plovers and longspurs, for example) that prefer ploughed fields, when available, to grasslands.

Do not assume that all the birds in a group are of one species. Many open country birds are gregarious outside the breeding season, and any rare vagrant that happens to be in the area is quite likely to attach itself to a group of some common local species.

Note that the presence of hedges and scattered trees will greatly increase the diversity of birds you can find.

SEASONAL CHANGES

In fall and winter, fields provide food for many species that migrate to grasslands after nesting in other habitats. If you pass through an area of open grassland or farmland regularly, from late summer through the winter you'll see a greater variety of species than at other times of the year, in particular more hawks, kestrels, sparrows, blackbirds, and finches. These numbers reflect both the population increase following the nesting season, and the migration of other species into a habitat that is good for feeding but would not be a suitable nesting habitat.

TALLGRASS TACTICS

Grasslands, with their unrestricted views, provide certain obvious advantages over woods and forests. However, these advantages do not apply to all birds all year round. In spring and summer, the males of most grassland species sing and are therefore fairly easy to find and identify, but during other seasons some birds, such as sparrows, can be hard to see, let alone identify.

If you are walking with a friend and flush a sparrow from the grass, watch where it comes back down. One of you can then keep an eye on the spot while the other walks part of the distance toward it. If the walker then stops and relocates the spot, the watcher can catch up. In this way you can walk up on the bird without ever losing sight of it, or at least where it landed.

ALPINE MEADOWS *support rosy-finches, ptarmigans, and several other high-country specialist birds.*

USING COVER

When you are out in open country with hedges, or with a bordering wood, walking along the hedge or beside the trees will make you less conspicuous. Furthermore, such areas are rich in birdlife.

GRASSLAND GEAR

Little is required in the way of specialized equipment for birding in grassland areas—just an efficient pair of binoculars. Spotting scopes do however come in handy in open areas where you may be some distance from a bird. Special mounts are available that allow you to clamp your scope to the glass of a half-open car window, enabling you to use the scope from your mobile blind.

GRASSLAND BIRDING *(left) requires a steady hand, as many species are easy to spot but hard to get close to. The Eastern Kingbird (above) is one of many birds that habitually perch on fence wires.*

Cattle Egret

Bubulcus ibis

While today the Cattle Egret is common across much of the south, 50 years ago it was almost unknown in North America. Its colonization of the New World has been remarkable. The first Cattle Egrets seen in the Americas were in Surinam in 1877, and to get there they had presumably crossed the Atlantic from Africa. In the New World they found cleared grasslands and cattle typical of their native environment. They crossed the Caribbean to Florida in the 1940s and a second front moved north through Central America in the 1950s. By the early 1970s, Cattle Egrets were well-established in the southern US, and their range seems to be still expanding.

This small heron is identified by its stocky shape and its habit of following cattle to feed on insects they flush up. Flocks have learned to accompany tractors for the same reason. For most of the year, Cattle Egrets are white overall with dark legs and a yellow bill. At the start of the breeding season they attain buffy plumes on their head, chest, and back; the bill becomes reddish; and the legs change color to orange.

winter plumage

breeding plumage

FIELD NOTES

- 18–21" (45.5–53.5 cm)
- Small and stocky
- Distinctive "heavy-jowled" look
- Breeding plumage: Golden buff wash on crown, lower breast, and back
- Platform of sticks in tree or reed bed, often with other herons
- 2–6; unmarked pale blue

J F M A M J J A S O N D

Black Vulture

Coragyps atratus

Acharacteristic bird of the open skies of the southeast, the Black Vulture is identified by its naked gray head, its broad wings with a large white patch on each wingtip, and its relatively short, squared tail. It flies with a distinctive flap-flap-flap-glide movement, the wingbeats hurried and the glides usually short, holding its wings flat or only slightly raised above the body while gliding. Its shape, combined with its way of flying, will enable you, with practice, to identify the Black Vulture at long range and to distinguish it from the Turkey Vulture (p. 170).

Black Vultures are social. Often you'll see groups of them soaring in tight circles or hopping and running with a gamboling gait at garbage dumps, fishing wharves, or on beaches where dead creatures wash up. If you look carefully, particularly in fall, you may notice that some Black Vultures have an all-gray bill while others have a distinct pale tip to their bill. The former are young of that year, the latter adults.

| J | F | M | A | M | J | J | A | S | O | N | D |

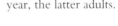

immature

adult

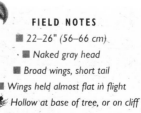

FIELD NOTES
- ◾ 22–26" (56–66 cm)
- ◾ Naked gray head
- ◾ Broad wings, short tail
- ◾ Wings held almost flat in flight
- ◾ Hollow at base of tree, or on cliff
- ◯ 1–3; pale greenish, usually marked with browns

Turkey Vulture

Cathartes aura

Although it withdraws from the northern part of its range in winter, migrating as far south as South America, the Turkey Vulture is a familiar sight in North American skies. It is best distinguished from the Black Vulture (p. 169) by its shape and flight manner. The Turkey Vulture has longer wings and tail. It glides and soars for long periods with its wings held in a shallow V-shape, tilting, or rocking, from side to side. It seldom flaps its wings, but when it does, the wingbeats are deep and smooth, not quick and hurried like those of the Black Vulture. From below, note also its two-tone wings.

Adults have naked reddish heads while juveniles have naked gray heads, similar to the Black Vulture. Generally, this species is seen singly or in small groups, and tends to fly lower than the Black, an indication of its ability to locate food by smell. In contrast, the Black Vulture hunts only by sight.

J F M A M J J A S O N D

two-tone wings

adult

juvenile

FIELD NOTES
- 26–30" (66–76 cm)
- Naked red head
- Broad wings, long tail
- Wings held in V-shape in flight
- Hollow at base of tree, in old log, or on cliff
- 1–3; whitish heavily marked with browns and grays

Northern Harrier

Circus cyaneus

The Northern Harrier, formerly called the Marsh Hawk, is widespread in grasslands and over open fields, especially in marshy areas. It hunts low to the ground, quartering back and forth with its wings held in a shallow V-shape, braking and turning with aerobatic agility. It perches readily on the ground or on fence posts, but, unlike many hawks, rarely if ever perches higher.

juvenile (showing facial disks)

J F M A M J J A S O N D

white rump

The Harrier's bold, white rump band and owl-like facial disks are good field marks. The male is gray overall with black wingtips; the larger female is mostly brown. Juveniles show a rich orangey color on their underparts.

In winter, several harriers may hunt over a small area, and communal winter roosts of up to 80 or 90 birds have been recorded. In display, the male flies high and tumbles and swoops while giving a rapid yelping chatter. For most of the year, however, harriers are silent.

FIELD NOTES

- 18–22" (45.5–56 cm)
- Long wings and tail
- White rump
- Slow sailing flight, often low over grassland or marsh
- Platform of sticks and grass on ground
- 3–9; bluish white, occasionally with brownish flecks

171

Swainson's Hawk

Buteo swainsoni

The Swainson's Hawk is noted for its remarkable long-distance migration, with most of the population spending the winter on the grasslands of Argentina. On their journey there, these birds move through Mexico and Central America in flocks that may number thousands, and often travel with Turkey Vultures and Broad-winged Hawks. The Swainson's Hawk returns to North America in March to nest in the grasslands and prairies of the west, and is a fairly common summer resident.

Like several North American hawks, the Swainson's comes in many different plumages, known as color morphs, and juveniles look different from adults. The most common plumage is the distinctive light morph of the adult. The Swainson's has long, relatively narrow and tapered wings, testimony to its long-distance migration. Often the wing linings are paler than the underside of the flight feathers.

The Swainson's hunts while soaring, its wings held in a distinct shallow V, and it often hangs in the wind. Flocks may gather at burning fields and dive spectacularly to snatch up grasshoppers flushed by the fire.

immature

dark morph

J F M A M J J A S O N D

FIELD NOTES

- 19–22" (48–56 cm)
- Longer, narrower, and more pointed wings than most other buteos
- Plumage very variable, but usually has dark "bib" contrasting with paler chin and underparts
- Platform of sticks, usually low in lone tree or bush
- 2–4; whitish, often marked with browns

gathering over grassfire

American Kestrel

Falco sparverius

Formerly known as the Sparrow Hawk, this familiar small falcon occurs throughout the Americas. It is a common sight perched on roadside wires or hunting, with its characteristic hovering flight, over fields and roadside verges. The pointed wings of the American Kestrel and other falcons distinguish them from hawks, which have broader, rounded wings.

The male American Kestrel, with his blue wings and orange-red tail, is one of the most attractive of all North American birds. The female's upperparts and tail are more uniform: orange-red, barred with black. As with many raptors, males are smaller than females.

One explanation for this difference in size is that it enables the male and female to hunt for different-sized prey, since any food of a fixed size may be insufficient to support both sexes. But why is the male not the larger bird? As female falcons and hawks do most, if

not all, of the incubating of the eggs, their larger size helps them stay at the nest for longer periods. Furthermore, the male feeds the female while she is at the nest, and the smaller prey that he catches tends to be more abundant than the larger prey caught by the female.

| J | F | M | A | M | J | J | A | S | O | N | D |

hovering over field

♂

♀

FIELD NOTES

- 10–11½" (25.5–29 cm)
- Small, common, widespread; hovers
- Orange-red back and tail
- Male: Blue-gray wings
- Cavity in tree, cliff, or building
- 3–7; cream blotched with browns

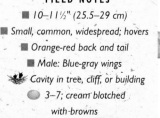

Northern Bobwhite

Colinus virginianus

The loud, sharp *bob-white!* or *h-hoo wheet!* call of the Northern Bobwhite is often heard in farmland and rural areas of the east where this bird lives in fields, brushy areas, and open woods. Populations at the northern edge of its range fluctuate, depending on how severe the winters are. In the west, this gamebird has been introduced into Washington state.

For much of the year, Bobwhites occur in groups, or coveys, of up to 25 birds, but in the spring the birds form territorial pairs. Bobwhites usually run for cover if disturbed, but, when startled, they

flush into the air with a whirr of their wings and fly a short distance out of sight across a hedge or into brush.

The female is less boldly patterned than the male and has a buffy brow and throat patch. A distinct race of Bobwhite, the so-called Masked Bobwhite, with a blackish face and throat, used to occur in the deserts of southern Arizona. It was wiped out in the early 1900s as a result of overgrazing of cattle, but attempts are being made to reintroduce it from Mexico.

J F M A M J J A S O N D

downy young

'Masked' form

eastern form ♀

FIELD NOTES

- 8–10" (20.5–25.5 cm)
- Small, mottled, strongly reddish in overall hue
- White throat
- Distinctive call
- 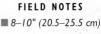 Well-hidden depression in ground, lined and concealed with grass
- 7–16; whitish

174

Killdeer

Charadrius vociferus

This striking and often noisy bird is actually a shorebird, but it is common across North America in farmland and other open areas such as playing fields, airfields, and riverbanks. Its name comes from its plaintive screaming and wailing cries, in particular the *kill-dee-eu* given in alarm or in display flight as the male circles with slow, deep wingbeats.

If you approach newly hatched Killdeer chicks too closely, the parents may give a broken-wing display, which is designed to distract predators. The adult Killdeer shuffles and runs along the ground, allowing you to come quite close, while holding out one wing as if it is broken and the bird cannot fly. Although interesting to observe, if this happens you should obviously move away to prevent further disturbance.

Killdeers are readily told from other plovers (which all tend to be found near water) by their two black chest bands and their long orangey tail with its black-and-white tip. Unlike many shorebirds, the Killdeer looks much the same in all plumages, although the downy chick has only a single black chest band.

Like other plovers, Killdeers feed with a distinctive stop-start action: standing still, then running and picking at the ground, then standing still again.

J F M A M J J A S O N D

FIELD NOTES
- 9½–10" (24–25.5 cm)
- Common and noisy
- Bright reddish rump
- Double black breast band
- Scrape in ground lined with small pebbles and grass
- 3–5; buff, marked with browns and black

broken-wing (distraction) display

175

Mourning Dove

Zenaida macroura

This elegant, medium-sized dove is common across North America in farmland, parks, gardens, open woodland, and irrigated desert areas. Flocks in fall and winter may number hundreds, especially in the south.

The Mourning Dove's name derives from its low, mournful, cooing call which may be written as *wh'hooo hoo hoo hooo*. It is overall a fairly plain dove, its long tapered tail being a field mark. The male is slightly brighter than the female and has a powdery blue-gray area on his nape and a rosy sheen on the sides of his neck. Juveniles have distinctly scaly-looking plumage and a shorter tail than the adults.

Like most doves of open country, the Mourning Dove is a strong, fast flier that flushes up with a whirring whistle of its wings. In display, single birds and pairs climb fairly high with slow wingbeats and then glide smoothly toward the ground with their wings held bowed down. Especially in dry regions, Mourning Doves may fly several miles to good feeding areas or the nearest water source, often at or before first light and again at dusk. Thus, if you are often out early or drive home at dusk through open country, you will soon come to recognize the birds' silhouettes.

♀

J F M A M J J A S O N D

FIELD NOTES
- 10–12" (25.5–30.5 cm)
- Pinkish brown overall
- Long, tapered, white-tipped tail
- Shallow bowl of sticks in tree or bush, or on ledge
- 1–4; white

♂

176

Barn Owl

Tyto alba

One of the most widespread birds in the world, the Barn Owl occurs in open country of rural and urban areas throughout much of the Americas, although it is absent from higher latitudes, including most of Canada. It is most frequently seen hunting at dusk or at night along highways, where the grassy verges and median strips are home to its main prey, rodents. Lit up by headlights, the Barn Owl's white underparts, combined with its silent, hovering flight, give it an almost ghost-like appearance.

Sadly, a combination of traffic casualties, the loss of trees and old buildings where the owls nest and roost, and, until recently, the effects of pesticides, have caused a decline in Barn Owl numbers in many regions. However, the use of nestboxes in some areas, for example around New York City, has helped maintain other populations of this beautiful species.

The Barn Owl belongs to the family Tytonidae, which is distinct from all other owl families in North America. One feature of this family is that the downy young molt directly into adult-like plumage. Another feature is their pectinate, or comb-like, central toenail, which is used for preening.

The Barn Owl has one of the most blood-curdling calls of any North American bird: a loud, hissing shriek, often given in flight.

J F M A M J J A S O N D

pectinate toenail

FIELD NOTES
- 14–16" (35.5–40.5 cm)
- Plain white below, mottled tan above
- Dark eyes set in white, heart-shaped face
- Cavity in tree, cliff, or old building
- 3–11; white

Barn Owl chicks

177

Common Nighthawk

Chordeiles minor

A sharp nasal *beehnk* heard at dusk may attract your attention skyward to a high-flying bird that suggests a swift in shape but is larger, with slower, more erratic flight. If you watch for a while it may dive steeply and at the bottom of the stoop make a low *boom* sound. This is the Common Nighthawk, a summer visitor to much of North America—from the open plains of the west to the cities of the east.

During summer, in the deserts and open dry lands of the southwest you'll find the very similar and closely related Lesser Nighthawk (*Chordeiles acutipennis*; 8–9" [20.5–23 cm]). This bird's song is a prolonged, thurring, toad-like trill and, unlike the Common Nighthawk's song, it is given while the bird is perched on the ground.

Identifying these two species by sight alone is difficult since, as with most night birds, their plumage camouflages them during the daytime, rather than acting as a visual signal, as is the case with other birds. Although hard to judge, the white bar on the nighthawk's wing is nearer the wingtip in the Lesser than in the Common. The Common looks longer-winged, its wings tend to be more pointed, and its flight is rangier and less fluttery.

| J | F | M | A | M | J | J | A | S | O | N | D |

Lesser ♂

Common ♂

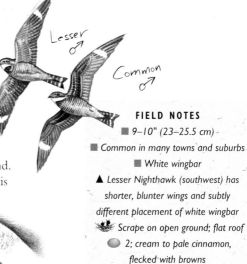

broad gape

FIELD NOTES

- 9–10" (23–25.5 cm)
- Common in many towns and suburbs
- White wingbar
- ▲ Lesser Nighthawk (southwest) has shorter, blunter wings and subtly different placement of white wingbar
- Scrape on open ground; flat roof
- 2; cream to pale cinnamon, flecked with browns

Eastern Kingbird

Tyrannus tyrannus

Kingbirds are large, conspicuous flycatchers of open country, and you'll often see them in summer on roadside wires and fences. Eight species of kingbirds nest in North America, and all of them are migratory, wintering from Mexico to South America. The Eastern Kingbird is common across much of North America and is a distinctive-looking bird with blackish upperparts, white underparts, and a bold white tip to its tail.

Eastern ♂ on wire

Although kingbirds are strongly territorial when nesting, in migration and in winter they form flocks that feed and roost together. Unlike many songbirds, kingbirds often migrate by day so that in spring and fall you may see a flock drop into a nearby tree, feed, and then move on.

The most spectacular kingbird in North America is the Scissor-tailed Flycatcher (*Tyrannus forficatus*; 7½–14" [19–35.5 cm]), a fairly small-bodied bird with a long, forked tail. The Scissor-tail nests in Texas and adjacent states where it is a common roadside bird in open ranchland. It usually shows only a soft pink wash on its belly when perched but in flight it reveals a bright pink flash on its flanks. Its spectacular tail is longest in the adult male, shortest in the immature.

J F M A M J J A S O N D

FIELD NOTES

- 7¾–8¼" (19.5–21 cm)
- Common and conspicuous
- Slate-gray above, white below
- Broad white band at tail tip
- Bulky cup of grass, weeds, in bush or tree
- 3–5; whitish, marked with browns

Scissor-tailed Flycatcher

179

Western Kingbird

Tyrannus verticalis

The Western Kingbird is common in summer across farmland of the midwest and west, and in many areas it may be found alongside the Eastern Kingbird (p. 179). The Western's distinctive features are its pale gray head and chest and its square-tipped black tail with white sides.

While these white sides can be hard to see, or even missing if the tail is molting, the nasal *pik* call will always enable you to identify it. All kingbirds in fact have distinctive calls, and their full songs, or "dawn songs" as they are often known, are given mainly at or before first light.

Another yellow-bellied kingbird, similar to the Western, is Cassin's Kingbird (*Tyrannus vociferans*; 8–9" [20.5–23 cm]). The Cassin's is typical of dry habitats of the interior west, and occurs north to southern Montana and central California. It is distinguished from the Western Kingbird by its dusky gray head and chest which offset a cottony white chin patch, or bib. Its tail is blackish and squared, with a paler tip, and lacks the bright white sides of the Western. The Cassin's call—a burry, slightly explosive *ch-beehr*—is also a good way to identify this bird.

| J | F | M | A | M | J | J | A | S | O | N | D |

Western

Cassin's Kingbird

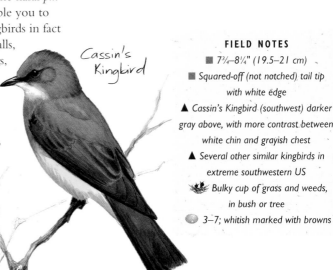

FIELD NOTES

- ■ 7¾–8¼" (19.5–21 cm)
- ■ Squared-off (not notched) tail tip with white edge
- ▲ Cassin's Kingbird (southwest) darker gray above, with more contrast between white chin and grayish chest
- ▲ Several other similar kingbirds in extreme southwestern US
- Bulky cup of grass and weeds, in bush or tree
- 3–7; whitish marked with browns

Horned Lark

Eremophila alpestris

M ale Horned Larks draw attention to themselves when singing their high-pitched tinkling song, either from a low rise on the ground or in a prolonged song flight high overhead. At other times, both males and females tend to be inconspicuous, blending well with their

chick   background and running away or crouching quietly when disturbed. If alarmed, they take off in a low, undulating flight, usually giving a few high-pitched tinkling call notes as they go.

The Horned Lark occurs in many open habitats, from the arctic tundra to the southwestern deserts, and from ploughed fields to beaches. In winter these birds may gather in flocks of over a hundred birds.

Like many widespread songbirds, the Horned Lark's plumage varies considerably from place to place. In all areas, however, the black mask, black chest band, and black

forehead band that runs into short "horns" in the male, are distinctive field marks.

The juvenile Horned Lark, with its pale-spotted upperparts and little trace of the distinctive face pattern, looks strikingly different from the adult and is often a source of confusion when first encountered.

J F M A M J J A S O N D

northern race

prairie race

FIELD NOTES

■ 6½–7½" (16.5–19 cm)

■ Whitish or yellowish face and throat

■ Black face pattern

▲ Numerous subspecies, varying slightly in color

🪺 Hollow in ground, lined with grass

🥚 2–5; grayish white speckled with browns

Black-billed Magpie

Pica pica

A striking, long-tailed bird, the Black-billed Magpie is found in farmland, rangeland, and open woodland of the interior west and northwest, where its raucous, chattering calls are a common sound.

A good example of biogeographic differentiation (the evolution of an isolated population into a separate species) is the closely related Yellow-billed Magpie (*Pica nuttallii*; 17–21" [43–53.5 cm]), which is common in the valleys of central California and is separated from the range of the Black-billed by high mountains that have little or no suitable habitat for magpies. The Yellow-billed Magpie is the only species of bird restricted to the state of California and, as its name suggests, it is readily identified by its yellow bill (which may be dusky in immatures). If you look closely you may also see a yellow crescent of naked skin below its eyes.

Magpies often form loose flocks of up to 20 birds outside the breeding season, and both species may also nest in loose colonies. In areas where magpies are common, their bulky nests, used year after year, are conspicuous features of the landscape.

J F M A M J J A S O N D

Yellow-billed

nest

FIELD NOTES
- 18–22" (45.5–56 cm)
- Black and white, with long tail
- Black bill
- ▲ Yellow-billed Magpie has yellow bill
- Bulky, dome-shaped structure of sticks at mid to upper levels in tree
- 5–13; greenish gray marked with browns

American Crow

Corvus brachyrhynchos

The American Crow is a familiar sight across most of North America in farmland and rural and urban areas. In the coastal northwest (north of Washington state) it is replaced by the very similar but slightly smaller Northwestern Crow (*Corvus caurinus*; 16" [40.5 cm]), which some ornithologists consider to be simply a subspecies of the American.

Crows are social birds, especially in winter when feeding and roosting flocks may number thousands. If you watch a flock of crows feeding, you may notice one or two birds positioned on posts or other prominent perches while the rest of the flock feeds. These sentinels keep watch for signs of danger and thus allow the flock to forage more efficiently.

Of the five crows in North America, the only other widespread species is the Common Raven (*Corvus corax*; 22–26½" [56–67 cm]) of the north and west. It is larger and more heavily built than the American Crow (ravens are simply large crows) and has a graduated, or wedge-shaped tail tip, unlike the squared-off tail tip of other crows. It also has a larger bill and shaggier throat than the American Crow.

American Crow

Common Raven

| J | F | M | A | M | J | J | A | S | O | N | D |

FIELD NOTES

- 16–20" (40.5–51 cm)
- Black
- Only common corvid across most of North America
- ▲ Common Raven (Canada and western US) is larger, with wedge-shaped tail, heavy bill
- ▲ Several other species of crows locally common in restricted ranges
- Bulky cup of sticks in tree, or on utility pole
- 3–7; greenish marked with browns and grays

Common Raven

183

Dickcissel

Spiza americana

Although a common summer resident in the prairie states and provinces of the midwest, the Dickcissel is notoriously unpredictable in its abundance in a given area from year to year, being common some years and rare or even absent in others.

J F M A M J J A S O N D

Dickcissels nest in grainfields and open weedy meadows where the males sing their buzzy *dick-cizz-l* song from fences or other low perches. In flight the Dickcissel gives a distinctive call: a wet, buzzy *dzzzrt*. Often these gregarious birds travel in vast flocks, especially during migration and when in their winter grounds in the tropics. At a distance, these flocks look like undulating clouds of insects.

While the male is relatively distinctive, the female and immature resemble a female House Sparrow. Note, however, the Dickcissel's longer and more conical bill, dark whisker mark, and orange-red shoulders. Young birds also often have dark streaks on their chest and flanks.

immature

FIELD NOTES

- 5¾–6¼" (14.5–16 cm)
- Yellowish eyebrow
- Stout grayish bill
- Reddish wingpatch
- Bulky cup of grass in clump of grass, hedge, or low bush
- 3–5; pale blue

flock of Dickcissels

Lark Sparrow

Chondestes grammacus

The attractive Lark Sparrow, a summer resident in farmlands, prairies, and rural areas, is one of the most readily identifiable sparrows, with its harlequin-like face pattern and bold white tail edging. Its name derives from its pleasant, lark-like song which is a varied series of rich chips, buzzes, and trills that may be given in a song flight.

Most sparrows fly fairly low when, for example, flushed up from the grass. Lark Sparrows, however, commonly fly overhead with a strong, gently undulating flight, and can often be spotted in the sky if you learn their distinctive, high-pitched, slightly metallic *tik* call.

Like most young sparrows, the juvenile Lark Sparrow has fine dusky streaking across its chest and shows a trace of the adult's distinctive head pattern, although brown replaces the adult's chestnut areas.

J F M A M J J A S O N D

Another sparrow with white in its tail is the Vesper Sparrow (*Pooecetes gramineus*; 5½–6" [14–15 cm]), widespread in summer in open grassy habitats across North America. It is streaky brown overall with orange-red shoulders and white tail sides, and it often shows a distinct, narrow, whitish eye-ring.

Lark Sparrow

Vesper Sparrow

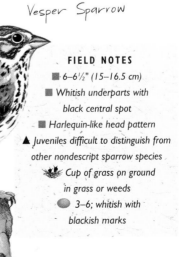

FIELD NOTES
- 6–6½" (15–16.5 cm)
- Whitish underparts with black central spot
- Harlequin-like head pattern
- ▲ Juveniles difficult to distinguish from other nondescript sparrow species
- Cup of grass on ground in grass or weeds
- 3–6; whitish with blackish marks

185

Lark Bunting

Calamospiza melanocorys

Driving across the prairie states and provinces in summer, you'll often see the handsome male Lark Bunting singing from fences or in his distinctive, hovering, song flight. As this species is not highly territorial, frequently several males sing in one small area.

The female is similar to several sparrows, but note her stout bill, which is black above and blue-gray below, and her whitish wing panel. After nesting, the male molts into a female-like plumage though with more black in the throat and more white in the wings. The only similar bird in this habitat in summer is the male Bobolink (p. 188), which has a blond hood and whitish rump.

In fall and winter, Lark Buntings form large flocks that may be seen feeding along roadsides in brushy and grassy ranchland. These flocks fly in a distinctive and fairly compact formation, with a general undulating movement. As they fly, the birds give their, soft, slightly nasal *whew* or *hoo-ee* call.

J F M A M J J A S O N D

winter ♂

winter ♂

♀

FIELD NOTES

■ 6¼–6¾" (16–17 cm)

■ Stocky

■ White wing patch

■ Stout bill

■ Summer male: Black

🪹 Cup of grass in depression in ground

🥚 3–7; pale bluish, sometimes with rusty spotting

Savannah Sparrow

Passerculus sandwichensis

One of the most widespread North American birds, the Savannah Sparrow is a typical streaky brown sparrow. It is found in fields, grasslands, marshes, and grassy dunes, and tends to be somewhat skulking. In spring, the male draws attention to himself with his song of a few high-pitched chips running into a trilled buzz, given from a low perch. At other times, you will most often see the Savannah Sparrow as a small, streaky brown bird that flushes up from close range, flies a short distance, and then drops back down to cover. However, unlike many grassland and marshland sparrows which are silent when flushed, the Savannah often calls as it flies off, giving a high-pitched *tsip*. It may also perch briefly on a grass stalk, low bush, or fence before dropping back to cover.

In most of its range, it has a small pinkish bill, streaked chest, and pale buffy or whitish eyebrow with a yellowish wash forward of the eyes.

| J | F | M | A | M | J | J | A | S | O | N | D |

Some birds of the northeast Atlantic coast (sometimes called the Ipswich Sparrow) are larger and paler overall with little or no yellow in their face, while those in the salt marshes of southern California are darker and more heavily streaked.

dark form

Ipswich form

pale form (deserts)

FIELD NOTES
- ■ 5–6" (12.5–15 cm)
- ■ Common and widespread
- ■ Brown and streaky
- ■ Pink bill and legs
- ■ Yellowish brow
- ▲ Very variable
- Cup of grass in hollow in ground
- 3–6; whitish to pale greenish blue, marked with browns

Bobolink

Dolichonyx oryzivorus

Named for the male's
bubbling *bob-o-link bob-o-
link…* song, this blackbird
nests in hayfields and open weedy
grasslands. The males often sing in a
fluttering display flight and may mate
with more than one female. This is
thought to reflect the female's
preference for a male with high
quality territory over males with poor territories.
Males with good territories are therefore able to
attract more than one mate.

J F M A M J J A S O N D

As with many northern-breeding
songbirds, after nesting the male molts
into a plumage resembling that of the
female and the immature: buffy
overall, streaked with dark brown
on the face, back, and sides. This
plumage suggests a sparrow, but note
the Bobolink's relatively large size
and its plain underparts with their
dark streaks only down the sides and not
extending across the chest. In all plumages the
Bobolink has a distinctly spiky-looking tail.

A good way to find Bobolinks during their
migration is to listen for their nasal *eenk* call
note which is often given in flight.

FIELD NOTES

- 6–7" (15–18 cm)
- Male: Entirely black below; white rump and shoulders; buff nape
- Female: Yellowish; heavily streaked above and on flanks
- Cup of grass in hollow in tall grass or crops
- 4–7; pale gray to brownish, marked with browns

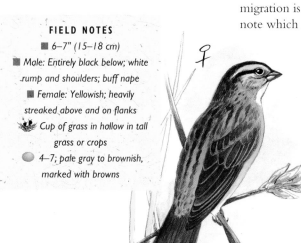

spiky tail

188

Eastern Meadowlark

Sturna magna

Eastern Meadowlarks are familiar and conspicuous songbirds of open country. In the midwest and southwest, their range overlaps that of their western counterpart, the Western Meadowlark (*Sturna neglecta*; 7½–9½" [19–24 cm]). Both species are commonly found in open fields. They are most often seen perched on fenceposts, and seldom on overhead wires.

white tail sides

J F M A M J J A S O N D

Identifying a silent meadowlark is a challenge, even for experts. The male Western can sometimes be distinguished from the Eastern by the more extensive yellow in his cheeks, but both meadowlarks are more easily identified by their songs and calls.

Eastern ♂

The Eastern sings a pleasant song usually of three or four plaintive whistled notes such as *see seer seee-u* or *see seeu see-u-seu*, while the Western Meadowlark's song is fluty and more complex, typically running into a warbled ending—*whee hir weedle-e whi-chee*. The two species also have distinct call notes, the Eastern giving a raspy *zzzrt* and the Western a low *chuk*.

Western ♂

As the birds fly, note the bright white tail sides of both species, often best seen as they take off or land.

Western ♀

FIELD NOTES

- ■ 7½–9½" (19–24 cm)
- ■ Bright yellow underparts
- ■ White tail sides
- ■ Bold, black V-shaped breast band
- ▲ Eastern and Western similar
- ❋ Cup of grass, often with dome, in depression in ground
- ● 3–7; whitish, marked with browns

189

Great-tailed Grackle

Quiscalus mexicanus

Until the early 1960s, the Great-tailed Grackle was considered the same species as the Boat-tailed Grackle (*Quiscalus major*; 13–16" [33–40.5 cm]) of the coastal US from New England to eastern Texas. However, studies conducted in Louisiana showed that the two nest alongside one another without interbreeding and they are now considered separate species.

The Great-tailed can be told by its larger size and pale yellow eyes. The Boat-taileds of the Gulf coast have pale brownish eyes (though Atlantic coast Boat-taileds often have pale yellowish eyes). The vocalizations and displays of the two also differ, although both have a varied repertoire of loud clucks, whistles, shrieks, and chatters. The Great-tailed is expanding its range in the southwest, following the spread of agriculture and irrigated urban areas. Except in Florida, the Boat-tailed occurs only along or near the coast, and is often associated with salt marshes.

J F M A M J J A S O N D

Boat-tailed ♂

Great-tailed

Great-tailed ♀

FIELD NOTES

- 10½–18½" (26.5–47 cm)
- Long, full tail
- Golden yellow eyes
- Flat crown
- Bulky cup of grass low to high in bush or tree
- 3–4; pale grayish with dark markings

190

Brown-headed Cowbird

Molothrus ater

The Brown-headed Cowbird's most famous or infamous attribute is that it is a brood parasite—the female lays eggs in the nests of other birds and takes no part in the rearing of her young. Brown-headed Cowbird eggs have been recorded in the nests of some 220 species, ranging from ducks to hummingbirds! The female cowbird has been estimated to lay an average of 80 eggs—40 per year for two years. Although only about 3 percent of eggs end up as adults, this still means that an average of 2.4 adults are produced by each female, so the species continues to increase in number.

Originally a bird of the Great Plains, where it lived around buffalo, this cowbird has spread dramatically across North America, following the clearance of forest for farms and pastures. This has allowed it to parasitize many more species, some of them poorly adapted to such behavior.

The male Cowbird makes a high-pitched whistle, while the female's spluttering chatter often gives her presence away. The female and juvenile Brown-headed Cowbirds are a plain gray-brown overall, though paler on the head and underparts. They both have a fairly stubby bill and a pale eye-ring.

J F M A M J J A S O N D

Bell's Vireo feeding cowbird chicks

FIELD NOTES

- 6½–7½" (16.5–19 cm)
- Stocky, with stubby bill and rather short tail
- Male: Black with brown head
- Female: Gray-brown, paler below
- Juvenile: Similar to adult female but streaked below
- Eggs laid in other species' nests
- Bluish white, densely speckled with browns

191

American Goldfinch

Carduelis tristis

The American Goldfinch is a common bird of weedy fields, farmland, open woodlands, and urban areas. In all these areas it is often found feeding on thistle seeds. While the summer male is one of the most colorful American birds, after breeding, both male and female molt into a more somber winter plumage like that of the immatures. In winter, American Goldfinches frequently visit garden birdfeeders to eat seeds.

In much of the southwest, the American Goldfinch is only a winter visitor and is replaced as a nesting bird by the Lesser Goldfinch (*Carduelis psaltria*; 4–4½" [10–11.5 cm]). Male Lessers in the west have green backs and a black cap, while those in the east have a black head and back. In all plumages, Lessers differ from American Goldfinches in having a

white flash at the base of the primaries on the closed wing, and in their pale yellowish (versus whitish) undertail coverts. Both species are accomplished singers and their pleasant twittering songs often include mimicry of other species' calls.

J F M A M J J A S O N D

Lesser

♀

♂ (western form)

FIELD NOTES

■ 4½–5" (11.5–12.5 cm)

■ Adult breeding male unmistakable

■ White undertail coverts and lack of streaking constant in all plumages

▲ Lesser Goldfinches have yellowish undertail coverts, greenish backs, and males are entirely black-capped

🪺 Cup of fine plant material, such as thistledown, in bush or tree

🥚 4–6; unmarked bluish white

at feeder

Wetlands

OVERHEAD There is always a good deal of traffic between wetlands areas, so watch out for passing flocks of birds such as American Wigeon, or geese flying in their distinctive V formations.

DEEP WATER Several species of ducks that dive for their food, such as Canvasbacks and scaups, tend to form rafts in deep water well away from shore. Loons and most grebes are generally found in deep water.

SHALLOWS Depending on the locality, look here for egrets, herons, phalaropes, stilts, avocets, and a variety of other birds that gather food while wading in shallow water.

MUD FLATS Many birds forage on mud flats. Some shorebirds, such as the Least Sandpiper, actually prefer freshwater to coastal environments.

WETLANDS
Lakes, Marshes, Reservoirs, Rivers, Swamps

Ranging from small local reservoirs and ponds in city parks to the Great Lakes and the famous Everglades of southern Florida, wetlands are a prominent feature of the North American landscape. The term "wetlands" is generally taken to refer to bodies of fresh water only, but when talking about bird habitats it is hard to make a firm distinction between these and salt marshes, river estuaries, and similar coastal environments.

Within each wetland environment, birds can gather their food in a remarkable range of ways, so wetlands are home to a notably broad spectrum of species. The bird population of a cold, deep, northern lake, for example, will be very different from that of a shallow, sun-baked prairie slough, or the cypress swamps of the deep south.

In general, northern wetlands tend to be rich in species of ducks, whereas southern wetlands are favored by a variety of herons, ibises, and similar large wading birds. Western and prairie wetlands support an especially wide range of ducks and shorebirds.

From the birder's perspective, wetlands tend to be characterized by their margins, the bird diversity they support increasing more or less in proportion with the extent of mud, reed beds, and water shallow enough to wade in.

Unfortunately, humans have tended to regard wetlands as wastelands rather than vital components of a healthy ecosystem, and short-sighted drainage and land reclamation have led to drastic reductions in the numbers of some wetland birds. For example, as a result of land reclamation programs at the lakes in the prairies of the Great Plains, traditionally a major nesting ground for waterfowl, numbers of these birds have declined dramatically in the past 100 years.

More recently, however, the surge in environmental awareness in much of North America has resulted in a growth in the conservation of wetland areas, and many are now protected as reserves and sanctuaries.

REED BEDS Rails and bitterns generally hide deep in the reed beds, but may forage along their margins when undisturbed. Reed beds are also home to some songbirds, such as Marsh Wrens, and may support nesting colonies of Yellow-headed or Red-winged blackbirds.

BIRDING *in* WETLANDS

Clearly delineated habitats and a diversity of highly visible species make wetland environments ideal places to study the social behavior of birds, their feeding tactics, and annual migration cycles.

Wetlands provide some of the most exciting habitats for birding because they contain all sorts of spectacular and easily observed species, such as pelicans, herons, egrets, geese, ducks, Ospreys, and shorebirds. Another appealing aspect of birding on an area of water is that it is a finite region, distinct from the surrounding land, enabling you to keep track of day-to-day changes in the diversity and numbers of birds present.

On a walk in the woods or fields you may see more warblers or sparrows one day than another but you will be unable to tell whether there are really more birds because at any one time many birds may be hidden from view. In contrast, if you see 20 ducks and 10 coots on a lake one day, and 50 ducks and no coots the next, you can be fairly certain that the variation is real rather than apparent.

PASSING THROUGH

Many wetlands are wintering areas or transit points for vast numbers of ducks and shorebirds that nest in Alaska and the Canadian arctic.

Southbound migrants appear as early as late June, heralding a stream of avian traffic that extends well into November. Some remain for the winter, others continue southward into Central or South America. In spring, some birds begin moving north again as soon as ice-free conditions permit, while many others are still moving north as late as early June.

It can be fascinating to note these day-to-day changes in your notebook, and over the years to compare arrival and departure dates for various species. You also may come to see how day-to-day changes relate to weather factors and thus learn how to predict which days are best for birding.

COEXISTENCE

The self-contained nature of many wetland habitats will also allow you to observe the intricacy with which the total resources of a habitat are parcelled out to different kinds of birds.

There is almost sure to be at least one small, short-legged species that forages over the muddy margins but does not actually wade (a sandpiper, perhaps).

WILDLIFE REFUGES *A huge range of highly visible birds can be observed in wetlands, from these ducks "dabbling" for food (below) to the White Ibis (right), seen here in a mangrove swamp.*

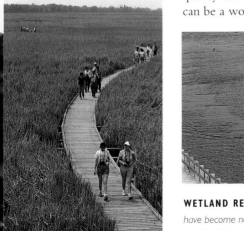

BIRD SPECTACULARS *Wetlands are the stage for many of the most spectacular sights in nature. Events such as the migrations of Snow Geese (right) attract birders from all around the country (above).*

Then there will be a slightly longer-legged species that can cover a wider area because it can wade in shallow water (yellowlegs, for example). And there will also be longer-legged birds that can reach deeper water to take full advantage of an even larger percentage of the wetland's total area (stilts or herons). Other birds—terns, for example—can cover the total surface area, but only at the cost of staying airborne for long periods. Some ducks habitually feed in the shallows, others "upend" in somewhat deeper water, while still others dive for food, exploiting resources that cannot be reached by

other birds. Birds such as rails have narrow bodies that enable them to slip easily between stems in reedbeds on the margins of the wetland.

More than other habitats, wetlands illustrate that, far from being distributed haphazardly, birds live in clearly structured communities. It can be absorbing to work out the way wetland birds are distributed and how they operate.

GETTING AROUND
Some wetland areas can be difficult to reach. Power-boats, of course, involve far too much noise to be of any use to the birder but—depending on the kind of wetland—puttering about quietly in a canoe or kayak can be a wonderful way of

observing waterbirds at close range without disturbing them unduly.

Alternatively, you may be able to find a causeway or dike to use as a vantage point to scan the wetland with your binoculars or spotting scope. Otherwise, wading may be the only way of exploring the marsh, but this often results in wet feet.

You can, of course, wear rubber boots or waders, but a little-known corollary of Murphy's Law states that the depth of the water you want to wade across is always one inch higher than the top of your boots. That's why experienced birders often keep a pair of sneakers and an old towel in the trunk of the car.

One final recommendation for wetland birding: don't forget the insect repellent!

WETLAND RESERVES *are so popular with visitors that boardwalks (left) and blinds have become necessary controls in their management. Canoes (above) can also provide effective and unobtrusive transport through these areas.*

Pied-billed Grebe

Podilymbus podiceps

Common across much of North America, this small, chunky grebe can be found on lakes and ponds with marshy vegetation. Generally, it avoids open water, such as stone-banked reservoirs or estuaries, but in winter it may be found occasionally in these habitats, especially if smaller lakes freeze over. Like all grebes, it dives well and can be elusive, especially in the nesting season when its presence

J F M A M J J A S O N D

may be given away only by varied whinnying and clucking calls coming from the reeds.

The Pied-billed Grebe is identified by its large head and thick pale bill which, in breeding birds, has a black vertical band, hence the name "pied-billed". The immature and non-breeding adult lack the black band on the bill and have a whitish throat. The downy young have black-and-white striped heads and often ride on their parents' backs.

An interesting aspect of grebe biology is that these fish-eating birds also consume many feathers—in fact, as much as half of the stomach contents of a grebe may be feathers. It is thought that the feathers form soft balls that protect the stomach against damage from the sharp fish bones that the grebe's gizzard is unable to break down.

juvenile

FIELD NOTES

- 11–13" (28–33 cm)
- Stocky, large-headed
- Stout bill: white with black ring in summer, otherwise dull yellowish
- Platform of aquatic vegetation, floating or anchored to reeds
- 2–10; bluish white

with chicks

Western Grebe

Aechmophorus occidentalis

This elegant grebe nests in colonies on lakes in much of the west. After breeding, most of the population migrates to spend the winter along the west coast, where you can also see non-breeding birds throughout the summer.

If you watch birds at a nesting lake long enough, you may be fortunate to see this species' spectacular and elaborate courtship display. This involves "rushing", when two or more birds run upright across the water, and the "weed dance", when two birds face one another with weed in their bills and make a number of ritualistic displays.

Until recently, it was widely believed that there were two forms of the Western Grebe: a dark form, with dark feathering extending below the eyes, and a light form, with white feathering extending above and in front of the eyes. However, studies have shown that the two rarely interbreed

and they are now considered separate species, the Western Grebe having the dark feathering, and the Clark's Grebe (*Aechmophorus clarkii*) the light.

The face patterns are best seen on breeding birds and most of the time you'll find it easier to identify the two species by the color of the bill. The Western has a greenish yellow bill while the Clark's has a brighter, orange-yellow bill.

Western

Clark's

J F M A M J J A S O N D

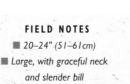

grebes 'rushing'

FIELD NOTES
- 20–24" (51–61cm)
- Large, with graceful neck and slender bill
- Blackish above, white below
- ▲ Clark's Grebe has brighter, orange-yellow bill
- Platform of aquatic vegetation, floating or anchored to reeds
- 2–7; unmarked bluish white

American White Pelican

Pelecanus erythrorhynchos

With a wingspan of up to 9½ feet (3 meters), this unmistakable bird is one of North America's largest, and there are few more spectacular sights than a flock of White Pelicans, wheeling and turning in unison. These birds nest mostly in colonies at large lakes in the interior west and then migrate to lagoons and estuaries along the coasts of the southern US and Mexico for the winter.

Unlike the coastal, saltwater Brown Pelican, which dives from the air, White Pelicans feed while swimming, putting their heads and bills under water to scoop up fish. Often several birds will swim together in a line, rounding up fish in shallow water and so maximizing their catch.

J F M A M J J A S O N D

During the nesting season, White Pelicans develop a horn-like growth on their bill. This growth is shed after the eggs have been laid. Immatures differ from adults in having a paler, grayish to flesh-colored bill, paler orange legs, and a brownish wash to their upperwing coverts. They resemble adults by the end of their second year.

bill showing 'horn'

FIELD NOTES

■ 57–65" (145–165 cm)

■ Large, mainly white, with large pouched bill—unmistakable

🪺 Depression in ground, sometimes built up with dirt

🥚 1–6; dull white

200

Great Blue Heron

Ardea herodias

Found in almost all wetland habitats, this is the most familiar large wading bird in North America. Like many conspicuous and widespread wading birds, the Great Blue Heron nests in relatively few colonies throughout its range, and non-breeding immatures occur in summer at many localities far from nesting populations.

Great Blue Herons are most often seen slowly stalking at the side of a lake or marsh, or standing still in fairly deep water where their long legs enable them to feed. In some areas you may see them feeding in fields or on lawns, where they hunt gophers and mice. If disturbed, the Great Blue takes off heavily and flies away with slow deep wingbeats, often giving a deep, throaty call as it goes.

J F M A M J J A S O N D

The Great Blue is unmistakable throughout most of its range, but in the Florida Keys you may find an all-white form, formerly considered a separate species. To distinguish this white form from the smaller Great Egret (p. 202), note the dull yellowish bill and pale legs of the heron.

The immature Great Blue has an all-dark crown and is duller overall than the adult. It attains full adult plumage when it is three years old.

white form

FIELD NOTES
- 40–50" (101.5–127 cm)
- Large, gray
- ▲ White form, locally common in southern Florida, may be confused with Great Egret but has pale legs
- 🌿 Platform of sticks in trees, on ground, or on cliffs
- 🥚 3–7; pale greenish

immature

Great Egret

Casmerodius albus

Formerly known as both the American Egret and the Common Egret, this is the large white heron seen across much of North America. These birds occur at lakes, lagoons, and along rivers and coasts, and like most herons, they nest in colonies which may include several other species of waterbirds.

Besides its size, the Great Egret's field marks are its bright yellow beak and its all-black legs and feet—note, however, that the space between the eye and the bill (the lore) on an adult becomes bright green for a brief period at the start of the breeding season.

Great Egrets feed by standing still and waiting, or by stalking slowly, and their statuesque posture while feeding distinguishes them from the Snowy Egret (p. 203).

In the second half of the nineteenth century, huge demand from the fashion industry for the plumes of breeding egrets caused egret populations to be devastated through hunting. Protective legislation introduced at the start of the twentieth century, following campaigns by the Audubon Society (whose symbol is the Great Egret) and others, has helped egret populations recover.

J F M A M J J A S O N D

FIELD NOTES
- 33–39" (84–99 cm)
- Large, white, with yellow bill
- Uses motionless, "stand-and-wait" hunting technique
- Platform of sticks in trees or reed bed
- 1–6; pale greenish

breeding plumage

Snowy Egret

Egretta thula

The Snowy Egret sometimes dashes around with its wings partly spread, and when it does, it presents a notable contrast to the much more sedate Great Egret. The rapid movement of the Snowy is thought to startle fish into revealing themselves, while the spread wings may shadow the water's surface, enabling the bird to see its prey more clearly.

Common to lakes, marshes, and coasts in North America, this small, white egret is identified by its all-black bill, yellow lores, and black legs with yellow feet or "golden slippers".

J F M A M J J A S O N D

In the southeast, especially along the coast, you'll also find the Little Blue Heron (*Egretta caerulea*; 20–24" [51–61 cm]). The adult is distinctive, with its overall dark bluish plumage. Immature Little Blue Herons are much harder to identify because they are all white and can easily be confused with Snowy Egrets. Unlike the Snowy, the Little Blue usually has a bicolored bill.

immature Little Blue

Little Blue Heron

FIELD NOTES

- 19–23" (48–58.5 cm)
- Small, white
- Black bill and legs, yellow feet
- Hunts briskly in shallow water
- Platform of sticks on ground, or in trees
- 1–6; pale greenish

203

Green Heron

Butorides virescens

Although widespread and common, this crow-sized heron tends not to be as conspicuous as the larger herons and egrets, since it prefers wooded marshes and pools and avoids wide open habitats. Nonetheless, if you walk quietly and are observant, you may well see Green Herons (formerly known as Green-backed Herons) hunched quietly at the edges of ponds and marshes. Often they are detected by their calls: a sharp barking *kyow!* which they give when flushed, and varied barking and clucking chatters.

In flight, the Green Heron is distinguished by its small size, compact shape, and dark plumage; and the yellow feet projecting beyond the tail are often quite conspicuous. Its main field marks are its chestnut-colored face and neck, its dark cap, and its yellow legs. In good light, the chalky greenish cast that gives the bird its name is visible on its back. This is most evident in breeding birds, which also have bright reddish orange legs. The immature is duller overall than the adult and has dark and pale streaking on its neck and chest.

J F M A M J J A S O N D

adult

FIELD NOTES

- 15–17" (38–43 cm)
- Small
- Yellowish legs
- Looks all dark at a distance
- Platform of sticks in reeds or trees
- 3–6; pale greenish

fishing

Black-crowned Night-Heron

Nycticorax nycticorax

As the name implies, this heron is mostly nocturnal, although it can often be seen during the day, feeding along the edges of lakes or coastal lagoons, or roosting in trees near water. The Black-crowned's barking *wok!* frequently draws attention to it at dusk when these birds leave their roosts and set out to hunt for food. (This is when most herons are heading in the opposite direction—back to their roosts.)

The Black-crowned stands with a characteristic hunched posture that helps distinguish it from the closely related, taller-standing Yellow-crowned Night-Heron (*Nycticorax violaceus*; 20–23" [51–58.5 cm]) of the southeast. In flight, note that the longer legs of the Yellow-crowned project noticeably beyond its tail whereas the feet of the Black-crowned can only just be seen. Immatures of these two species look very similar, being brown overall with pale spotting on their upperparts. They are often best told apart by their shape, but note also that the Yellow-crowned's thicker bill is all-black while the immature Black-crowned has a yellowish base to its bill.

Yellow-crowned

Black-crowned

J F M A M J J A S O N D

Yellow-crowned

immature Black-crowned

FIELD NOTES

- ■ 22–25" (56–63.5 cm)
- ■ Adult: black cap and back, gray wings, white underparts
- ▲ Immature easily confused with Yellow-crowned Night-Heron and American Bittern
- ❀ Platform of sticks in trees, in marshes
- ● 1–6; pale greenish

205

Snow Goose

Chen caerulescens

Few sights in the bird world are as breathtaking as a cacophonous blizzard of thousands of Snow Geese taking to the air or alighting in a field. After breeding in the arctic tundra, this goose migrates south to spend the winter at traditional wintering grounds in parts of the US, and in southwest British Columbia.

Because of the commercial value of geese to hunters, a large part of the work of many wildlife refuges across North America involves protecting populations of Snow and other geese during the migrations in fall and early spring, as well as in winter. Visiting these refuges, especially in the hunting season before the great majority of geese disperse away from the safety of protected sites, is the best way to see Snow Geese and many other waterfowl.

blue form

The Snow Goose comes in two forms (morphs): the more common white form and the blue form, at one time considered a separate species known as the Blue Goose. Blue morph Snow Geese occur mainly in the midwest and on the Great Plains.

The immature Snow Goose is dirty whitish overall in the white form and dusky brownish overall in the blue form. Many immatures do not attain adult-like plumage by spring.

J F M A M J J A S O N D

immature (white form)

FIELD NOTES

- 25–30" (63.5–76 cm)
- White form: Plain white with black wingtips
- Blue form: Dark bluish gray with (adults only) white head
- Depression in ground lined with grass and down
- 4–7; creamy white

Canada Goose

Branta canadensis

Perhaps the most familiar goose to most North Americans, the Canada Goose is famous for its geographic variation—some of the largest subspecies are nearly twice as big as the smallest.

From eight to eleven subspecies are generally recognized. For practical purposes these can be broken down into small, medium, and large birds. In general, the smaller races, which are a quarter the size of the largest birds, give higher-pitched, yelping or cackling calls, and the larger birds give more drawn-out honking calls. The small races are therefore often known as "cackling geese", whereas the larger races are known as "honkers".

All Canada Geese have the diagnostic white "chinstrap" and are varying shades of brownish below. The young look much like the adults.

J F M A M J J A S O N D

The large and medium-sized races are fairly widespread whereas the small cacklers breed only in the far north and winter locally in the west and midwest.

As with other geese, Canada Geese often fly in a distinctive V-formation that aids streamlining, and family parties stay together throughout the winter.

'cackling' Canada Goose

'honker'

FIELD NOTES

- 22–45" (56–114.5 cm)
- Black head and neck
- White patch under chin
- Depression in ground built up with grass and lined with feathers
- 2–12; dull white

207

Wood Duck

Aix sponsa

That the Wood Duck is now common in much of eastern North America is a tribute to a highly successful conservation policy. Early in the twentieth century, Wood Ducks were threatened with extinction through over-hunting, drainage of wetlands, and felling of forests. Their rarity led to a moratorium on hunting for 23 years, from 1918 to 1941, and a program of close habitat management. Since Wood Ducks nest in tree cavities, nestboxes have also played a particularly important role in re-establishing the species in many areas.

Many people's first encounter with a Wood Duck is hearing a rising squeal and seeing a pair of ducks with long, squared-off tails rise up from a wooded

pond and circle overhead. If this happens and you remain still, they may land nearby, giving you the opportunity of viewing one of the most handsome birds you are likely to encounter in wetlands.

The ornate male is unmistakable for much of the year. After nesting he molts into a drab female-like plumage but keeps his distinctive red bill. Good field marks of the female are her bushy pointed crest and her bold white eye-ring.

J F M A M J J A S O N D

chicks
leaving
nest

♀

FIELD NOTES
- 17–19" (43–48 cm)
- Male: Unmistakable, with bold, intricate pattern and bright colors
- Female: Dull; grayish head with white patch around eye
- Hollow in tree
- 9–12; off-white

Mallard

Anas platyrhynchos

The Mallard is the most widespread and familiar duck in the Northern Hemisphere. Since it is often tame and found in city parks, it can provide an excellent opportunity to learn the important basics of duck breeding biology, plumage, and molt—lessons that will serve you well when identifying less familiar species.

Mallards are the ancestors of all breeds of domestic or farmyard ducks except the Muscovy. Wild and feral birds may interbreed in parks, giving rise to an array of plumages ranging from typical male Mallards, with their green head, white neck band, and mahogany breast, to birds that are mostly white. Females are dull and mottled like most female dabbling ducks.

In the east you'll also find the closely related Black Duck (*Anas rubripes*; 21–24" [53.5–61 cm]). As this bird sometimes interbreeds with the Mallard, some ornithologists consider it a subspecies of the Mallard. The male does not have brightly colored plumage—both sexes resemble dark female Mallards. Black Ducks, however, have white on only the trailing edge of their deep blue speculum. The Mallard's speculum has a white border on both sides.

J F M A M J J A S O N D

dabbling Mallard

speculum

American Black Duck

FIELD NOTES

■ 20–23" (51–58.5 cm)

■ Male: Glossy green head, mahogany breast, narrow white collar

▲ Female difficult to distinguish from Black Duck, but Mallard has white on both sides of speculum

🪺 Cup of leaves and grass on ground, lined with down

🥚 5–14; greenish white

209

Green-winged Teal

Anas crecca

Teals are small dabbling ducks, and the Green-winged Teal is common across North America. It nests in tall grass and reeds around lakes and marshes, and in winter it favors muddy channels in marshes and estuaries for feeding. Non-breeding Green-winged Teals often occur in fairly large flocks that fly rapidly in tightly grouped formation. They associate with other dabbling ducks while feeding, but, although a single teal may fly with Mallards or other ducks, the species tend to separate in flight.

The handsome, full-plumaged male is unmistakable, while the female is told from most ducks by her small size. In flight, she is readily separated from the Blue-winged and Cinnamon teals by her brownish (not pale bluish) forewings and the bright green inner square on the speculum (wingpatch).

J F M A M J J A S O N D

While swimming, the three teals can look very similar, but note the female Green-winged's relatively small bill and whitish undertail coverts.

breeding ♂

♀ Green-winged Teal & ducklings

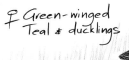

FIELD NOTES

■ 14–15" (35.5–38 cm)
   ■ Very small
   ■ Male: Chestnut and bottle-green head
   ▲ Female difficult to distinguish from other teals, but has plain head, whitish undertail coverts, and green speculum
   🪶 Depression in ground lined with grass
   🥚 7–15; cream

Northern Pintail

Anas acuta

After the Mallard and perhaps the Lesser Scaup, the elegant Pintail is one of the most abundant ducks in North America. Like most dabbling ducks, Pintails nest mainly on freshwater lakes and marshes in the north and west. They migrate south in winter to the west and south coasts, where large groups may be found in favored estuaries and coastal lagoons.

The Pintail's long neck enables it to feed, by up-ending, in deeper water than other dabbling ducks. In nuptial plumage, the male, with his attenuated, pin-like central tail feathers making up almost a quarter of his total length, is unmistakable.

The female is generally paler and grayer than other dabbling ducks, and has something of the male's elegant, long-necked and long-tailed appearance. In flight, the female Pintail's best field mark is the white edge on the brown speculum (wingpatch) of her upperwing.

J F M A M J J A S O N D

FIELD NOTES

- 20–26" (51–66 cm)
- Slim and elegant
- Long slender neck
- Male: Brown head, white foreneck
- Female: Plain head, pointed tail, gray legs
- Depression in ground lined with grass, leaves
- 6–12; cream

♀

up-ending

breeding ♂

♀

211

Blue-winged Teal

Anas discors

Common across much of North America, although less so along the west coast, the Blue-winged Teal is one of the long-distance migrants of the duck world, with some birds flying as far as Argentina in the winter. In parts of the west, you are likely to find the closely related Cinnamon Teal (*Anas cyanoptera*; 15–16" [38–40.5 cm]).

The males of these two species are readily separable in nuptial plumage: the male Blue-winged has a bold white crescent on his slaty blue face, and the poorly named male Cinnamon

Teal is chestnut (not cinnamon) overall. Females, juveniles, and non-breeding males of these two species are difficult to tell apart and can puzzle even expert birders. Note that the Cinnamon Teal is often a warmer brown overall and has a broader, more spatulate bill that suggests the Northern Shoveler. In flight, both are readily told from the Green-winged Teal by their pale bluish forewings, which are brightest in the adult males.

FIELD NOTES

- 15–16" (38–40.5 cm)
- Male: Slaty gray face with white crescent
- Female: Pale spot at base of bill
- Basket-like structure of dead grass on ground
- 6–15; creamy white

212

Northern Shoveler

Anas clypeata

By virtue of its shovel-like bill, the Northern Shoveler is one of the most distinctive North American ducks. In profile the heavy bill is longer than the head—a distinguishing mark among the dabbling ducks. The size of the bill causes the bird to hold its head slightly drooped in flight. When feeding (usually in shallow water), the Northern Shoveler extends its neck forward and dabbles its bill just under the water's surface. The small comb-like teeth along the sides of the bill are used as a strainer, retaining food items.

The male Northern Shoveler in nuptial plumage is one of the most handsome North American ducks. The female, like other female dabblers, is mottled brown overall.

Unlike most dabbling ducks, the immature Northern Shoveler does not attain adult male plumage until late winter. You may therefore see the distinctive immature male plumage—similar to a dull adult but with a mottled whitish crescent forward of the eyes—right through the New Year.

♂ immature

FIELD NOTES

- 17–20" (43–51 cm)
- Large, spatulate bill
- Male: Green head, white chest, chestnut flanks
- Female: Plain, sober-hued, best identified by distinctive bill
- Depression in ground, lined with grass
- 6–14; pale buff color

spatulate bill

213

Lesser Scaup

Aythya affinis

Lesser Scaups are a common sight on lakes and reservoirs across much of North America in winter, when they may form large flocks and associate with other diving ducks. Large numbers also spend the winter in protected estuaries and lagoons along both coasts. In summer, they nest mainly on small prairie lakes. Like other diving ducks, scaups spend much of the day sleeping because they feed at night, their bill tucked into their back.

The closely related Ring-necked Duck (*Aythya collaris*; 16–18" [40.5–45.5 cm]) may be found with Lesser Scaups, although it tends not to occur in large flocks and prefers less open habitats, such as small ponds and lakes in woodlands.

| J | F | M | A | M | J | J | A | S | O | N | D |

Unlike dabbling ducks, diving ducks run along the water to take off. In flight, the scaup shows a white wingstripe compared with the pale gray stripe on the Ring-necked Duck's wings. The female Ring-necked lacks the bold white patch at the base of the scaup's plain bill. She has a gray face, narrow white eye-ring, and banded bill. In all plumages, note the distinctive head and bill shapes of these two species.

Lesser Scaup ♀

Ring-neck

FIELD NOTES

- 15–17" (38–43 cm)
- White, not gray, wingbar
- ▲ Ring-necked Duck has high-peaked crown as opposed to Lesser Scaup's more rounded head
- Hollow in ground lined with grass and down
- 6–15; dark olive-buff

214

Bufflehead

Bucephala albeola

The sprightly, fast-flying Bufflehead is the smallest North American diving duck. Unlike most diving ducks, however, it can take off from the water without running along the surface. Buffleheads are common in winter on lakes, reservoirs, coastal lagoons, and in estuaries and sheltered harbors. They usually occur in small flocks and readily associate with other diving ducks.

The females and first-winter males are identified by their small size and the white patch on the sides of the head. In flight, the male shows the white inner half of his upperwings, whereas the female and immature have a white patch on the secondary wing feathers.

In the same genus is the Common Goldeneye (*Bucephala clangula*; 17–20" [43–51 cm]), which occurs in much the same range and habitats as the Bufflehead. Frequently, the two species are

seen side by side. The adult male Goldeneye is identified by the large, round white spot in front of his eyes. The female and immature have a brown knobby head. By midwinter the immature male often shows a whitish spot in front of his eyes.

| J | F | M | A | M | J | J | A | S | O | N | D |

Common Goldeneye

FIELD NOTES
■ 14–16" (35.5–40.5 cm)
■ Male: Tubby with big, dark green and white head
■ Female: Dark gray head with horizontal white cheek patch
🪺 Cavity in tree, often old Flicker hole
🥚 6–11; cream

215

Ruddy Duck

Oxyura jamaicensis

The distinctive Ruddy Duck is a compact duck with a "stiff" tail that is often held cocked, especially when the bird is sleeping. In winter both sexes have pale cheeks, but the female's cheeks have a dark bar across them. The male attains his full chestnut breeding plumage by March, and this is lost again by the end of the summer.

Many ducks dive but the Ruddy sinks slowly below the surface, scarcely leaving a ripple. In display, the male "bubbles", striking his bill against his inflated chest to disperse bubbles into the surrounding water.

Ruddies are common in many areas: they nest on marshy ponds and lakes with reedy edges, and spend the winter on lakes, lagoons, and reservoirs. Throughout the year, non-breeding birds may occur in flocks which tend to keep somewhat apart from other ducks. Although strong fliers, Ruddy Ducks take to the air infrequently. In flight their upperparts are uniformly dark, lacking the white markings found on many other ducks.

J F M A M J J A S O N D

diving

winter ♀

winter ♂

FIELD NOTES
- 14–16" (35.5–40.5 cm)
- Dumpy shape
- Prominent "stiff" tail, carried flat or cocked
- Male: Mainly chestnut, with blue bill, black cap, white cheeks
- Female: Brownish gray body, horizontal dark bar across cheek
- Basket-like structure of marsh grass anchored to reeds
- 5–10; creamy white

Osprey
Pandion haliaetus

From a distance, an Osprey circling high over the water, with its crooked wings and whitish underparts, may suggest a large gull. Note, however, the dark wrist marks on the Osprey's blunter-tipped wings, and its dark eyestripe. Also, unlike gulls, the Osprey hovers. If you watch for a while, you may witness the spectacular sight of an Osprey diving feet-first into the water, coming up with a fish and carrying it off aligned head first, in its talons.

While today the Osprey is common in summer across much of North America, from the 1950s through the 1970s many populations declined drastically. This was largely as a result of the misuse of pesticides—such as DDT, which caused thinning of birds' eggshells and thus reproductive failure. The banning of DDT in the early 1970s, and the provision of nesting platforms, helped the Osprey recover.

The male and female Osprey look alike, although the female often has a necklace of brown streaks across her chest. The juvenile is distinguished in fall by the extensive pale tips on the feathers of its upperparts.

J F M A M J J A S O N D

dark wrist mark

FIELD NOTES
- 22–26" (56–66 cm)
- Dark brown above, white below
- Dark wrist marks on underwing
- Carries wings in distinctive arched posture
- Bulky platform of sticks in tree, on cliff, or on ground
- 2–4; pinkish, heavily marked with browns

artificial nest-platform

217

Bald Eagle

Haliaeetus leucocephalus

Although the Bald Eagle is considered a threatened species in many areas, if you live in the northwest you have a good chance of seeing this impressive raptor along the coast or at large lakes. In fall, Bald Eagles gather at favored feeding grounds, in particular certain salmon-spawning grounds in Alaska and British Columbia, where up to 3,000 eagles may gather. Elsewhere, in the east and south, Bald Eagles are local and uncommon, although for the most part their populations are increasing following a decline linked, like the decline of the Osprey, to pesticides such as DDT.

In 1782 the Bald Eagle won the contest between it and the Wild Turkey to become the national bird of the US, and was picked for its fierce demeanor. In fact, Bald Eagles tend to be quite timid and often feed on carrion. They hunt mostly from perches overlooking water, and plunge like Ospreys to catch fish with their talons before returning to a perch to eat them.

J F M A M J J A S O N D

In flight, at a distance, the Bald Eagle can be told from the Turkey Vulture (p. 170) by its more massive, barn-door-like shape, and its broader wings that are held flat rather than distinctly raised, as is the case with the Turkey Vulture. The immature Bald Eagle is mostly dark brown, with some whitish mottling under its wings. After four years it attains the white-headed, white-tailed adult plumage.

adult

immature

adult

immature

FIELD NOTES

■ *30–40" (76–101.5 cm)*

■ *White head and tail*

▲ *Immatures easily confused with Golden Eagle*

❋ *Bulky mass of sticks in tree, on cliff*

● *1–3; dull white*

American Coot

Fulica americana

The widespread American Coot is one of the most common and conspicuous birds on North American lakes and ponds. Unlike ducks, which tend to be wary and fly off when you approach them, coots seem tolerant of people and will nest even at small ponds in city parks. They swim with a slight head-jerking motion that will enable you to pick them out at long range from swimming ducks, and they have to patter and splash frantically along the water's surface to gain momentum for flight.

In winter, coots may gather in large groups, or "rafts", on open water, but in the nesting season they can be quite shy, keeping to dense reeds and only giving away their presence by their gruff clucks and chatters.

J F M A M J J A S O N D

The juvenile coot looks very different from the adult. It lacks a bare forehead shield and is paler and grayer overall, with a whitish face and neck. By winter, the young resemble adults.

In marshes and ponds, especially in the east and south, you'll also find the Common Moorhen (*Gallinula chloropus*; 13–14" [33–35.5 cm]), which skulks more than the coot and is rarely seen on open water or in groups. The moorhen is readily told from a coot by its red and yellow bill and the white stripe along its sides. Like coots, moorhens feed while walking along the shores of ponds and while swimming.

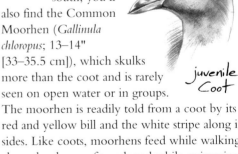

juvenile Coot

Common Moorhen

FIELD NOTES

- ■ 14–16" (35.5–40.5 cm)
- ■ Mainly black
- ■ White bill
- 🪺 Platform of marsh plants, anchored to reeds
- ⬭ 6–12; pale buff with dark speckling

219

Spotted Sandpiper

Actitis macularia

At first glance, this small bird, with its brown and white plumage and white wingstripe, may appear like any typical sandpiper, but certain characteristics make the Spotted one of the most distinctive North American shorebirds. If you watch a Spotted Sandpiper for more than a few seconds, you'll notice that it walks with a persistent bobbing action, wagging its rear end up and down and often continuing to bob when standing still. And in flight, the Spotted's wingbeats are stiff and shallow, so that the wings are flicked quickly and held bowed below the body.

The Spotted is also set apart from other small sandpipers by the fact that it does not occur in large flocks and tends to be found alone rather than with other shorebirds. During migration and in winter, you may find Spotteds at lakes, estuaries, reservoirs, and rocky coasts, as well as along rivers, which is where they nest in summer.

The spots for which this species is named are only present in the summer plumage. The base of the bill and the legs are yellowish to dull pinkish in winter, as opposed to bright orangey pink in nesting birds.

breeding

J F M A M J J A S O N D

FIELD NOTES

- 6½–7" (16.5–18 cm)
- Underparts spotted in summer, plain whitish in winter
- Teeters and bobs almost constantly
- Flies with rapid shallow beats of stiff, slightly bowed wings
- Hollow in ground, hidden by grass
- 1–4; buff marked with browns

winter

222

Belted Kingfisher

Ceryle alcyon

The machine-gun-like rattling call of the Belted Kingfisher is a distinctive sound in wetlands across North America, and will attract your attention to a medium-sized bird with a large, bushy head and stout, pointed bill. The male has a single blue-gray band across his white underparts, while the female has a rusty band below the gray band.

Kingfishers are often seen perched on trees or wires overlooking water, from where they plunge head-first to catch fish in their bills. They also hunt by hovering, often fairly high over the water, swooping down when they spot a fish.

Juvenile kingfishers are taught to fish by their parents, who drop dead fish into the water for the young to retrieve. After about ten days training, the young have learned to catch live food and are then chased away from the territory by the parents.

Kingfishers are solitary through the winter, when they may often be seen along seacoasts, and some birds overwinter as far north as ice-free water allows.

J F M A M J J A S O N D

diving for fish

FIELD NOTES

- 12–13" (30.5–33 cm)
- Large shaggy head
- Heavy, pointed bill
- White underparts with blue-gray band across chest
- Female: Additional chestnut band across lower chest
- Burrow excavated in bank
- 5–8; unmarked white

223

Eastern Phoebe

Sayornis phoebe

Phoebes are relatively hardy flycatchers that overwinter in North America, at least in the south, when other flycatchers migrate to the tropics. In part this is because they eat insects associated with year-round habitats, such as ponds and streams, rather than with short-lived spring and summer foliage. In much of the north and east, a familiar sight in summer is an Eastern Phoebe perched on a post or tree over water, attracting attention to itself with its high-pitched, sharp *peek!* call.

Like many small flycatchers, the Eastern Phoebe is fairly nondescript, which is a help when identifying it, since it lacks even the pale eye-ring and distinct pale wingbars of most small flycatchers. Other useful field marks are its dark head and the way that it wags, or dips, its tail down (not up) while perched.

J F M A M J J A S O N D

In the southwest its counterpart is the closely related Black Phoebe (*Sayornis nigricans*; 6–7" [15–18 cm]) which has the same habits and a very similar call note to the Eastern Phoebe. The Black Phoebe is almost all black, with a white belly. The juvenile has distinct cinnamon wingbars.

juvenile Black Phoebe

Black Phoebe

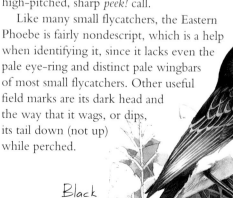

FIELD NOTES
- 6¼–6¾" (16–17 cm)
- Dingy white underparts
- Dark head
- Alert, upright stance
- Persistently jerks tail slowly downward
- Cup of mud and grass on rock ledge, or building
- 3–8; whitish

Tree Swallow

Tachycineta bicolor

In summer, Tree Swallows are common in most wooded habitats near water, especially where dead branches provide nest sites. (Tree Swallows also use nestboxes readily.) During migration, in fall, Tree Swallows may be seen in vast flocks that cloud the sky like insect swarms. As they eat berries in addition to insects, these swallows are able to overwinter in areas north of where purely insectivorous swallows can survive.

Most adult Tree Swallows are readily told from other North American swallows by their steely blue upperparts and white underparts. However, juveniles and immatures are brownish above and may have a dusky wash across the chest, and females too, at least in their first summer, are brownish above rather than glossy blue. Thus they may be confused with the two North American species of brown-backed swallows, the Bank

Swallow (*Riparia riparia*; 4¾–5¼" [12–13 cm]) and the Northern Rough-winged Swallow (*Stelgidopteryx serripennis*; 5–5½" [12.5–14 cm]), both of which nest in holes in banks or cliffs. The smaller Bank Swallow has a clean-cut brown chest band, while the Rough-winged has a dusky throat and a squarer-tipped tail.

J F M A M J J A S O N D

juvenile Tree Swallow

Rough-winged Swallow

Bank Swallow

Tree Swallow

FIELD NOTES

- ◼ 5¼–5¾" (13–14.5 cm)
- ◼ Glossy green-blue upperparts, white underparts
- ▲ Females and immatures may be confused with Bank and Northern Rough-winged swallows (see above)
- 🕊 Cup of grass in cavity
- 🥚 4–6; white

225

Common Yellowthroat

Geothlypis trichas

The bright warbled *witchety-witchety-witchety* song of the Common Yellowthroat often gives away the presence of this attractive warbler, which is common in summer in marshes and damp meadows and, during migration, in brushy fields and gardens often far from water. Another way to locate Yellowthroats is to learn their call note, a fairly gruff *chek*. If you then "spish" (make a lisping sound like *psssh-psssh...*), Yellowthroats will often respond by hopping up and flying toward you to investigate the noise. No one knows why birds respond to spishing this way, but it seems to work particularly well with Yellowthroats.

The male is readily identified by his bold black mask, bordered above by a narrow band that may be white, gray, or pale yellow. The female is fairly nondescript: her upperparts are olive and her underparts yellow, the yellow being brightest on the bib and on the undertail coverts. Young males in fall look like females but often show traces of the black mask.

J F M A M J J A S O N D

♀

immature
♂

FIELD NOTES

- ◼ 4½–5¼" (11.5–13 cm)
- ◼ Male: Olive above, bright yellow below, with bold black mask
- ▲ Female similar to other female and immature warblers, but note ground-haunting habits, plain tail, and yellowish throat and upper chest
- Bulky cup of grass, on or near ground in marshy vegetation
- 3–5; whitish speckled with browns

226

Red-winged Blackbird

Agelaius phoeniceus

Red-winged Blackbirds are a familiar sight across North America, where they nest in marshes, roadside ditches, grainfields, and damp meadows. In winter, they may form flocks of thousands, even millions, which swarm over fields to feed, often in company with cowbirds, grackles, and other blackbirds.

In spring, the male Red-winged can often be seen singing his song, a strangled gurgle, from a roadside perch or in a low fluttering flight. As he sings, he displays his brilliant red shoulders, or "epaulets", which are bordered with a yellowish band.

J F M A M J J A S O N D

The female is dark brown and heavily streaked, especially on the underparts. Young males resemble females until their second year.

The closely related and very similar Tricolored Blackbird (*Agelaius tricolor*; 7–9" [18–23 cm]) is found only in California and adjacent Oregon and northern Baja. The male Tricolored is distinctive in that his dark red shoulders are bordered by a white band rather than a yellowish band, but telling the female Tricolored and Red-winged blackbirds apart is a challenge even for experts.

Red-winged ♀

FIELD NOTES

■ 7–9½" (18–24 cm)

■ Male: Black with brilliant red shoulder patch

▲ Tricolored Blackbird has white, not yellow, edge on red shoulder patch. Females very similar.

🪺 Cup of grass attached to reeds or tall grass

🥚 3–5; pale blue with dark markings

Tricolored ♂

Red-winged ♂

227

Yellow-headed Blackbird

Xanthocephalus xanthocephalus

The unmistakable male Yellow-headed Blackbird is one of the most striking songbirds you are likely to see in a wetland habitat. As with many blackbirds, the female is smaller and more somberly colored than the male: she is dark brown overall with a yellow face and chest, and lacks the male's bold white forewing patch. Juveniles of both sexes have a golden-buff head and chest but soon molt into an adult-female-like immature plumage. The juvenile male tends to be brighter than the female and by spring looks similar to the adult male.

Yellow-headed Blackbirds are rare in the east but common in western and central North America. They nest in large, dense colonies, and often the reed beds are filled with the sound of thousands of them making their strangled, honking gurgles that pass for songs. In migration and winter, Yellow-heads remain highly gregarious and may join with other blackbirds feeding in fields. Also, as is frequently the case with winter blackbirds, males and females may form separate flocks, so you may come across a flock of thousands of male Yellow-headed Blackbirds— truly an incredible sight!

J F M A M J J A S O N D

FIELD NOTES
- 7½–10" (19–25.5 cm)
- Male: Black with bright yellow head and upper chest
- Female: Dark brown overall with yellow face and chest
- Deep basket of grass woven into reeds
- 3–5; pale grayish, marked with browns

228

S e a s h o r e s

ESTUARIES and SALT MARSHES
Many shorebirds such as Dunlins and Whimbrels prefer open estuarine mudflats, exposed at low tide, on which to forage. At high tide, they may retire to salt marshes or pebbly banks to roost in dense flocks.

SANDY BEACHES When not feeding offshore, terns are fond of loafing in large flocks on beaches. Sanderlings habitually forage along the shore, and gulls patrol tidelines for carrion. Another beach specialist is the endangered Piping Plover.

CLIFFS AND STACKS are prime nesting sites for colonies of cormorants, alcids (especially murres and puffins), and some species of gulls.

SEASHORES
Beaches, Sand Dunes, Coastal Cliffs, Estuaries, Mangroves

The seashore—where the land meets the sea—is a clearly defined but wonderfully varied environment. From the icy winter shores of Maine to Florida mangroves and sun-scorched Texas beaches, the American coastline encompasses a vast array of places where birds can live.

The most obvious seashore habitats are cliffs, surf-washed rocks, sand beaches, muddy estuaries, and mangroves.

SURF Depending on location, the surf zone just offshore may host feeding cormorants and Brown Pelicans, and—particularly in winter—rafts of scoters, grebes, murres, and loons.

While there is considerable overlap, certain bird groups are associated with particular habitats: cormorants with cliffs, terns with beaches, shorebirds with estuaries, and so on. Largely confined to the southeast, mangrove swamps represent a particularly specialized environment with a distinctive bird community, and are especially attractive to long-legged wading birds such as egrets, ibises, and spoonbills.

Climate, of course, affects the habitat and the type of food available to birds, and thus influences the species found in different coastal surroundings. Alcids and gulls, for example, tend to favor colder environments and are thus associated with northern coasts; terns are more common along warmer southern shores.

The sea itself provides a variety of bird habitats, though as these are defined by factors such as depth, temperature, and salinity they are less easily recognized by humans. For example, the truly pelagic birds—especially the tubenoses, such as albatrosses and shearwaters— seldom come any closer to land than the limits of the continental shelf, and there is a noticeable difference between offshore and inshore bird communities. The sea off the Pacific coast is especially rich in birdlife, with large populations of breeding auks and cormorants in summer augmented by numerous sea ducks, such as scoters, in winter.

BIRDING *at* SEASHORES

Seashores are demanding birding environments. You may study your garden or local patch for the sheer pleasure of watching birds going about their daily affairs, but seacoasts are where you go for the thrill of having your identification skills challenged and extended.

Birding would not be the fun it is if all birds were easy to identify, and seashores are where you will come up against three of the five most challenging groups of birds: gulls, migratory shorebirds, and seabirds (the fourth and fifth groups are the flycatchers and the fall warblers).

GULLS

Everyone knows a seagull when they see one, but the sheer number of species makes positive identification difficult. In addition, each gull takes between two and four years to reach maturity, each year giving rise to a different plumage. And to compound the problem further, most species have distinct winter and summer plumages (and this sometimes applies to the immatures as well!). Thus the birder is faced with a quite bewildering array of alternatives. Working through all these possibilities is the real problem; once you've done that, making a positive identification just takes time. At least gulls are (usually) fearless enough to let you look at them closely.

Critical points you should note when trying to identify a strange gull are:
- color and shape of bill
- leg color
- wingtip pattern
- whether it has a dark tail band

SHOREBIRDS

Migratory shorebirds are less cooperative than gulls. They are generally extremely wary, and habitually congregate in large flocks, often of mixed

COASTAL HABITATS *are often dominated by gulls, like this mixed group loafing on a rock platform in Monterey Bay (above) and the soaring Laughing Gull (right). In more remote parts of North America, such as Alaska's Pribilof Islands, you will find more exotic species including the Parakeet Auklet (above right).*

AT THE SEASHORE *the spotting scope (left) really comes into its own. Its greater power is particularly useful when it comes to identifying small shorebirds such as Sanderlings (below) as they scuttle before the surf.*

pecies, making them difficult to single out for study. Identification often has to be made at long distance. Like gulls, there are many species. In breeding plumage they are generally very distinctive, but juveniles and birds in winter plumage are often similar. In a few cases the similarities are such that positive identification depends almost literally on a feather-by-feather analysis or a detailed examination of the extremely subtle variations in relative size and form. For the most part, however, you are half way there if you carefully note:

• leg color
• length and shape of bill
• pattern of upperwing (if any)
• whether it has a white rump

SEABIRDS

The third problematic group is the seabirds, especially the tubenoses. There are two difficulties with tubenoses. Firstly, these are pelagic birds that generally remain far offshore. Viewing opportunities from land are therefore limited, and few of us get out to sea often enough to become familiar with them. Secondly, many species have similar plumage, differing, rather, in nuances of flight style and body proportions, which are difficult to describe in words.

You really need on-the-spot, one-to-one help from an expert to master identification of these birds. Birding groups in many cities and towns along the coast regularly organize pelagic trips, chartering a boat to ferry birders far out to sea to look at tubenoses. In such a group, you are sure to find experts familiar with seabirds.

TIDES

Birds living on either land or sea can, like us, run their lives according to the cycle of day and night, but birds living at the interface between the two must pay attention to the tides. Many feed at low tide and sleep while the tide is high; others do the opposite. If you live on the coast or often go birding at the seashore, you'll be aware of the importance of tides.

Low tide is generally the best time for birding, being when birds come together to feed on exposed beaches and mud flats. But in places with an extensive inter-tidal zone you may choose to go birding when the tide is rising, as it will push birds in close enough for you to see them clearly. In some areas, shorebirds gather at high-tide roosts where you can watch them before the tide recedes

and they set off again to feed. Local knowledge will help you make the most of your trip.

SEASHORE GEAR

Tidal flats, estuaries, and similar localities are places where the spotting scope really comes into its own, giving you greater "reach" than most binoculars can deliver. Many coastal birds are wary and highly mobile, and it is often more difficult to follow a particular bird at the seashore than it is in, say, grasslands. You will be called upon to exercise your identification skills at greater distances than in almost any other habitat.

Magnifications somewhere between 20x and 40x are probably best for seashore conditions. If you go much above this you start to magnify atmospheric conditions rather than birds. A spotting scope is almost useless without a tripod, especially on seashores where it may be windy and wet. For more information on spotting scopes and tripods, see p. 64.

Common Loon

Gavia immer

In the north, Common Loons are often seen nesting on large freshwater lakes, where their loud, yodeling calls are a sign of summer. Some of these birds also spend the winter on inland waters, especially the Great Lakes. For most people, however, loons are birds of the coasts.

All loons in winter are dark above and white below, and it is important to note the shape of the head and bill. The Common Loon has a large, angular head and a stout, straightish bill. These features, along with a distinct whitish area around its eyes in winter, distinguish it from the smaller Pacific Loon (*Gavia pacifica*; 22–26" [56–66 cm]), which nests in the far northwest and is common along the Pacific coast in winter.

The Pacific Loon has a puffier, more rounded head, and a slighter bill than the Common.

In summer the adult Pacific has a pale gray head and hindneck, and a blackish foreneck bordered by white stripes, while the Common Loon has a black head and neck with two striped white cross-bands.

Pacific Loons tend to fly low over the ocean and, unlike Commons, often occur in fair-sized flocks. Common Loons can also be distinguished in flight by their large feet that stick out behind them like paddles.

Common (winter)

J F M A M J J A S O N D

Common (breeding)

Pacific (breeding)

FIELD NOTES
- 26–33" (66–84 cm)
- Pointed bill
- Large, angular head
- Rides low in water
- Darker than most other loons
- ▲ Difficult to distinguish from several other loon species in winter
- Bowl of grass and twigs, on land or anchored to vegetation
- 1–3; olive-brown with fine dark flecks

234

Sooty Shearwater

Puffinus griseus

In August and September, you may look offshore from a beach in California, Oregon, or Washington and see large flocks of long-winged, all-dark birds gliding and skimming the surface of the sea— "shearing" the waves. You may also see them milling around, or sitting in "rafts" on the water, looking from a distance like a dark slick. These are Sooty Shearwaters, among the most abundant birds in the world.

Sooties nest on islands in the southern oceans and after breeding (in US winter) migrate north to the North Pacific and North Atlantic oceans. They are common off both coasts, more so off the west, and are most numerous in summer,

| J | F | M | A | M | J | J | A | S | O | N | D |

although small numbers of non-breeding immatures remain in North American waters year-round.

If you take a boat trip offshore in the Pacific, the Sooty Shearwater will be among the seabirds you are most likely to encounter, and it serves as a useful comparison with other species. If you get a good view of a Sooty, you'll note that when it banks up and shows its underside there is a silvery flash under the wings. Like other shearwaters and petrels, the Sooty has a "tubenose"—the nostrils are encased in tubes on top of the bill—through which salt from the sea water that the bird drinks is exuded.

tubenose bill

raft of sooties

FIELD NOTES

■ 17–18" (43–45.5 cm)

■ Conspicuous white underwings

▲ Several similar all-dark shearwater species off west coast

🪹 Burrow in ground

🥚 1; white

235

Brown Pelican

Pelecanus occidentalis

In the 1960s and 1970s, the Brown Pelican had become a rare sight along the US coasts. This drastic decline resulted from the use of pesticides such as DDT which caused eggshell thinning and reproductive failure. With the banning of DDT in North America, Brown Pelican populations have recovered and today this impressive bird is again common along southern coasts. If you look off the beaches you can often see pelicans flying low in lines, gliding just above the waves, and if you live near a fishing harbor you will almost certainly be familiar with tame pelicans sitting around on the wharves.

Brown Pelicans feed by plunge-diving from flight, either at a shallow angle, as they skim the water, or more steeply from high overhead. In fact, the adult Brown Pelican is overall silvery gray with a whitish head and neck. Prior to nesting, the hindneck of adults becomes dark reddish on Atlantic coast birds, or a darker reddish brown on Pacific coast birds. Immatures are brownish overall and take three years to attain adult plumage.

J F M A M J J A S O N D

winter

FIELD NOTES

- 44–54" (112–137 cm)
- Very large
- Huge pouched bill
- Plumage silvery gray
- Platform of sticks and grass in tree or on cliff
- 2–3; chalky white

summer

Double-crested Cormorant

Phalacrocorax auritus

The Double-crested Cormorant is the most widespread cormorant in North America, being found at inland lakes across the continent as well as *Double-crested* along both coasts. It is most common at estuaries and lakes adjacent to the coast and rarely ventures far offshore.

At a distance, you can tell cormorants from loons by the way cormorants hold their hooked bills tilted up a *Brandt's* little, and by the way they jump as they dive. Also, cormorants don't hold their necks drooped like loons when flying.

For most of the year, adults, like other cormorants, are blackish overall. Before nesting, the adults attain tufted white crests on either side of the head (hence the name). Immatures are dark brown with a pale foreneck and chest. The extensive bright yellow-orange throat pouch is a field mark in all plumages.

Along the Pacific coast, you'll also find the similar Brandt's Cormorant (*Phalacrocorax penicillatus*; 29–33" [73–84 cm]), strictly a bird

of salt water. The adult Brandt's has a blue-gray throat pouch bordered by a band of buffy feathers. To distinguish between these birds in flight, note that the Double-crested holds its head raised, giving it a kink-necked look, while the Brandt's holds its head and neck out in a straight line.

| J | F | M | A | M | J | J | A | S | O | N | D |

Brandt's

Double-crested

FIELD NOTES

■ 28–32" (71–81 cm)
■ Orange throat pouch (all year)
■ Carries neck kinked in flight
■ Breeding adult: Two wispy crests on crown (whitish in west, black in east)
🪹 Platform of sticks and seaweed on cliff or in tree
🥚 2–7; chalky pale blue

237

White Ibis

Eudocimus albus

Whate Ibises are gregarious wading birds that inhabit coastal saltmarshes, mangrove swamps, and adjacent freshwater lagoons in the southeastern US. Unlike herons, they fly with rapid, shallow wingbeats interspersed with glides, and they hold their neck outstretched. They may be seen flying in lines or V-shaped formations, especially early and late in the day when commuting to and from roosting sites. The downward-curving bill and probing feeding action distinguish the White Ibis from egrets.

In the breeding season, adult White Ibises develop a bright red wattle under their bill. The immature looks mostly brown, but in flight its white rump and uppertail coverts are conspicuous. Note the black wingtips of the adult as it flies.

Another spectacular wading bird found in similar habitats along the Gulf coast of the southern US is the unmistakable Roseate Spoonbill (*Ajaia ajaja*; 28–31" [71–79 cm]). The immature spoonbill is overall whitish with only a faint pinkish tinge, and attains the bright plumage and naked head of the adult over three years.

J F M A M J J A S O N D

White Ibis

adult

immature

Roseate Spoonbill

FIELD NOTES
- 21–25" (53–63.5 cm)
- Almost entirely white
- Dull pink to scarlet (depending on season) legs and curved bill
- Immatures: Brown above, white below; curved, dull pink bill
- Platform of sticks in tree
- 3–4; greenish white, spotted with browns

Surf Scoter

Melanitta nigra

Surf Scoters are a common sight off beaches along both Atlantic and Pacific coasts of North America, mainly in winter. As the name suggests, they can often be seen feeding in the surf of breaking waves, or sleeping in rafts just beyond the surf zone. Small numbers also occur in estuaries, harbors, and lagoons along the coast. In summer, Surf Scoters nest on the tundra of the far north, although some non-breeding immatures remain on the coasts throughout the year.

The distinctive male is one of the most handsome ducks. The all-brown female and immature may be confused with the closely related but generally less abundant White-winged Scoter (*Melanitta fusca*; 20–23" [51–58.5 cm]).

Note, however, that the whitish mark forward of the eye on the Surf Scoter is shaped like a vertical rectangle, while on the female White-winged it is a rounder spot. Also, the female Surf Scoter has a steeper forehead and flatter crown than the White-winged. In flight, or when scoters sit up and flap their wings, the bold white wingpatch on the White-winged is a good field mark.

White-winged ♂

Surf ♀

White-Winged ♀

J F M A M J J A S O N D

FIELD NOTES
- 18–20" (45.5–51 cm)
- Breeding male: Black; colorful bill; white forehead and nape
- Breeding females, immatures, winter males: Brown; two white spots on head
- ▲ White-winged Scoter has white patch on wing (revealed in flight)
- Depression in ground, built up with weeds
- 5–8; buff

raft of Surf Scoters

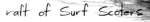

239

Black-bellied Plover

Pluvialis squatarola

This, the largest North American plover, is common on beaches and mud flats along coasts from August to May, with fewer birds present in June and July. During migration, some birds occur inland at lakes and on ploughed fields.

winter

Golden

The Black-bellied Plover is often located by its plaintive *clee-oo-ee* call. As well as the black belly, breeding adults attain a black face and throat bordered by a bold white stripe. Winter birds and juveniles are overall grayish above and whitish below.

breeding

American Golden

Black-bellied

In flight, note the white rump, bold white wingbar, and black axillars or "armpits" that distinguish the Black-bellied from the American Golden-Plover (*Pluvialis dominica*; 9½–10" [24–25.5 cm]). Goldens nest in the far north and spend the winter in South America. They occur as migrants in fields and at lakes through the center of North America in spring, and along the Atlantic coast in fall. Their upperparts in flight appear uniform, and their underwings are plain gray.

| J | F | M | A | M | J | J | A | S | O | N | D |

winte

Black-bellied

breeding

FIELD NOTES

- 10½–11½" (26.5–29 cm)
  - White rump
  - Bold white wingbar
  - Black "armpits"
- Breeding plumage: Bold black underparts
- Scrape in ground, lined with grass
- 3–4; buffy brown with dark markings

240

Willet

Catoptrophorus semipalmatus

For much of the year, this large sandpiper is dull grayish overall and when standing it resembles many other shorebirds. However, when it takes to the air the Willet is immediately distinguished by its flashy black-and-white wing pattern. Its loud shrieking *will-will-et* call will identify it in the breeding season.

| J | F | M | A | M | J | J | A | S | O | N | D |

Willets are common on beaches and at estuaries and lagoons along both coasts from July to May. They also nest along much of the Atlantic and Gulf coasts, as well as at lakes and marshes in the interior west. After nesting, females leave their chicks in the care of the male bird and set off on their migration, so the first southbound migrants you see are likely to be females. Breeding birds are more variegated than birds in plain winter plumage, having dark and white streaking and barring on the face, neck, and chest, and dark markings on the back. As with other shorebirds, juveniles can be distinguished from adults in fall by their neat, fresh plumage (as opposed to the worn, faded, breeding plumage of the adults), which is brownish above with fine pale flecks.

FIELD NOTES

- 12½–14" (31.5–35.5 cm)
- Noisy, conspicuous
- Unmistakable in flight—bold black and white patches clearly visible
- Summer: Mottled above and below
- Winter: Smooth grayish above, whitish below
- Scrape in ground, lined with grass
- 4–5; olive marked with browns

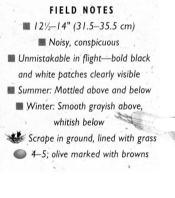

winter

breeding

241

Whimbrel

Numenius phaeopus

A rapid, piping, whistled *kee hee-hee-hee-hee-hee* call often draws attention to a flock of these birds flying overhead. Whimbrels are fairly common from July to May along beaches and at estuaries and lagoons along both coasts; smaller numbers occur in June, and some migrate through the interior in spring. They nest in the arctic tundra.

All plumages of the Whimbrel look similar. Overall it is medium-sized and grayish brown, like other curlews, but it is identified by its dark head stripes; fairly short, downward-curving bill; and an absence of cinnamon coloring in its plumage.

J F M A M J J A S O N D

The larger and longer-billed Long-billed Curlew (*Numenius americanus*; 18–23" [45.5–58.5 cm]) lacks bold, dark head stripes and shows bright cinnamon under its wings. It nests in marshes and grasslands in the interior west and winters mainly on beaches, at lagoons, and in grasslands along both coasts of the southern US and through Mexico. If you compare it with the similar-looking Marbled Godwit (p. 243), you will see that the bills are different. Juvenile Long-billed Curlews are often much shorter-billed than adults and can be mistaken for Whimbrels.

Long-billed

Whimbrel

Long-billed Curlew at nest

FIELD NOTES
- ■ *14–17" (35.5–43 cm)*
- ■ *Moderately long, curved bill*
- ■ *Grayish plumage*
- ▲ *Long-billed Curlew is much bigger, has plain head, and long, curved bill*
- 🪹 *Scrape in ground*
- 🥚 *3–5; olive marked with browns*

Marbled Godwit

Limosa fedoa

Marbled Godwits are common from July to May along the west coast on beaches and at estuaries and coastal lagoons. They are less common on the east and Gulf coasts. Small numbers of non-breeding immatures also spend the summer along the coasts while the adults are nesting in wet meadows in the northern prairies. Flocks of migrants flying overhead can often be picked out when you learn their nasal, slightly laughing *ah-ahk* calls— quite unlike the calls of curlews.

Like the Whimbrel and Long-billed Curlew, the different aged and seasonal plumages of the Marbled Godwit are quite similar, although if you look closely you'll note that the underparts of breeding birds have dark bars, while those of juveniles and winter birds are plain. The Marbled Godwit's plumage looks like that of the Long-billed Curlew, including the cinnamon wingpatches revealed in flight, and sleeping birds of these two species can be almost impossible to tell apart. However, once you see the bill shape, identification is no longer a problem.

J F M A M J J A S O N D

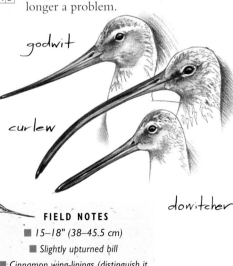

godwit

curlew

dowitcher

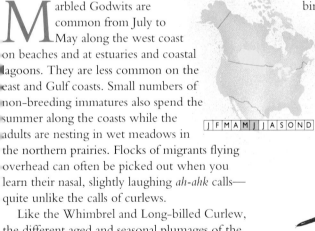

flock of Marbled Godwits

FIELD NOTES

- 15–18" (38–45.5 cm)
- Slightly upturned bill
- Cinnamon wing-linings (distinguish it from other North American godwits)
- Scrape in grass
- 3–5; olive marked with browns

243

Ruddy Turnstone

Arenaria interpres

As the name indicates, turnstones use their short, slightly wedge-shaped bills to turn over stones, seaweed, and other beach debris to look for prey. The chunky, medium-sized Ruddy is a distinctive shorebird, seen frequently on sandy beaches, rocky coasts, and jetties throughout the year, most commonly from August to May. It tends to avoid muddy shores and estuaries. In summer, it nests on the arctic tundra.

The breeding adult is strikingly marked, while juveniles and winter birds are duller: note their plump shape, short bill, reddish legs, and dark circular patches at the sides of the chest.

| J | F | M | A | M | J | J | A | S | O | N | D |

On the west coast you'll also find the Black Turnstone (*Arenaria melanocephala*; 8½–9" [21.5–23 cm]), which favors rocky coasts and headlands. The Black is darker overall than the Ruddy, and has a solidly dark chest and duller, grayish to pale pinkish legs. In flight, both turnstones display a bold, angular pattern of white patches on their upperparts, and both have distinctive dry, chattering or rattling calls.

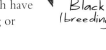

Ruddy
(breeding)

Black
(breeding)

Black
Turnstone

Ruddy Turnstone
(winter)

FIELD NOTES

■ 8½–9" (21.5–23 cm)

■ Distinctive tortoise-shell pattern of black, white, and orange-red

■ Blackish bib

■ Reddish legs

▲ Black Turnstone has largely dark head and chest

 Scrape in tundra

● 3–4; olive marked with dark browns

244

Sanderling

Calidris alba

A group of Sanderlings feeding at the tideline is a common sight on sandy beaches. Watch for them running after the receding waves to pick at food washed up, then racing back up the beach ahead of the advancing waves. Like many arctic-nesting shorebirds, Sanderlings are most common on the coast from August to May, with smaller numbers, mainly non-breeding immatures, present during June and July.

Among small sandpipers, winter Sanderlings are characteristically pallid. Breeding birds and juvenile Sanderlings look quite different from winter birds. In breeding plumage (seen on migrants in May) the face, chest, and upperparts are overall bright reddish, while juveniles have a white face and underparts; a dark cap; and dark, spangled upperparts.

J F M A M J J A S O N D

The Sanderling is an exception among sandpipers in that it is the only one that lacks a hind toe.

The Dunlin (*Calidris alpina*; 7¾–8½" [19.5–21.5 cm]) is a common, equally widespread sandpiper, similar in size to the Sanderling but with a longer, slightly downward-curving bill. Its winter plumage is brownish gray above (and on the chest), darker than the Sanderling, and spring adults have a black belly patch. Dunlins favor mud flats and estuaries and often occur in large flocks.

nderling chicks

juvenile Sanderling

breeding

FIELD NOTES

■ 7–7½" (18–19 cm)

■ Pale gray with bold white wingbar

■ Black bill and legs

■ Trots up and down beach, staying just out of reach of waves

▲ Other small sandpipers usually darker with less distinct wingbars

❀ Scrape in ground, lined with moss

● 3–4; olive marked with browns

Dunlin (winter)

245

Western Sandpiper

Calidris mauri

Least (winter)

Small sandpipers, of which there are five common species in North America, are known as "peeps". Two of these winter in North America—the Western Sandpiper and the Least Sandpiper.

The Western is common in winter on both coasts at estuaries, lagoons, and on mudflats. In some areas, huge flocks occur, wheeling in flight over the water like rippling silvery sheets, or covering the mudflats with a carpet of intense, twittering activity.

The Western is identified by its long, slightly downward-curving bill and its black legs. Winter Westerns are grayish above, and white below. Juveniles, common in August and September, have reddish and pale gray upperparts.

| J | F | M | A | M | J | J | A | S | O | N | D |

Breeding adults have a reddish cap and cheeks, and dark spots down their sides.

The other peep common in winter is the Least Sandpiper (*Calidris minutilla*; 5¼–5¾" [13–14.5 cm]). Although Leasts prefer drier and marshier areas than Westerns and are more commonly seen inland, the two species often occur together. Note the Least's browner plumage and yellowish legs.

FIELD NOTES

■ 6–6½" (15–16.5 cm)

■ Tapered bill with faint droop at tip

■ Often has orange-red tinge along shoulders

▲ Difficult to distinguish from other small sandpipers

🪹 Scrape in ground, lined with grass

🥚 4; buff marked with browns

Laughing Gull

Larus atricilla

The Laughing Gull is common along the Atlantic and Gulf coasts, where it occurs on beaches, at estuaries, and in fields. For a gull, it is at the small end of medium-sized, and is termed a "three-year gull"—it molts into its adult plumage in three years (see p. 232). Characteristic features of the adult are its size, dark gray back, and the dark bill that droops slightly at the tip. Breeding birds attain a blackish hood, while winter birds have a whitish head with a dusky smudge behind the eye. Juveniles are brownish above and have a brownish chest band. They attain a gray back in their first winter, and by their second winter they are similar to adults.

| J | F | M | A | M | J | J | A | S | O | N | D |

The closely related Franklin's Gull (*Larus pipixcan*; 14–15" [35.5– 38 cm]) migrates up the center of North America, from its winter grounds in the southern hemisphere, to nest on the northern prairies. The adult has bold white markings on its wingtips in contrast to the solid black wingtips of the Laughing Gull.

Franklin's (breeding)

Laughing (winter)

Franklin's (winter)

1st winter Laughing

FIELD NOTES

- ■ 15–17" (38–43 cm)
- ■ Slate gray with black-tipped wings
- ■ Comparatively long slender bill, red in breeding adult
- ■ Winter adult: White head with light gray wash across nape
- ▲ Two successive immature plumages
- Scrape in ground, built up with seaweed
- 3–4; olive marked with browns

Herring Gull

Larus argentatus

The Herring Gull is a large, four-year gull (see p. 232) common on the coast, especially the Atlantic coast, as well as at lakes and reservoirs across much of North America. You'll see it feeding at fishing harbors and on beaches, as well as at garbage dumps and in ploughed fields away from the coast. In the afternoons, watch for birds flying inland to bathe in fresh water. Later in the day a steady procession of birds flying toward their communal roosts is a common sight.

spot

J F M A M J J A S O N D

The adult Herring Gull is distinguished by its large size, pale gray back, black wingtips, and pink legs; note also that its bill has a red spot near the tip. Like other large white-headed gulls, winter adults have extensive dusky mottling on their head and chest. First-year birds are mottled brownish and have a blackish bill. They attain a pale gray back in their second year. In their third year they look similar to adults but usually have some black near the bill tip, less white on the wingtips, and some black still in the tail.

FIELD NOTES

- 22–27" (56–69 cm)
- Pinkish legs
- Yellow bill with red spot on lower mandible
- Black wingtips with white spots
- ▲ Intricate series of three immature plumages
- Scrape in ground built up with weeds
- 2–3; pale bluish to brownish, with dark markings

2nd winter

1st winter

Ring-billed Gull

Larus delawarensis

Found throughout much of North America—on beaches, estuaries, inland lakes, reservoirs, and even supermarket parking lots—the Ring-billed Gull is a medium-sized, three-year gull (see p. 232). This bird is often quite tame and will beg and scavenge at picnic tables and on beaches.

J F M A M J J A S O N D

FIELD NOTES

■ 17–20" (43–51 cm)

■ Yellow bill with narrow black band

■ Greenish yellow legs

▲ Two successive immature plumages

🪶 Scrape in ground, built up with grass

🥚 2–4; buff marked with browns

The adult is distinctive, with its pale, silvery gray back, yellow bill with a black ring, and greenish yellow legs. Like virtually all juvenile gulls, the young Ring-billed is overall mottled brownish. In its first winter it attains a gray back, and the legs and black-tipped bill are pale pinkish. By its second winter the immature looks similar to the adult but lacks the bold white spots in the wingtips and usually shows some black in the tail. Non-breeding immatures remain on coasts away from the nesting range.

Close up, the immatures look like immature Herring Gulls (p. 248), but note the Ring-billed's smaller and lighter-looking bill, and smaller overall size.

adult

immature (1st winter)

249

Western Gull

Larus occidentalis

Found along much of the Pacific coast throughout the year, the Western Gull is a large, four-year gull (see p. 232). The adult has pink legs and a dark gray back (always obviously darker than that of the Herring Gull). The plumage stages from juvenile to adult parallel those of the Herring Gull (p. 248).

In the Pacific northwest, the Western is replaced by the closely related Glaucous-winged Gull (*Larus glaucescens*; 22–28" [56–71 cm]), which in winter occurs south along the Pacific coast to California. The adult Glaucous-winged has pink legs, a pale gray back, and gray, not black, wingtips; the immature always has paler wingtips than the Western.

In some areas, especially along the coast of northern Washington state, Western and Glaucous-winged gulls hybridize extensively at mixed colonies. Not surprisingly, some ornithologists consider these two large gulls to be a single species.

J F M A M J J A S O N D

Glaucous-winged
adult

Glaucous-winged
(1st winter)

Western
(1st winter)

FIELD NOTES

- 21–26" (53.5–66 cm)
- Slate gray mantle and upperwings
- Pink legs
- ▲ Three successive immature plumages
- ▲ Hybridizes with Glaucous-winged Gull
- Shallow scrape built up with weeds and grass
- 1–5; buff to pale gray, with dark markings

Great Black-backed Gull

Larus marinus

The largest gull in the world, the Great Black-backed Gull is a voracious feeder and readily eats fairly large young ducks and other birds, which it can swallow whole in a few gulps. The Great Black-back inhabits the harbors, beaches, and rocky coasts of the northeast. It is expanding its breeding range south, and in winter it is occasionally seen on the Gulf coast. Some birds can be found year-round on the Great Lakes.

This is a four-year gull (see p. 232), readily identified by its large size and massive bill. Among the common, large eastern gulls, the adult's black back is distinctive. The first-year bird looks like other immature large gulls, but note that compared with a young Herring Gull (p. 248) its upperparts are more neatly checkered, its tail has a black band of wavy lines rather than a solid dark band, and its head often looks whiter. The second-year bird has dark gray feathers on its back.

| J | F | M | A | M | J | J | A | S | O | N | D |

with prey

FIELD NOTES

- 25–31" (63.5–79 cm)
- Very large (bigger than most raptors)
- Large, stout yellow bill with red spot on lower mandible
- ▲ Three successive immature plumages
- Scrape in ground, built up with seaweed
- 1–4; olive marked with browns

1st year

2nd year

3rd year

251

Caspian Tern

Sterna caspia

A deep, throaty, slightly scratchy *rrah* call often draws attention to an adult Caspian Tern flying overhead. This is the largest tern, about the size of a medium-sized gull, and is readily identified by its stout, carrot-red bill, black cap, and the large dark patch under each wingtip, visible when the bird is in flight.

Caspian Terns are locally common in summer at beaches and coastal lagoons, as well as at lakes and along inland rivers. In late summer, you may see juveniles accompanying their parents on migration, following after them and begging with high-pitched whistles that are quite different from the adult's deep call.

The slightly smaller Royal Tern (*Sterna maxima*; 17–19" [43–48 cm]) is common on the southeast coast and also occurs on the coast of southern California. It has a stout, bright-orange bill and lacks the Caspian's big dark patch under the wingtips. For much of the year, Royal Terns have a large white forehead patch; on the Caspian this area is streaked dark gray and white.

J F M A M J J A S O N D

Royal Tern
(winter)

Caspian Tern
(winter)

FIELD NOTES
- 20–22" (51–56 cm)
- Large, gull-like
- Long, stout red bill
- Scrape in sand, often lined with grass
- 1–4; buff, marked with browns

Caspian
(summer

Royal
(summer)

252

Forster's Tern

Sterna forsteri

The Forster's Tern nests at interior lakes and marshes, as well as along the Atlantic and Gulf coasts. It is the only tern commonly seen in winter at lagoons and estuaries along both coasts—most species migrate south to Mexico or beyond. In winter and immature plumages, when the bill is black, the bold, black mask is a field mark. Breeding birds have an orangey red bill with an extensive black tip. In most plumages, the pale silvery upper surface of the wings is a good field mark.

The similar Common Tern (*Sterna hirundo*; 11½–13½" [29–34 cm]) nests along the northeast coast as well as at lakes in the northern interior and is a common migrant along both coasts. Breeding Commons have a red bill with a small black tip, and lack the silvery upperwings of the Forster's. Immatures and winter adults have dark bills. Unlike the Forster's, their dark mask extends around the back of the head in a partial cap, and, when at rest, they show a dark bar along the shoulder.

J F M A M J J A S O N D

Common
(summer)

Forster's
(summer)

FIELD NOTES

- ■ 12½–17" (31.5–43 cm)
- ■ Summer: Black cap; orange-red bill and legs; pale upperwings, lacking noticeable markings
- ▲ In winter difficult to distinguish from Arctic and Common Terns, but normally only Forster's present in winter in US
- On floating raft of reeds, or scrape in ground
- 2–5; buff marked with browns

Forster's Tern
(winter)

253

Common Murre

Uria aalge

Alcids are heavy-bodied, small-winged pelagic birds, 20 species of which occur in North America, most of them in the Pacific Ocean. The Common Murre is the most widespread member of this family. Murres nest in large colonies on rocky headlands and offshore islands and spend the winter at sea. Away from colonies, they are most often seen flying fast and low over the sea, or swimming singly or in loose groups in inshore waters, where they dive for fish.

Overall, Common Murres are similar to small loons but are stockier and shorter-necked. The summer adult has a dark head and neck while the immature and winter adult have a white face and neck with a dark stripe below the eye. The males accompany the young after they fledge, and adult-juvenile "pairs" are a common sight in late summer.

J F M A M J J A S O N D

The other auk most commonly seen off the west coast is the Pigeon Guillemot (*Cepphus columba*; 13–14" [33–35.5 cm]) which stays close to land throughout the year. Summer birds are all-black with a white wing patch; winter birds and juveniles are peppered black and white, with a less conspicuous white wingpatch.

juvenile

adult

FIELD NOTES
- 16–17" (40.5–43 cm)
- Brownish black above, white below
- ▲ Thick-billed Murre (far north) larger and blacker with stouter bill; white underparts rise to sharp point on throat (straight across in Common Murre)
- ▲ Winter birds difficult to distinguish
- Bare cliff ledge
- 1; white to brown, marked with dark browns

Pigeon Guillemot (summer)

Deserts

DESERTS
Scrublands, Chaparral, Mesas, Sagebrush Plains

Strictly speaking, deserts are areas where less than 10 inches (25 centimeters) of rain falls during a year. Though the scarcity of water in deserts usually results in vegetation that is low and sparse, vegetation is lacking altogether only in extremely arid environments.

Rainfall in deserts may be extremely erratic, or fall mainly in winter (sometimes as snow) or largely in summer. In some deserts, water is available most often in the form of spring snowmelt from nearby mountains. Clearly, vegetation varies according to the amount and frequency of rainfall and provides in turn a wide range of bird habitats.

North American deserts are mainly restricted to the interior west and southwest, which are protected from the influence of rain-bearing weather systems by the massive chain of mountain ranges—the Rockies, the Sierra Nevada, and the Cascades—running up the western fringe of the continent. To the east, they merge more or less imperceptibly with the shortgrass plains.

You'll find the true cactus deserts in the southwest, from southeastern California across to southern Texas. Farther north, in the interior, deserts and desert-like conditions prevail east of the Sierra Nevada and the Cascades through the Great Basin all the way up to the interior of southern British Columbia. These regions lack the diverse, tall cacti of the southern deserts, and are often dominated by sagebrush.

Chaparral is a dense, semiarid, evergreen scrub which is almost entirely restricted to California.

SAGE FLATS are favored by several bird species, such as Sage Grouse, that are uncommon or rare in other habitats.

WATER HOLES Even tiny rock-shaded puddles can provide a focal point for a wide range of desert birds that will travel from far afield to find water.

OVERHEAD Vultures and some hawks spend much of the day soaring, especially where mesas and similar formations provide strong thermals.

MESAS AND CANYONS are good places to look for birds such as Rock Wrens, Say's Phoebes, and even Mountain Bluebirds.

SAGUAROS provide nesting sites and a source of food for a variety of bird species ranging from Gila Woodpeckers to Elf Owls and White-winged Doves.

BIRDING *in* DESERTS

The extremely harsh climate and localized vegetation of deserts support a specialized and distinctive community of bird species, many of which seldom occur in any other type of habitat.

Woodland and wetland birds move around the continent enough for you to have some hope of seeing many of them, at least as vagrants or casual visitors, in your local marsh or woodlot. To see certain bird species you have to go to the desert. Most birders who don't live in the southwest will therefore, sooner or later, want to travel to desert country to see this particular avifauna for themselves.

Deserts have been aptly described as very cold places where the sun is very hot. Chilly nights may be followed by noon-time temperatures approaching 100° Fahrenheit (38° Celsius). Being out and about early is important, particularly in spring and summer, as most desert birds suspend their activities through the heat of the day. By mid-morning, birds that have been active earlier seem to melt into their surround-ings, and can be difficult to locate.

As in woodlands and grass-lands, finding birds by song is therefore important. Because vegetation is sparse, territories can be large and many birds, such as thrashers, have songs that carry long distances. Limited vegetation usually means you can walk in a fairly direct line towards a singing bird, but always be aware of where the trail is and where you parked your car.

WHERE TO LOOK
Keep scanning the skies. A vulture or hawk soaring high in the air may be looking for lunch—but the bird will also be a good deal cooler up there than it is on the ground.

Keep an eye open for water, a scarce commodity in deserts. An intermittent stream or a small pool with shade trees can be a really active spot for birds throughout the heat of the day, and from the birder's point of view it sure beats walking around under the blazing sun and not seeing anything.

DESERT GEAR
A wide-brimmed hat or baseball cap not only protects you from the sun, but by shading your face it makes spotting birds in the harsh glare just that little bit easier. An effective sunscreen is very important, and remember to protect the back of your neck. A water-bottle hooked to your belt or a couple of soft drinks slung into a knapsack is by no means a bad idea either.

SOUTHWESTERN DESERTS
combine spectacular scenery (above) and exotic birds such as the Roadrunner (right) in a memorable experience for visiting birders.

Desert birds have a way of leading you on, and you may well find yourself much farther away from your car than you intended to be!

If you happen to live in, or do most of your birding in, a desert area, this may influence your choice of binoculars (p. 62). In the deep shade of woodland or forest, wide angles and big, bright images are important, both for locating the bird in the field of view and enjoying the image when you have it. But wide angles and large images come at the cost of sizeable chunks of glass inside the binoculars, and glass is very heavy. As light is seldom a problem in desert regions during the day, you may find that binoculars with a narrower field of view and less magnification will deliver the kind of image you are comfortable with, and they will be easier to carry around.

DESERT BIRDS *include the Cactus Wren (right), and the Gambel's Quail (below left). Many desert species use saguaros (below) as sources of food and nesting sites.*

HOT SPOTS *When birding in deserts (above), make sure you protect yourself from the frequently fierce sun by wearing a hat and applying an effective sunscreen.*

California Quail

Callipepla californica

The crowing *ka KA-kwah* or *chi CA-go* of the California Quail is a familiar sound throughout much of that state. These attractive, plump birds are common in chaparral; scrub and open woodland; desert edges; and in suburban areas, where they will come to seed put out in gardens. In the absence of introduced predators, such as feral cats, they can become quite tame. In wilder areas you may see them as they flush up in a twittering whir of wings from close-by in the brush.

Through much of the year, California Quail occur in groups, or coveys, of 10 to 20 or more birds. In spring, these break up into pairs and the males give their crowing song from fence posts and atop bushes.

The closely related Gambel's Quail (*Callipepla gambelii*; 9½–10½" [24–26.5 cm]) is found only in deserts of the interior southwest, from southeastern California to western Texas. It looks and sounds like the California Quail but is a little paler and grayer and has chestnut sides and a creamy belly. The two species seldom occur together.

JFMAMJJASOND

Gambel's

Gambel's

FIELD NOTES
- 9–10" (23–25.5 cm)
- Black forward-tilted head plume
- Brown flanks, streaked white
- Prominent black scales on belly
- ▲ Gambel's Quail (southwest) has chestnut flanks
- Scrape in ground, lined with leaves and grass
- 6–17; cream, spotted with browns

White-winged Dove

Zenaida asiatica

Common in summer in the southern deserts, especially alongside streams, White-winged Doves are often found nesting in large colonies. Around these colonies the White-winged's display flight can be a common sight: the bird climbs up with clapping wingbeats, then glides back down again.

On hot summer days this dove's slightly burry cooing *who koo-koo-koo* or *Who cooks-for you?* call can be heard almost continually, even when many birds are silent. A longer, more complex series of moaning coos that slows toward the end of the song may also be heard. In winter, most White-winged Doves migrate south to warmer latitudes in Mexico.

Like Mourning Doves in open habitats, White-winged Doves may fly long distances each day to drink from the nearest creek or pool. In flight, the bold white band on their wings is a striking field mark. Their tail is shorter and broader than the Mourning Dove's tail and has bold white corners, easily seen as the bird lands or takes off.

J F M A M J J A S O N D

nest

White-winged Dove

Mourning Dove

FIELD NOTES

■ 10½–12" (26.5–30.5 cm)

■ Large white wing patches

🪺 Platform of twigs in bush or tree

🥚 1–4; creamy white

Greater Roadrunner

Geococcyx californianus

This large, ground-dwelling cuckoo is so unmistakable that it has even found its way into the world of cartoons. Many people who know the cartoon character are surprised to learn that such a bird really exists! Although typical of the southwestern deserts, Roadrunners also occur in open woodland, chaparral, and farmland where they run after snakes, lizards, and rodents, which they dispatch with their stout, pointed bills.

J F M A M J J A S O N D

sunbathing

FIELD NOTES
- 20–24" (51–61 cm)
- Unmistakable
- Platform of sticks in low tree or cactus
- 2–6; chalky white

Most people encounter a Roadrunner by chance as it runs along or across a road. If you set out to track down a Roadrunner, you may find it quite a challenge. Listen for their low, moaning, slightly dove-like "song" of five to eight coos that descends from high to low pitch, or scan the tops of bushes, fence posts, or rocks early in the day when Roadrunners perch up high to sunbathe.

The male and female look alike, and the young can be told by the gray, rather than blue and red, naked facial skin. If you see a Roadrunner fly, note the bold band of white across the wing and the long tail with bold white spots at the feather tips.

Roadrunner and rattler

Anna's Hummingbird

Calypte anna

The wiry, high-pitched, often prolonged warble of the Anna's Hummingbird is a common sound in chaparral and other scrub, and in suburban parks and gardens. This song makes the Anna's an exception among North American hummingbirds, as no other North American hummer sings. In the tropics, however, most hummers sing, so it is really the North American species, which use display flights instead of song to attract mates, that are in the minority. The Anna's also uses a display flight, during which the male makes steep dives from high in the air. The male is identified by his iridescent reddish gorget (throat patch) and forecrown.

With the planting of flowering trees beside roads and houses in the desert, the breeding range of the Anna's has recently expanded into southern Arizona.

In the deserts of southern California and Arizona you'll also find the closely related Costa's Hummingbird (*Calypte costae*; 3–3½" [7.5–9 cm]). The male has an elongated purple gorget (throat patch) and forecrown and can often be found by tracking down the very high-pitched, thin, whining whistle that he gives while making high oval loops in his display flight. Females of both Anna's and Costa's look like females of other small hummingbirds and even experts have difficulty telling them all apart.

Anna's ♀

osta's ♂

FIELD NOTES
- 3½–4" (9–10 cm)
- Male: Rose-red head and throat
- ▲ Female very difficult to distinguish from Black-chinned and Costa's, but is larger, usually has darker, grayer breast, and streaks of rose-red on throat
- Cup of lichens, spiders' silk, plant down
- 2; white

J F M A M J J A S O N D

263

Scrub Jay

Aphelocoma coreulescens

S crub Jays are common in chaparral and suburban areas of California, and in arid scrublands of the interior west. Usually you'll find them singly or in pairs, often perching conspicuously on roadside wires or atop bushes. From their perches they keep an eye out for lizards and insects which they then fly down to seize. They're also notorious nest raiders, pouncing on the eggs or nestlings of many songbirds.

An isolated population of Scrub Jays, sometimes considered a separate species, exists in central

J F M A M J J A S O N D

Florida. These Florida Scrub Jays are renowned for being cooperative breeders, a group of birds, usually related, helping to raise the brood of the one nesting pair in the group.

Male and female Scrub Jays look alike. The juvenile has duskier, less blue, upperparts which bear only a trace of the adult's dark mask.

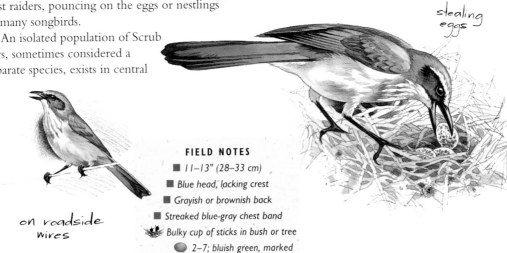

stealing eggs

on roadside wires

FIELD NOTES
■ 11–13" (28–33 cm)
■ Blue head, lacking crest
■ Grayish or brownish back
■ Streaked blue-gray chest band
■ Bulky cup of sticks in bush or tree
● 2–7; bluish green, marked with browns and greens

Bushtit

Psaltriparus minimus

A tiny, active, fluffy ball of feathers with a long tail, the Bushtit is common in chaparral, open woodland, and suburban parks and gardens. It is usually detected by following up an excited-sounding, high-pitched twittering. As often as not, you'll then find not one Bushtit but a flock of 10 to 25 or more birds that feed in an acrobatic, chickadee-like manner, swinging from foliage to pick under leaves and in spider's webs. Flocks tend to feed in a tree or bush for a while and then move on, flying across a trail or other open area, allowing the observer to count just how many birds are creating all that twittering fuss.

Males have dark eyes and females have pale eyes. Coastal Bushtits have a brownish cap while interior birds have a grayish cap. Some male birds in West Texas and southern Arizona have black cheeks.

The Verdin (*Auriparus flaviceps*; 4–4¼" [10–11 cm]) is a superficially similar bird of the southern deserts. Usually it occurs singly or in pairs, and it is identified by its yellow head. The young Verdin, however, is overall pale grayish and is told from the longer-tailed Bushtit by its sharply pointed (not small and stubby) bill.

nest

J F M A M J J A S O N D

FIELD NOTES

■ 4¼–4½" (11–11.5 cm)

■ Tiny, plain, strongly gregarious

■ Grayish above, paler below

■ Brown cap (coastal birds) or gray cap (interior birds)

🕸 Gourd-shaped hanging pouch with entrance hole near top

🥚 5–13; white

Verdin

Bushtit ♀

Black-cheeked form ♂

265

Cactus Wren

Campylorhynchus brunneicapillus

In the southern deserts, throughout the year and at any time of day, a loud, gruff, prolonged chattering *grru grru grru…* or *cha-cha-cha…* can be heard. This is the sound of the Cactus Wren, the largest North American wren and an exception in a family of small, somewhat skulking birds typified by the House Wren (page 109).

J F M A M J J A S O N D

Cactus Wrens tend to be conspicuous and are found in pairs or small groups, foraging in cacti and small bushes. Sometimes they feed on the ground, where they dig like thrashers in the sand with their bills. They sing from a prominent perch atop a bush or post and build conspicuous, bulky, domed nests of sticks, typically in a cactus. Each Cactus Wren builds several such nests—one for the eggs and the others for sleeping in. These birds also occur in brush alongside rivers and streams, and in residential areas where they may nest in man-made structures.

The juvenile Cactus Wren lacks the adult's bold patch of black blotches on the chest, and its underparts are buffy white with evenly spaced fine dusky spots.

Cactus Wren nest

FIELD NOTES
- 7–7½" (18–19 cm)
- *Strongly barred wings and tail*
- *Conspicuous white eyebrow*
- *Bulky dome of sticks in cactus or bush*
- *3–7; cream speckled with browns*

juvenile

266

Rock Wren

Salpinctes obsoletus

Rock Wrens, as the name suggests, are found in rocky areas, from steep-walled canyons to broken, rocky and stony slopes, and even at times on sea cliffs. Your first encounter with one may be hearing its bright, springy *ch-reer* call or its song: a varied series of buzzes, trills, chips, and whistles, each usually repeated a few times, suggesting a quiet mockingbird song. This will lead to what is, at first sight a small, rather plain bird which typically bobs or hops over the rocks. A closer view will reveal subtly attractive plumage, with fine silvery flecks on the upperparts and fine dusky streaks on the underparts. The most distinctive feature is the Rock Wren's fairly long tail, with a blackish subterminal band and pale cinnamon tail corners.

Often in the same habitat, particularly on cliffs and in canyons, you'll come across the Canyon Wren (*Catherpes mexicanus*; 5–5½" [12.5–14 cm]) whose presence is also most often given away by its call— a springy, nasal *bzeeihr*—or by its song—a beautiful, descending series of whistles that cascades from canyon walls but can be hard to trace. The bright white bib and orange-red tail of this handsome bird are good field marks.

J F M A M J J A S O N D

cocked tail

Canyon Wren

FIELD NOTES

- 5¼–5¾" (13–14.5 cm)
- Grayish above
- Cinnamon rump and tail
- Very pale underparts
- Faintly streaked chest
- Cup of grass in burrow or rock crevice
- 4–10; white flecked with browns

267

Curve-billed Thrasher

Toxostoma curvirostre

The Curve-billed Thrasher is a common and relatively conspicuous thrasher found in deserts, brushy riverside washes, and residential areas of the southwest. It is often seen perched on cacti or posts by the roadside, or flying low between bushes or across the road. As it lands and fans its tail, note the pale tips to the tail corners.

Like many birds, Curve-billed Thrashers are often heard before they are seen: listen for a bright, emphatic *whit whuit!* or *whit whuit whuit* call, and a varied, rich to slightly scratchy warbling song that may be prolonged and often includes repetition of phrases. The song carries a long way and often you'll be able to spot the bird atop a cactus or other prominent perch from quite far off.

Good field marks of the Curve-billed Thrasher are the all-black bill which usually appears downward-curving; the bright orange eyes; and the diffuse dusky motttling, or spotting, on the chest. Young birds look similar to adults but their eyes are duller and their bill can be notably shorter and barely curved.

J F M A M J J A S O N D

adult

juvenile

FIELD NOTES
- 10–11" (25.5–28 cm)
- Mottled chest
- Moderately long, all-dark, strongly curved bill
- Bulky cup of twigs and grass in cactus or bush
- 2–4; pale bluish green, spotted with browns

Phainopepla

Phainopepla nitens

This attractive crested bird, whose name means "shining robe", is a member of a small family of birds found from the US southwest (one species) to Central America (three species). Members of this family all have "silky" plumage (hence the common name of the family), and are closely related to the waxwings (p. 112).

J F M A M J J A S O N D

Phainopeplas are most often seen perched prominently atop bushes and trees, or flying over open areas with a weak, jerky flight, which reveals the male's striking white wingpatches. Overall, males are black and females are gray.

The best places to look for Phainopeplas are desert washes and thickets with mesquite trees and a source of berries. In addition to berries, Phainopeplas eat insects, which they catch on the wing. Phainopeplas are not particularly vocal, but their mellow *whiut?* call is distinctive and may help locate them. Their song is a short, quiet warble that does not attract attention. Juveniles resemble females; in their first summer males can be blotched black and gray.

FIELD NOTES
- 6¾–7¾" (17–19.5 cm)
- Small spiky crest and long tail
- Red eyes
- Male: Black, with white wingpatch noticeable only in flight
- Female: Plain gray
- Cup of fine plant material saddled in tree
- 2–4; whitish marked with browns

269

Pyrrhuloxia

Cardinalis sinuatus

The name Pyrrhuloxia derives from two Greek words—*pyrrhos*, meaning "flame-colored", and *loxos*, meaning "slanted"—which allude to the bird's pinkish red plumage and curved, parrot-like bill. The Pyrrhuloxia inhabits thorny desert washes, agricultural land with brushy hedges, suburban areas, and thickets. It resembles the Northern Cardinal (p. 114) and its song of loud, rich whistles, given from a prominent perch atop a tree or from a phone wire, sounds like the song of the Cardinal. In fact, where these two closely related species occur together it can be very difficult to identify them by their songs. If not singing, the Pyrrhuloxia can be hard to find: listen for a slightly metallic, Cardinal-like *tik* call, and a scratching sound in the leaf litter that may give away its presence.

Pyrrhuloxias sometimes form small flocks in winter when, like Northern Cardinals, they visit garden birdfeeders. The Pyrrhuloxia is a distinctive bird, grayer than the female Cardinal and with a yellowish bill and spikier crest. As with the Cardinal, the juvenile resembles the female but has a grayish bill.

J F M A M J J A S O N D

♀

♂

♂ Cardinal

FIELD NOTES
- 7½–8½" (19–21.5 cm)
- Short, deep, arched bill
- Cup of twigs and grass in bush
- 2–5; greenish white, marked with browns

Black-throated Sparrow

Amphispiza bilineata

The Black-throated Sparrow is an attractive sparrow found in rocky deserts with cacti and low bushes—habitats often shared with the Cactus Wren (p. 266) and the Verdin (p. 265). It is best found by tuning into its high-pitched, thin, tinkling calls. On tracking these calls down, you'll find the birds running on the ground with their tails cocked, or flying low from bush to bush. Alternatively, if you make a "spishing" sound (see p. 72) this will often bring the birds into sight as they pop up and look about to see where the sound came from.

The Black-throated's song is a high-pitched warble with intermittent trills, normally given from a low bush.

In sandier deserts with sagebrush, and also in chaparral, you'll find the closely related Sage Sparrow (*Amphispiza belli*; 5½–6¼" [14–16 cm]) which is similar to the Black-throated in its calls and behavior. Its song is a jangling or tinkling warble. Sage Sparrows of California's chaparral are notably darker than the paler, sandier-colored birds of the Great Basin sagebrush flats.

Juveniles of these two species lack the adult's bold markings, and both have fine dusky streaks on their pale chests. Note that the Black-throated has a long, bold, whitish eyebrow while the Sage has a short whitish brow mostly forward of the eye.

| J | F | M | A | M | J | J | A | S | O | N | D |

e Sparrow juvenile

Black-throated juvenile

Sage ♂

FIELD NOTES

- 5¼–5¾" (13–14.5 cm)
- Black bib
- Bold triangular patch on chest
- White eyebrow (conspicuous even in juvenile)
- Cup of fine twigs and grass in bush or cactus
- 2–4; bluish white

271

Hooded Oriole

Icterus cucullatus

This slender, relatively long-tailed oriole is a summer resident in desert washes and oases; farmland with scattered trees; and suburban areas. The key to finding Hooded Orioles is palm trees, especially fan palms. In these trees, the oriole slings its pouch-like nest of palm fibers under a frond. Some palms have dense crowns and the bird can be hard to see, so it's useful to learn the Hooded Oriole's call note—a whistled, rising *wheet*. The Hooded also makes a dry, chattering rattle, similar to other orioles. Its song is a varied, fairly fast-paced warble.

Another good place to look for these orioles is in flowering trees, where the birds probe for nectar. Hooded Orioles also visit hummingbird feeders in yards. Males in the west are paler, more golden-yellow than the brighter, orange males of south Texas. The females also show this color difference, though to a lesser extent. Young males in their first year resemble females but have a black bib like the adult male.

J F M A M J J A S O N D

fan palm

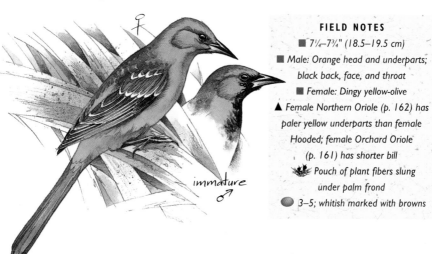

♀

immature ♂

FIELD NOTES

■ 7¼–7¾" (18.5–19.5 cm)

■ Male: Orange head and underparts; black back, face, and throat

■ Female: Dingy yellow-olive

▲ Female Northern Oriole (p. 162) has paler yellow underparts than female Hooded; female Orchard Oriole (p. 161) has shorter bill

Pouch of plant fibers slung under palm frond

3–5; whitish marked with browns

RESOURCES
DIRECTORY

FURTHER READING

This is by no means a complete list of books but should provide a solid foundation of references on which a beginning birder can build. The following abbreviations have been used: ABA (American Birding Association), AOU (American Ornithologists' Union), and Soc. (Society).

Understanding Birds

The Audubon Society Encyclopedia of North American Birds, by John K. Terres (Knopf, 1980). A wealth of information and outstanding photos.

Audubon to Xantus, by Barbara and Richard Mearns (Academic Press, 1992). Fascinating accounts of the lives of those people for which many species are named.

The Birder's Handbook: A Field Guide to the Natural History of North American Birds, by Paul R. Ehrlich, David S. Dobkin and Darryl Wheye (Simon and Schuster, 1988). Combines comprehensive information on the nesting and breeding habits of all North American species with over 250 essays.

Bird Wise, by P.M. Hickman (New England Press, 1988). A well-illustrated, activity book for 6 to 11 year olds.

Manual of Ornithology: Avian Structure and Function, by N. Proctor, P.J. Lynch (Yale University Press, 1993). A detailed, well-illustrated analysis of bird anatomy.

Backyard Birding

Attracting Birds to your Backyard, by C. Heimerdinger and S.H. Spofford (Publications Intel Ltd., 1991). Recommended by the American Birding Association.

The National Audubon Society North American Birdfeeder Handbook, by Robert Burton (Dorling Kindersley, 1992). Comprehensive coverage of this topic along with profiles of common garden birds.

Going Birding

The Birder's Catalogue, by Sheila Buff (Simon & Schuster, 1989). Good introduction to all aspects of birding, from bird sounds to bird art.

Birding for Beginners, by Sheila Buff, (Lyons & Burford Publishers, 1993). An excellent all-round introduction, with good advice on identification.

Field Guides

The Audubon Society Master Guide to Birding. 3 vols. Edited by John Farrand, Jr. (Knopf, 1983). Great photographs and descriptions by experts of all North American species.

Birds of North America by Chandler S. Robbins, Bertel Bruun, Herbert S.L. Zim, and Arthur Singer (Golden Press/Western Publishing, 1993). Rightly a bestseller. Good text and maps.

A Field Guide to Advanced Birding, by Kenn Kaufman (Houghton Mifflin, 1990). Essays and sketches analyzing 34 potential identification problems.

A Field Guide to Birds Coloring Book, by Roger Tory Peterson (Houghton Mifflin, 1982). Introduction to birds for kids, with simple species profiles and line drawings for coloring.

A Field Guide to Eastern Birds; *A Field Guide to Western Birds*, by Roger Tory Peterson (Houghton Mifflin, 1990). 2 vols. These superb guides to the birds of North America remain classics. They are easy to read and full of useful information, maps, and color illustrations.

A Field Guide to the Birds of North America. Edited by the National Geographic Society. 2d ed. (National Geographic Soc., 1987). Excellent single-volume field guide.

Eastern Birds: A Guide to Field Identification of North American Species, by James Coe (Golden Press, 1994). A beginner's guide to the most widely distributed eastern species, with good artwork.

Gulls: A Guide to Identification, by P.J. Grant. 2d ed. (Buteo Books, 1986). The last word in Palearctic and Nearctic gull identification.

Identification Guide to North American Passerines, by P. Pyle et al. (Slate Creek Press, 1987). Good technical information to assist aging, sexing, and naming perching birds in the hand.

Peterson First Guide to the Birds, by Roger Tory Peterson (Houghton Mifflin, 1986). An unintimidating bird book that presents 118 of the most conspicuous American birds.

Seabirds, by P. Harrison. 2d ed. (Houghton Mifflin, 1985). Descriptions of all known seabirds. Good color plates.

Shorebirds, by Hayman, P.J. Marchant, and Prater. (Houghton Mifflin, 1986). Exhaustive and generously illustrated coverage of the world's shorebirds.

Annotated Checklists

The American Ornithologists' Union Check-list of North American Birds. Edited by AOU (AOU, 1983). 6th ed. Lists all species in North America, from Panama to the Arctic islands and the Hawaiian Islands.

The American Birding Association Checklist. Edited by ABA (ABA, 1990). 4th ed. Standard checklist covering the US and Canada only. Available as a booklet or on computer disk.

Birds of the World: A Checklist, by J.F. Clements. 4th ed. (Facts on File, 1991). Includes information on the status and distribution of almost 9,700 known bird species.

Birdfinding Guides
GENERAL
Where the Birds Are, by John O. Jones (Wm. Morrow and Company, 1990).

The Birder's Guide to Bed and Breakfasts: United States and Canada, by Peggy Van Hulsteyn (John Muir Publishers, 1993).

Birdfinding in Forty National Forests and Grasslands, by ABA and US National Forest Service (ABA, 1994).

WESTERN US
Hawaii
Enjoying Birds in Hawaii, by H. Douglas Pratt (Mutual Publishing, 1993).
Alaska
Birdwatching in Eastcentral Alaska, by M.I. Springer (Falco, 1993).

A Bird Finder's Guide to the Kenai Peninsula, by George C. West (Birchside Studios, 1994).
Washington
Birding in Seattle and King County, by Eugene S. Hunn (Seattle Audubon Soc., 1982).

Birding in the San Juan Islands, by Mark G. Lewis and Fred A. Sharpe (The Mountaineers Books, 1987).

Birds of the Tri-Cities and Vicinity, by Howard R. Ennor (Lower Columbia Basin Audubon Soc., 1992).

Guide to Bird-finding in Washington, by Terence R. Wahl and Dennis R. Paulson (T.R. Wahl, 1991).
Oregon
The Birder's Guide to Oregon, by Joseph E. Evanich, Jr. (Portland Audubon Soc., 1990).

Birding Oregon, by Fred L. Ramsey (Audubon Soc. of Corvallis, 1981).
California
A Birder's Guide to Southern California, by Harold R. Holt and ABA (ABA, 1991).

Birder's Guide to Northern California, by LoLo and Jim Westrich (Gulf Publishing, 1991).

Birding Northern California, by Jean Richmond (Mount Diablo Audubon Soc., 1985).

Birding at the Bottom of the Bay, by Santa Clara Valley Audubon Soc. (Santa Clara Valley Audubon Soc., 1990).

San Francisco Peninsula Birdwatching, by Sequoia Audubon Soc. (Sequoia Audubon Soc., 1984).

Nevada
Southern Nevada Birds, A Seeker's Guide, by Carolyn K. Titus (Red Rock Audubon Soc., 1991).
Arizona
A Birder's Guide to Southeastern Arizona, by Harold R. Holt (ABA, 1989).

Birds in Southeastern Arizona, by William A. Davis and Stephen M. Russell (Tucson Audubon Soc., 1990).
Montana
A Birder's Guide to Montana, by Terry McEneaney (Falcon Press, 1993).
Wyoming
A Birder's Guide to Wyoming, by Oliver K. Scott and ABA (ABA, 1993).

Birds of Yellowstone, by Terry McEneaney (Roberts Rinehart Publishers, 1988).

Finding the Birds of Jackson Hole, by Bert Raynes and Darwin Wile (Darwin Wile Publisher, 1994).
Colorado
A Birder's Guide to Colorado, by Harold R. Holt and James A. Lane (ABA, 1988).
New Mexico
New Mexico Bird-finding Guide, by Dale A. and Marian A. Zimmerman, and John N. Durrie (New Mexico Ornithological Soc., 1992).

CENTRAL US
South Dakota
A Birdwatcher's Guide to the Black Hills and Adjacent Plains, by Richard A. Peterson (Richard A. Peterson, 1993).
Kansas/Missouri
A Guide to Bird Finding in Kansas and Western Missouri, by John L. Zimmerman and Sebastian T. Patti (University Press of Kansas, 1988).
Oklahoma
Guide to Birding in Oklahoma, by Tulsa Audubon Soc. (Tulsa Audubon Soc., 1986).
Texas
A Birder's Guide to the Rio Grande Valley of Texas, by Harold R. Holt and ABA (ABA, 1992).

A Birder's Guide to the Texas Coast, by Harold R. Holt and ABA (ABA, 1993).

Birder's Guide to Texas, by Edward A. Kutac (Gulf Publishing, 1989).

Birder's Guide to Rockport-Fulton, by Rockport Chamber of Commerce and Audubon Outdoor Club. (Rockport/Fulton Area Chamber of Commerce, 1989).
Minnesota
A Birder's Guide to Minnesota, by Kim R. Eckert (Kim R. Eckert, 1983).
Missouri
A Guide to the Birding Areas of Missouri, by Audubon Soc. of Missouri (Audubon Soc. of Missouri, 1993).
Louisiana
A Bird Finder's Guide to Southeast Louisiana, by Dan Purrington, et al. (Orleans Audubon Soc., 1987).
Wisconsin
Wisconsin's Favorite Bird Haunts, by Daryl D. Tessen (Wisconsin Soc. for Ornithology, 1989).
Illinois
Bird-finding in Illinois, by Elton Fawks and Paul H. Lobik (Illinois Audubon Soc., 1975).

Chicago Area Birds, by Steven Mlodinow (Chicago Review Press, 1984).
Mississippi
Birder's Guide to Alabama and Mississippi, by Ray Vaughan (Gulf Publishing Company, 1994).

Birds and Birding on the Mississippi Coast, by Judith A. Toups and Jerome A. Jackson (University Press of Mississippi, 1987).
Michigan
Birdfinding Guide to Michigan, edited by C. Roy Smith, Michigan Audubon Soc. (Michigan Audubon Soc., 1994).

Enjoying Birds in Michigan, by Michigan Audubon Soc. (Michigan Audubon Soc., 1989).
Ohio
Birding in Ohio, by Tom Thomson (Indiana University Press, 1983).
Tennessee
Bird-finding in Tennessee, by Michael Lee Bierly (Michael Lee Bierly, 1980).

EASTERN US
Visitor's Guide to the Birds of the Eastern National Parks, by Roland Wauer (John Muir Publishers, 1992).
New England
Bird Finding in New England, by Richard K. Walton (David R. Godine Publishers, 1988).

Maine
*A Birder's Guide to the Coast of
Maine,* by Elizabeth C. and Jan
E. Pierson (Down East
Enterprise, 1981).
Vermont
Guide to Bird-finding in Vermont,
by Walter G. Ellison
(Vermont Institute of
Natural Science, 1983).
New York
*Where to Find Birds in New York
State: Top 500 Sites,* by Susan
Roney Drennan (Syracuse
University Press, 1981).
Massachusetts
*A Birder's Guide to Eastern
Massachusetts,* by the Staff of
Bird Observer (ABA, 1994).
Birding Cape Cod, by Cape
Cod Bird Club and
Massachusetts Audubon Soc.
(Massachusetts Audubon
Soc., 1990).
Birding Nantucket, by Edith
Andrews and Kenneth
T. Blackshaw (Edith
Andrews, 1984).
Rhode Island
Bird Walks in Rhode Island, by
Adam J. Fry (Countryman
Press, 1992).
Pennsylvania
Birds of Erie County, by Jean
and James Stull and Gerald
McWilliams (Allegheny
Press, 1985).
*A Guide to the Birds of Lancaster
County,* by Lancaster County
Bird Club (Lancaster County
Bird Club, 1991).
*Where to Find Birds in Western
Pennsylvania,* edited by David
B. Freeland (Audubon Soc. of
Western Pennsylvania, 1975).
New Jersey
Bird-finding Guide to New Jersey,
by William J. Boyle, Jr.
(Rutgers University Press,
1989).
**Southeastern Pennsylvania/
southern New Jersey/
Delaware**
Birding the Delaware Valley Region,
by John J. Harding and Justin
J. Harding (Temple University
Press, 1980).
Delaware/Maryland/Virginia
*Finding Birds in the National
Capital Area,* by Claudia Wilds
(Smithsonian Institution Press,
1992).
North Carolina/Virginia
*Birds of the Blue Ridge
Mountains,* by Marcus B.
Simpson, Jr. (University of
North Carolina Press, 1992).

South Carolina
Finding Birds in South Carolina, by
Robin M. Carter (University
of South Carolina Press, 1992).
*Birder's Guide to Hilton Head
and Low Country,* by Hilton
Head Island Audubon Soc.
(Hilton Head Island Audubon
Soc., 1989).
*A Birding Guide to the South
Carolina Lowcountry,* by
W. David Chamberlain and
D.M. Forsythe (Charleston
Natural History Soc., 1988).
Georgia
A Birder's Guide to Georgia, edited
by Kenneth T. Blackshaw and
Joel R. Hitt (Georgia
Ornithological Soc., 1992).
Florida
A Birder's Guide to Florida, by
James A. Lane and Harold R.
Holt (ABA, 1989).

CANADA
A Bird-finding Guide to Canada,
edited by J.C. Finlay
(Hurtig Publishers, 1984).
British Columbia
*A Birder's Guide to British
Columbia,* by Keith Taylor
(Keith Taylor Birdfinding
Guides, 1993).
*A Birder's Guide to Vancouver
Island,* by Keith Taylor
(Keith Taylor Birdfinding
Guides, 1990).
*A Bird Watcher's Guide to the
Vancouver Area,* by the
Vancouver Natural History
Soc. (Cavendish Books, 1993).
Alberta
*A Birdfinding Guide to the Calgary
Region,* edited by John F.
McDonald (Calgary Field
Naturalists' Soc., 1993).
Manitoba
A Birder's Guide to Churchill, by
Bonnie Chartier and ABA
(ABA, 1994).
*Birder's Guide to Southeastern
Manitoba,* by Manitoba
Naturalists Soc.
(Manitoba Naturalists
Soc., 1988).
*Birder's Guide to Southwestern
Manitoba,* by Cal Cuthbert,
et al. (SWN Birder's Guide,
1990).
Ontario
*A Birdfinding Guide to the
Toronto Region,* by Clive E.
Goodwin (C. & J. Goodwin
Enterprises, 1988).
Bird-finding Guide to Ontario, by
Clive E. Goodwin (University
of Toronto Press, 1982).

Quebec
Birdfinding in the Montreal Area,
by Pierre Bannon (Centre de
Conservation de la Faune
Ailée, 1991).
*Birdwatching Itinerary of the Gaspé
Peninsula,* by Sylvie Girard
(Club Ornithologique de
Gaspésie).
**New Brunswick/Prince
Edward Island**
Birding in Atlantic Canada: Acadia,
by Roger Burrows (Jesperson
Press, 1992).
Nova Scotia
*Birding in Atlantic Canada: Nova
Scotia,* by Roger Burrows
(Jesperson Press, 1988).
Birding Nova Scotia, edited by
J. Shirley Cohrs and Nova
Scotia Bird Soc. (Nova
Scotia Bird Soc., 1985).
Newfoundland
*Birding in Atlantic Canada:
Newfoundland,* by Roger
Burrows (Jesperson Press,
1989).

Magazines
GENERAL
*American Birds/Audubon Field
Notes,* 700 Broadway, New
York, NY 10003
Bird Watcher's Digest, PO Box
110, Marietta, OH 45750
Birder's World, 44 E. 8th Street,
Suite 410, Holland, MI 49423
Birding, American Birding
Association, PO Box 6599,
Colorado Springs, CO 80934
Living Bird, 159 Sapsucker
Woods Road, Ithaca, NY
14850
WildBird, PO Box 52898,
Boulder, CO 80322

WESTERN US
Western Birds, Western Field
Ornithologists, 6011
Saddletree Lane, Yorba Linda,
CA 92686

CANADA
Birds of the Wild, PO Box 73,
Markham, ON L3P 3J5
Birders Journal, 8 Midtown Drive,
Suite 289, Oshawa, ON L1J 8L

BIRDING HOTLINES

Birding hotlines generally allow you to report or listen to reports on interesting or rare sightings in your area. The numbers below are state- or province-wide unless otherwise indicated.

WESTERN US

Alaska (907) 338-2473
Washington (206) 526-8266
  Southeastern (208) 882-6195
Oregon (503) 292-0661
  Northeastern (208) 882-6195
California
  Arcata (707) 826-7031
  Los Angeles (213) 874-1318
  Monterey (408) 375-9122
    Updates: (408) 375-2577
  Morro Bay (805) 528-7182
  Northern California
    (510) 524-5592
    To report: (510) 528-0288
  Orange County
    (714) 563-6516
  Sacramento (916) 481-0118
  San Bernadino (909) 793-5599
  San Diego (619) 479-3400
  Santa Barbara (805) 964-8240
Idaho
  Northern (208) 882-6195
  Southeast (208) 236-3337
Nevada
  Southern (702) 649-1516
  Northwest (702) 324-2473
Utah (801) 538-4730
Arizona
  Phoenix (602) 832-8745
  Tuscon (602) 798-1005
Montana (406) 626-2473
Wyoming (307) 265-2473
Colorado (303) 279-3076
New Mexico (505) 662-2101

CENTRAL US

Nebraska (402) 292-5325
Kansas (913) 372-5499
  Kansas City (913) 342-2473
Oklahoma (918) 669-6646
  Oklahoma City
    (405) 373-4531
Texas (713) 992-2757
  Austin (512) 483-0952
  Northcentral (817) 261-6792
  Lower Rio Grande Valley
    (210) 565-6773
  San Antonio (210) 733-8306
  Sinton (512) 364-3634
Minnesota (612) 827-3161
  Duluth (218) 525-5952
Iowa (319) 338-9881
  Sioux City (712) 262-5958
Missouri (314) 445-9115
  Kansas City (913) 342-2473
  St. Louis (314) 935-8432

Arkansas (501) 753-5853
Louisiana
  Baton Rouge (504) 293-2473
  New Orleans (504) 246-2473
Wisconsin (414) 352-3857
  Madison (608) 255-2476
    (except M–F: 9am–3pm)
Illinois
  Central Illinois (217) 785-1083
  Chicago (708) 671-1522
Mississippi
  Coast (601) 467-9500
Michigan (616) 471-4919
  Detroit (810) 477-1360
  Sault Ste. Marie
    (705) 256-2790
Indiana (317) 259-0911
Ohio
  Cincinnati (513) 521-2847
  Cleveland (216) 321-7245
  Columbus (614) 221-9736
  Blendon Woods Park
    (614) 895-6222
  SW Ohio (513) 277-6446
  NW Ohio (419) 875-6889
  Youngstown (216) 742-6661
Kentucky (502) 894-9538
Tennessee (615) 356-7636
  Chattanooga (615) 843-2822
Alabama (205) 987-2730

EASTERN US

Maine (207) 781-2332 (M–F:
  5pm-8am; w/ends: 24 hrs)
  Downeast/Central
    (207) 244-4116
New Hampshire
  (603) 224-9900 (M–F: 5pm–
  9am; w/ends: 24hrs)
Vermont (802) 457-4861 (M–F:
  5pm–9am; w/ends: 24 hrs)
  To report: (802) 457-2779
New York
  Albany (518) 439-8080
  Buffalo (716) 896-1271
  Cayuga Lake Basin
    (607) 254 2429
    To report: (607) 277-5455
  Lower Hudson Valley
    (914) 666-6614
  New York (212) 979-3070
  Rochester (716) 461-9593
  Syracuse (315) 682-7039
Massachusetts
  Boston (617) 259-8805
  Western Mass. (413) 253-2218
Connecticut (203) 254-3665

Rhode Island (401) 949-3870
  To report: (401) 949-5454
Pennsylvania
  Allentown (610) 252-3455
  Philadelphia (215) 567-2473
  Western Pennsylvania
    (412) 963-0560
  Wilkes-Barre
    (717) 825-2473
  SE/SC Pennsylvania
    (215) 383-8840
New Jersey (908) 766-2661
  Cape May (609) 884-2626
**Maryland/District of
  Columbia** (301) 652-1088
Delaware (215) 567-2473
Virginia (804) 238-2713;
  (301) 652-1088
North Carolina (704) 332-2473
South Carolina (704) 332-2473
Georgia (404) 509-0204
Florida (813) 984-4444

CANADA

British Columbia
  Vancouver (604) 737-9910
  Victoria (604) 592-3381
Alberta
  Calgary (403) 237-8821
  Edmonton (403) 433-2473
Saskatchewan
  Regina (306) 761-2094
Ontario (519) 586-3959
  Durham (905) 668-3070
  Ottawa (613) 761-1967
  Sault Ste. Marie
    (705) 256-2790
  Toronto (416) 350-3000
    (then enter 2293)
  Windsor/Detroit
    (313) 477-1360
  Windsor/Pt. Pelee
    (519) 252-2473
  Hamilton (905) 648-9537
  Long Point Bird Observatory
    (519) 586-3959
Quebec
  Montreal
    (in French) (514) 355-7255;
    (in English) (514) 355-6549
  Eastern Quebec (in French)
    (418) 660-9089
  Sagueny/Lac St. Jean
    (in French) (418) 696-1868
  Bas St. Laurent (in French)
    (418) 725-5118
  Western Quebec (in French)
    (819) 778-0737
New Brunswick
  (506) 382-3825
Nova Scotia (902) 852-2428

ORGANIZATIONS *and* OBSERVATORIES

Joining a birding organization is the best way to make contact with people with similar birding interests. Most of the following groups publish newsletters, organize field trips, and have periodic meetings featuring guest speakers. Observatories are basically research centers, but they also organize activities and events that will be of interest to birders, and, of course, they are great places to go birding.

Organizations

GENERAL

American Birding Association, PO Box 6599, Colorado Springs, CO 80934

Cornell Laboratory of Ornithology, 159 Sapsucker Woods Road, Ithaca, NY 14850

WESTERN US

Hawaii
Hawaii Audubon Soc., PO Box 22832, Honolulu, HI 96813

Washington
Washington Ornithological Soc., PO Box 85786, Seattle, WA 98145

Oregon
Oregon Field Ornithologists, PO Box 10373, Eugene, OR 97440

California
Western Field Ornithologists, c/o Treasurer, 6011 Saddletree Lane, Yorba Linda, CA 92686

Utah
Utah Ornithological Soc., PO Box 1042, Cedar City, UT 84721

Utah Field Ornithologists, 2226 East 40th South, Salt Lake City, UT 84103

Colorado
Colorado Field Ornithologists, 1782 Locust Street, Denver, CO 80220

New Mexico
New Mexico Ornithological Soc., University of New Mexico, Department of Biology-NMOS, Albuquerque, NM 87131

CENTRAL US

North Dakota
North Dakota Birding Soc., PO Box 9019, Grand Forks, ND 58202

South Dakota
South Dakota Ornithological Soc., 1620 Elmwood Drive, Brookings, SD 57006

Nebraska
Nebraska Ornithologists' Union, 3018 O Street, Lincoln, NE 68510

Kansas
Kansas Ornithological Soc., c/o Editor, *KOS Bulletin*, 1729 E. 11th Avenue, Winfield, KS 67156

Oklahoma
Oklahoma Ornithological Soc., PO Box 65, Ada, OK 74821

Texas
Texas Ornithological Soc., PO Box 38157, Houston, TX 77238

Minnesota
Minnesota Ornithological Union, Bell Museum of Natural History, 10 Church Street, SE, Minneapolis, MN 55455

Iowa
Iowa Ornithologists' Union, c/o Treasurer, 1601 Pleasant Street, West Des Moines, IA 50265

Missouri
Audubon Soc. of Missouri, Treasurer, 1800 South Roby Farm Road, Rocheport, MO 65279

Arkansas
Arkansas Audubon Soc., 2426 South Main Street, Malvern, AR 72104

Louisiana
Louisiana Ornithological Soc., 88 Egret Street, New Orleans, LA 70124

Wisconsin
Wisconsin Soc. for Ornithology, W330 N8275 W. Shore Drive, Hartland, WI 53029

Illinois
Illinois Ornithological Soc., PO Box 1971, Evanston, IL 60204

Mississippi
Mississippi Ornithological Soc., c/o 308 Lewis Lane, Oxford, MS 38655

Indiana
Indiana Audubon Soc., 901 Maplewood Drive, New Castle, IN 47362

Ohio
The Ohio Cardinal, c/o 520 Swartz Road, Akron, OH 44319

Kentucky
Kentucky Ornithological Soc., 9101 Spokane Way, Louisville, KY 40241

Tennessee
Tennessee Ornithological Soc., PO Box 402, Norris, TN 37828

Alabama
Alabama Ornithological Soc., c/o Treasurer, 702 Royce Circle, Huntsville, AL 35803

EASTERN US

Maine
Maine Audubon Soc., Gilsland Farm, Falmouth, ME 04105

New Hampshire
Audubon Soc. of New Hampshire, 3 Silk Farm Road, PO Box 528-B, Concord, NH 03302

New York
Federation of New York State Bird Clubs, c/o Cornell Laboratory of Ornithology, 159 Sapsucker Woods Road, Ithaca, NY 14850

New York City area
The Linnaean Soc. of New York, 15 W. 77th Street, New York, NY 10024

Massachusetts
Bird Observer of Eastern

Massachusetts, 462 Trapelo
Road, Belmont, MA 02178
or PO Box 236, Arlington,
MA 02174

Massachusetts Audubon Soc.,
South Great Road, Lincoln,
MA 01773

Connecticut

Connecticut Ornithological
Association, 314 Unquowa
Road, Fairfield, CT 06430

Rhode Island

Rhode Island Ornithological
Club, c/o 411 Burt Street,
Taunton, MA 02780

New Jersey

New Jersey Audubon Soc.,
790 Ewing Avenue, Franklin
Lakes, NJ 07417

Urner Orthnithological Club,
c/o Newark Museum,
43–9 Washington Street,
Newark, NJ 07101

**Southeast Pennsylvania/
southern New Jersey/
Delaware**

Delaware Valley Ornithological
Club, c/o Academy of Natural
Sciences, 19th and Parkway,
Philadelphia, PA 1910

Delaware/Delmarva Peninsula

Delmarva Ornithological Soc.,
PO Box 4242, Greenville,
DE 19807

Maryland

Maryland Ornithological Soc.,
Cylburn Mansion, 4915
Greenspring Avenue,
Baltimore, MD 21209

Washington DC area

Audubon Naturalist Soc., 8940
Jones Mill Road, Chevy
Chase, MD 20815

Virginia

Virginia Soc. of Ornithology,
520 Rainbow Forest Drive,
Lynchburg, VA 24502

West Virginia

Brooks Bird Club, 707
Warwood Avenue, Wheeling,
WV 26003

North Carolina

Carolina Bird Club, PO Box
29555, Raleigh, NC 27626

South Carolina

Carolina Bird Club, PO Box
29555, Raleigh, NC 27626

Georgia

Georgia Ornithological Soc.,
PO Box 1684, Cartersville,
GA 30120

Florida

Florida Ornithological Soc.,
Department of Ornithology,
Florida Museum of Natural
History, University of Florida,
Gainesville, FL 32611

CANADA

British Columbia

British Columbia Field
Ornithologists, PO Box 1018,
Surrey, BC V3S 4P5

Alberta

Federation of Alberta
Naturalists, Box 1472,
Edmonton, AB T5J 2N5

Saskatchewan

Saskatchewan Natural History
Soc., Box 4348, Regina,
SK S4P 3W6

Manitoba

Manitoba Naturalist's Soc.,
302–128, James Avednue,
Winnipeg, MB R3B 0N5

Ontario

Ontario Field Ornithologists,
Box 1204, Station B,
Burlington, ON L7P 3S9

Quebec

Province of Quebec Soc. for
Protection of Birds, PO Box
43, Station B, Montreal
PQ H3B 3J1

Association Quebecois de
Groupe d'Ornithologues,
4545 Pierre-de-Coubertin,
CP 1000, Succ. M, Montreal
PQ H1B 3R2

New Brunswick

New Brunswick Federation
of Naturalists, 277 Douglas
Avenue, St. John,
NB E2K 1E5

Nova Scotia

Nova Scotia Bird Soc.,
c/o Nova Scotia Museum
1747 Summer Street,
Halifax, NS B3H 3A6

Prince Edward Island

Natural History Soc. of PEI,
PO Box 2346, Charlottetown,
PEI C1A 1R4

Newfoundland

Newfoundland Natural History
Soc., PO Box 1013, St. John's,
NF A1C 5M3

Observatories

California

Point Reyes Bird Observatory,
4990 Shoreline Highway,
Stinson Beach, CA 94970

San Francisco Bay Bird
Observatory, PO Box 247,
Alviso, CA 95002

Michigan

Whitefish Point Bird
Observatory, HC 48, PO Box
115, Paradise, MI 49768

Massachusetts

Manomet Observatory for
Conservation Sciences,
PO Box 1770, Manomet,
MA 02345

New Jersey

Cape May Bird Observatory,
PO Box 3, Cape May Point,
NJ 08212

Ontario

Long Point Bird Observatory,
PO Box 160, Port Rowan,
ON N0E 1M0

Toronto Bird Observatory,
c/o Eric Machell, 10 Bateman
Court, Whitby, ON L1P 1E5

**Professional Societies
and Journals**

Association of Field Ornithologists, c/o Ornithological
Societies of North America,
PO Box 1897, Lawrence, KS
66044. (Society Journal: *Journal
of Field Ornithology*)

American Ornithologists'
Union, c/o Ornithological
Societies of North America,
PO Box 1897, Lawrence,
KS 66044. (Society Journal:
The Auk)

Colonial Waterbird Society, c/o
Robert Baker, 8096 River
Bay Drive West, Indianapolis,
IN 46240

Cooper Ornithological Society,
c/o Ornithological Societies
of North America, PO Box
1897, Lawrence, KS 66044
(Society Journal: *The Condor*)

Hawk Migration Association of
North America, c/o Treasurer,
377 Loomis Street, Southwick,
MA 01077

International Council for Bird
Preservation (BirdLife
International)—US Section,
c/o World Wildlife Fund,
1250 24th Street, NW,
Washington, DC 20037

Wilson Ornithological Society,
c/o Ornithological Societies
of North America, PO Box
1897, Lawrence, KS 66044.
(Society Journal: *The Wilson
Bulletin*)

INDEX and GLOSSARY

I n this combined index and glossary, bold page numbers indicate the main reference, and italics indicate illustrations and photographs.

CAPTIONS

Page 1: The Anna's Hummingbird is one of the most common and familiar hummers on the west coast.

Page 2: The Black-bellied Whistling-duck is found only in the extreme south of Texas.

Pages 4–5: A flock of Sandhill Cranes congregating at their winter quarters.

Pages 6–7: The Virginia's Warbler is easily confused with at least two other warblers in the southwest.

Pages 8–9: Chasing waves on beaches, the Sanderling is more easily identified by behavior than appearance.

Pages 10–11: Atlantic Puffins nest on grassy, cliff-top slopes along the northeastern coast.

Pages 12–13: After decades of scarcity, the Brown Pelican is gradually recovering its numbers.

Pages 44–5: A Northern Cardinal with Common Goldfinches at a winter birdfeeder.

Pages 58–9: The beautiful Roseate Spoonbill occurs only in coastal wetlands in Florida and westward along the Gulf Coast.

Pages 84–5: The Green Heron is common in the wetlands of the eastern US, but less so in the west.

Page 95: A group of starlings *(top inset)* perched on powerlines. A Blue Jay *(bottom inset)* sits on a birdfeeder.

Page 121: A Virginia's Warbler *(top inset)* foraging deep in deciduous forest. A Blue-gray Gnatcatcher *(bottom inset)* in the Everglades National Park, Florida.

Page 163: A Horned Lark *(top inset)* perches on a rock beside some California poppies. Two male prairie-chickens *(bottom inset)* compete at a lek.

Page 193: A male Barrow's Goldeneye duck *(top inset)* paddles with ducklings in Grand Teton National Park, Wyoming. A flock of Roseate Spoonbills *(bottom inset)* feeding in mangroves on Sanibel Island, Florida.

Page 229: A flock of White Ibises *(top inset)* fly above coastal waters. A lone Avocet *(bottom inset)* feeds at the water's edge as the sun sets.

Page 255: A tiny Rock Wren *(top inset)* sits on a desert ledge. A pair of Turkey Vultures *(bottom inset)* perch imposingly on top of a cactus.

Page 273: A Brown Pelican and its young at the nest.

ACKNOWLEDGEMENTS

The publishers wish to thank the following people for their assistance in the production of this book:
Walter Boles (Australian Museum), Julia Burke, Angela Dow, Jason Forbes, Selena Hand, Diane Harriman, Greg Hassall, Veronica Hilton, Toni Hope-Caten, Lynn Humphries, Tracy Tucker, Lesa Ward.

PICTURE AND ILLUSTRATION CREDITS

(t = top, b = bottom, l = left, r = right, c = center. A = Auscape International Pty Ltd; AA/ES = Animals Animals/Earth Scenes; BAL = Bridgeman Art Library, London; BC = Bruce Coleman Limited; BPL = Boltin Picture Library; Cornell = Cornell Laboratory of Ornithology; Culver = Culver Pictures, Inc.; DJC = DJC & Associates; DRK = DRK Photo; IB = The Image Bank; J = Jacana; MEPL = Mary Evans Picture Library; MP = Minden Pictures; NHPA = Natural History Photographic Agency; NS = Natural Selection; NW = North Wind Picture Archives; OSF = Oxford Scientific Films Ltd; PA = Peter Arnold, Inc.; PE = Planet Earth Pictures; PI = Positive Images; PN = Photo/Nats, Inc.; PR = Photo Researchers, Inc.; S = Scala; SB = Stock Boston; TPL = The Photographic Library of Australia; TS = Tom Stack & Associates; V = Vireo; VU = Visuals Unlimited; WC = Woodfin Camp & Associates.)

1 John Cancalosi/A. 2 Cortez G Austin/PN. 3 Thomas Buchholz/BCL. 4-5 Wendy Shattil & Bob Rozinski/OSF. 6-7 D & M Zimmerman/V. 8-9 William M Smithey Jr/PEP. 10-11 Frans Lanting/MP. 11 Stephen J Krasemann/DRK. 12-13 Alan Briere. 14-15 Robert Morton & David Wood. 16t NW; bl Jean Vertut; bkgr NW. 17tl C M Dixon; tr David Woo/SB; c by permission of the Linnean Society of London; b Lawrence Migdale. 18t Louvre, Paris/BAL; cr David Kirshner; b William E Ferguson. 19t & cr David Kirshner; b Gunter Ziesler/BCL. 20tl Giraudon/BAL; tr B Henry/V; bl John Gerlach/AA/ES; bc Wayne Lankinen/DRK; bkgr NW. 21t MEPL; c Steven Holt/V, b Will & Deni McIntyre/PR. 22t Frans Lanting/BCL; c & b David Kirshner. 23t Frank Knight; cl Jim Zipp/PR; cr Thomas Kitchin/TS; bl Frank Knight; br Lee Boltin/BPL. 24tl Art Resource, NY/S; c Geoff Avern/Australian Museum; bl Michael Melford/IB; br Frank Knight. 25 David Kirshner. 26tl John Shaw/A; cr A Morris/V; bl Stephen J Krasemann/DRK. 27tl Stephen J Krasemann/DRK; tr Wayne Lankinen/DRK; b J Carmichael, jr/IB. 28tl Joe McDonald/TS; tr R J Erwin/NHPA; cl Jordan Coonrad; b Andrew J. Purcell/BC. 29t Frank Knight; cr Palazzo Vecchio, Firenze/S; b NW; bkgr MEPL. 30t J White/ET Archive; c Jim Brandenburg/MP; b Maslowski Productions/PR. 31tl NW; tr Mary Clay/PE; c1 Mary Clay/TS; c2 Gary Milburn/TS; b Brian Kenney/PE. 32tr S J Lang/V; bl Dieter & Mary Plage/BC; br Robert Mancini. 33tl Johann Schumacher/V; tr S J Lang/V; b Robert Mancini. 34t C M Dixon; b Dr Scott Nielsen/BC. 35tl Diana L Stratton/TS; tr Priscilla Connell/PN; cl Phil Dotson/PR; br Thomas Kitchin/TS. 36t A & E Morris/V; b Erich Hartmann/Magnum. 37tl Jim Brandenburg/MP; tr Wayne Lankinen/BC; cl Cornell. 38tl C M Dixon; bkgr Steve Maslowski/VU; bl Anne Bowman; br Steve Kaufman/DRK. 39tl Don Enger/AA/ES; tr Roger Tidman/NHPA; b Wide World Photos/AP. 40 tl Michael Melford/IB; c1, 2 & 3 Breck P Kent/AA/ES; bl Diana L Stratton/TS; bkgr Stephen J Krasemann/DRK. 41t Life Magazine ©Time Warner/Nina Leen; c Tom J Ulrich; b Wayne Lankinen/DRK; 42t Jonathan Blair/WC; c D Robert Franz/PE; b John Eastcott/PE. 43cr Anne Bowman. 44-45 Tom Vanderschmidt/AA/ES. 46tl J H Robinson/PR; tr Harry Haralambou/PI; cr Daniel J Cox/DJC; bl Culver. 47 Casa del Bracciale d'Oro, Pompeii/S; b John Cancalosi/BC. 48 Colin McRae Photography; tl George H Harrison/Grant Heilman Photography; bl Ron Austing. 49br Daniel J Cox/DJC. 50 Colin McRae Photography; tl Sam Fried/V; bl Stephen J Krasemann/DRK; 51 Colin McRae Photography; cl George H Harrison/Grant Heilman Photography; br Robert A Tyrrell/OSF. 52tr Phillips, The International Fine Art Auction/BAL; bl Gay Bumgarner/PN; br Mary Clay/PE. 53tr Jane Burton/BC; cl C M Dixon; br Jim Brandenburg/MP; bkgr Joe McDonald/TS. 54 Colin McRae Photography; tl Jerry Howard/PI; bl Stephen J Krasemann/NHPA. 55tr Jack Dermid/OSF; cr Ron Austing; bl Lang Elliott/Cornell. 56tr Casa del Bracciale d'Oro, Pompeii/S; bkgr NW; br Grace Davies/Envision. 57t C C Lockwood/AA/ES; c Patti Murray/AA/ES; b Robert Mancini. 58-59 John Hall/AA/ES. 60tl, r, & cl Colin McRae Photography; cr Jiri Lochman; bl Susan Day. 61t Hellio-Van Ingen/J/A; b Colin McRae Photography. 62tl Paul Resendez/PI; tr Colin McRae Photography; b Dennis Frates/PI; inset Brock May/PR. 63t,& c Stephen J Krasemann/DRK; b David Wood. 64tr Tom Bean/DRK; cr William H Mullins/PR; cc Colin McRae Photography; b Jim Brandenburg/MP. 65tl William M Smithey, Jr/PE; tr Jack Wilburn/A/ES; bl Richard Day; br Stephen J Krasemann/DRK. 66t Culver; c Ron Austing; b Stephen J Krasemann/DRK. 67tl Jerry Howard/PI; tr Leonard Lee Rue/PR; cl John Cancalosi/DRK; bl J H Robinson/PR. 68t Marie Read/BC; c Jon Mark Stewart/Biological Photo Service; b Frans Lanting/MP. 69t Frank Knight; b George Holton/PR. 70tl Steve Maslowski/PR; cl A Morris/V; bl Charlie Ott/BC. 70-71 illust Frank Knight; 71tr Dr Scott Nielsen/DRK; cr Jean-Paul Ferrero/A; br John Cancalosi/BC. 72t Colin McRae Photography; cr John Shaw/TS; br Cynthia Berger/Cornell; bkgr NW. 73tl Haroldo Castro; bl Colin McRae Photography; tr Rod Planck/TS; bl Steve Pantle. 74tl Art Resource, NY/S; bl Colin McRae Photography. 75tl Candice Cochrane/PI; tr Colin McRae Photography; cr Mark Catesby/BPL; bl Cornell; bc Culver; br NW. 76tl & r Colin McRae Photography; bl & r Joe McDonald/AA/ES. 77t Courtesy R Gunz & Co Pty Ltd & Cannon Australia; bl Alan Briere; br Daniel J Cox/DJC. 78tl Julie O'Neil/PN; cl Ron Austing; bl Alan Briere. 79 tr NW; tl Richard Day; bl Jim Kahnweiler/PI; bc William H Mullins/PR; br Frans Lanting/ MP. 80tl Daniel J Cox/DJC; bl Culver; br NW. 81tr Ron Austing; bl Annie Griffiths Belt/DRK; br Tom McHugh/PR. 82 tr John Shaw/NHPA; cl Kenneth W Fink/PR; cc Mary Clay/PN; cr Anthony Mercieca/NS; br John Cancalosi/DRK. 83tl Tom McHugh/PR; tc Stephen J Krasemann/DRK; tr Liz Ball/PN; cr Jeff Lepore/PR; br M P Kahl/DRK; bkgr Steve Travaskis. 84-85 John Shaw/NHPA. 86tl John Shaw/A; b Frank

Huber/OSF; 86-93 bkgr Frans Lanting/MP. 87tl A & E Morris/V; tr & 88tl; Peter Gasson/PE;. 89t John Shaw/A; c1 Gil Lopez-Espina/NS; c2 John Cancalosi/A; b Frank Schneidermever/OSF. 90tl Gordon Langsbury/BC; tr Joseph Van Wormer/BC; bl Francois Gohier/A. 91tl Francois Gohier/A; tr Bob & Clara Calhoun/BC; bl Wayne Lankinen/BC; br John Cancalosi/A. 92bl Mark Schumann/PE; bc Wayne Lankinen/BC; br Glenn Jahnke/Root Resources. 93tl Stan Osolinski/OSF; tr Stephen J Krasemann/NHPA. 95 bkgr Jerry Howard/PI; t Frans Lanting/MP; Richard Hutchings/PR. 96-97 Tim Hayward. 98t Daniel J Cox/OSF; cl D Newman/VU; br G Dremeaux/V. 99tl Bullaty-Lomeo Photo; tc Galen Rowell/Mountain Light; tr John Cancalosi/A; b Julie O'Neil/PN. 100 Manfred Danegger/A. 101 Ron Austing. 102 Nick Bergkessel/TPL. 103 F K Schleicher/V. 104 Tom Ulrich/OSF. 105 Hans Reinhard/BC. 106 Wayne Lankinen/BC. 107 John Shaw/BC. 108-9 Robert P Carr/BC. 110 S J Lang/V. 111 John Shaw/A. 112 Wayne Lankinen/BC. 113 A Morris/V. 114 J Cancalosi/A. 115 P La Tourette/V. 116-7 A & E Morris/V. 118 Dr Scott Nielsen/BC. 119 A & E Morris/V. 120 R Villani/V. 121 bkgr Catherine Ursillo/PR; t D & M Zimmerman/V; b Eric A Soder/NHPA. 122-3 Louis Alach. 124t J Krasemann/DRK; cr C R Sams II & J F Stoik/V; br Michael Leach/OSF; bl Roger Tidman/NHPA. 125t Tom Ulrich/OSF; c1 Dick Scott/A; c2 Roger Tidman/NHPA; b Francis Lepine/AA/ES. 126 Leonard Lee Rue/BC. 127 Brian Hawks/A. 128 John Cancalosi/A. 129 Tom & Pat Leeson/DRK. 130 Stan Osolinski/OSF. 131 Dick Scott/A. 132 John Cancalosi/A. 133 R & N Bowers/V. 134 S J Lang/V. 135 Mary Clay/PE. 136 Ron Austing. 137 A & E Morris/V. 138 W Greene/V. 139 Marie Read/BC. 140 Bob & Clara Calhoun/BC; 141 P La Tourette/V. 142 B Schorre/V. 143 A & E Morris/V. 144-5 B Schorre/V. 146 A & E Morris/V. 147 Will Troyer/VU. 148 A & E Morris/V. 149 Sid Lipschutz/V. 150 B Schorre/V. 151 A & E Morris/V. 152 Bob & Clara Calhoun/BC. 153 Stephen J Krasemann/DRK. 154 Stephen J Krasemann/J/A. 155 Hector Rivarola/A. 156 Bob & Clara Calhoun/BC. 157 Wayne Lankinen/BC. 158 Jack Dermid/BC. 159 Wayne Lankinen/BC. 160 Marie Read/BC. 161-2 B Schorre/V. 163bkgr R J Erwin/DRK; t Franz J Camenzind/PE; b Richard Thom/VU. 164-5 Louis Alach. 166t Leonard Lee Rue/BC; bl Paul Rezendes/PI; cr Marie Read/BC; Joe McDonald/TS. 167t Lone E Lauber/OSF; bl Michael Sacca/AA/ES; br Rod Planck/NHPA. 168 Jean-Louis le Moigne/A. 169 Werner Layer/A. 170 Francois Gohier/A. 171-2 Bob & Clara Calhoun/BC. 173 Francois Gohier/A. 174 Leonard Lee Rue/BC. 175 Gens/J/A. 176 S J Lang/V. 177 George McCarthy/BC. 178 Francois Gohier/A. 179 Robert P Carr/BC. 180 Leonard Lee Rue/BC. 181 C B Frith/BC. 182 John Shaw/A. 183 Stephen J Krasemann/J/A. 184 A & E Morris/V. 185 Wayne Lankinen/BC. 186 Tom Ulrich/OSF. 187 Bernd Thies/BC. 188 W Greene/V. 189 A & E Morris/V. 190 Cyril de Klemm/A. 191 M P Kahl/BC. 192 Wayne Lankinen/BC. 193bkgr Helen Cruickshank/V; t Scott McKinley/PE, b Jeff Foott/A. 194-5 Tim Hayward. 196 t Wayne Lynch/DRK; bl R Glover/BC; br Stephen J Krasemann/BC. 197tl Joe/ Carol McDonald/TS; tr Helen Cruickshank/V; bl & r Stephen J Krasemann/PA. 198 Dr Scott Nielsen/BC. 199 G Nuechterlein/V. 200 Erwin & Peggy Bauer/BC. 201 John Shaw/A. 202 John Shaw/BC. 203 Jeff Foott/A. 204 John Shaw/A. 205 Rinie Van Meurs/BC. 206 Erwin & Peggy Bauer/A. 207 Jack Dermid/A. 208 W Greene/V. 209 Tom Walker/A. 210 Gordon Langsbury/BC. 211 Erwin & Peggy Bauer/A. 212 Dr Scott Nielsen/BC. 213 J R Woodward/A. 214-5 Dr Scott Nielsen/BC. 216 Erwin & Peggy Bauer/A. 217 Fritz Polking/A. 218 John Shaw/A. 219 Dr Scott Nielsen/BC. 220 J L G Grande/BC. 221 T H Davis/V. 222 Dr Scott Nielsen/BC. 223 A & E Morris/V. 224 Johann Schumacher/V. 225 F K Schleicher/V. 226-7 A & E Morris/V. 228 Stephen J Krasemann/ J/A. 229bkgr Brett Froomer/IB; t Brian Alker/PE; b Hermann Brehm/BC. 230-1 Robert Morton. 232t Francois Gohier/A; bl Francois Gohier/PR; cr John Shaw/TS; br A & E Morris/V. 233tl Frans Lanting/MP; tr Stephen J Krasemann/DRK. 234 Erwin & Peggy Bauer/A. 235 T H Davis/V. 236-7 Francois Gohier/A. 238 Werner Layer/A. 239 H Clarke/V. 240 A & E Morris/V. 241 John Shaw/A. 242 Winfried Wisniewski/A. 243 A & E Morris/V. 244 Doug Wechsler/V. 245-6 A & E Morris/V. 247 Jean-Louis Dubois/A. 248 Gordon Langsbury/BC. 249 John Shaw/A. 250 Francois Gohier/A. 251 Philippe Prigent/A. 252 Helen Cruickshank/V. 253 A & E Morris/V. 254 M & A Boet/A. 255 D & M Zimmerman/V; t Rob Curtis/ V; b Francois Gohier/A. 256-7 Tim Hayward. 258t Tom Bean; bl Larry Ulrich/DRK; br C Allan Morgan/DRK; bkgr Pat O'Hara. 260 J Hoffman/V. 261 John Cancalosi/BC. 262 Jeff Foott/BC. 263 Bob & Clara Calhoun/BC. 264 Francois Gohier/A. 265 P La Tourette/V. 266 John Cancalosi/BC. 267 Bob & Clara Calhoun/BC. 268 John Cancalosi/BC. 269 Jeff Foott/BC. 270 John Cancalosi/DRK. 271 Charlie Oti/BC. 272 Bob & Clara Calhoun/BC. 273t Frans Lanting/M; inset Francois Gohier/J/A. 274-287 Steven Bray.

Illustrations in the Field Guide section are by **Helen Halliday** page trim; **Terence Lindsey** 113, 117, 127, 154, 155, 180; **Robert Mancini** 100, 101, 106, 107, 110, 111, 114, 115, 118, 119, 120, 128, 129, 132, 133, 136, 137, 140, 141, 144, 145, 148, 149, 152, 153, 156, 157, 159 160, 161, 162, 170, 171, 174, 175, 178, 179, 182, 183, 186, 187, 190, 191, 200, 201, 204, 205, 208, 209, 210, 211, 212, 213, 216, 217, 219, 220, 221, 222, 224, 225, 226, 234, 235, 238, 239, 242, 243, 245, 246, 247, 249, 250, 251, 253, 254, 260, 261, 264, 265 266, 268, 269, 271, 272; **Maurice Pledger** 62, 241, 262; **Trevor Weekes** 102, 103, 104, 105, 108, 109, 112, 113, 116, 117, 126, 127, 130, 131, 134, 135, 138, 139, 142, 143, 146, 147, 150, 151, 154, 155, 158, 159, 168, 169, 172, 173, 176, 177, 180, 181, 184, 185, 188, 189, 192, 198, 199, 202, 203, 206, 207, 210, 211, 214, 215, 218, 223, 227, 228, 236, 237, 240, 244, 245, 248, 249, 252, 263, 267, 270.